THE MOGULS

By *Norman Zierold*

Norman Zierold

THE MOGULS

Coward-McCann, Inc.   New York

For RITA SENF, TOM DAWSON, *and* VIRGINIA RICE

Contents

Illustrations follow pages 98 and 258.

Preface

THEY came from the ghettos of Kiev and Minsk and Warsaw, and from little towns like Laupheim in Germany and Ricse in Hungary and Krasmashhilz in Poland. In turn-of-the-century America they took new names as they began to make their way in a new land—names like Mayer, Goldfish, Warner, Zukor, and Selznick. They worked at petty trade, in menial occupations, among them a cloth sponger, a junk dealer, a glove salesman, a furrier, a pool hustler—and a jeweler who went bankrupt.

One by one they were drawn to the field of entertainment, first to nickelodeons where for a small coin you could see a peep show, have your fortune told, learn your weight. And then to an extraordinary new medium called motion pictures. It was a daring thing, in those early days, to invest money in a device which was said to cause a permanent squint in the viewer, to be the occasion for the debauchery of innocent girls. But for this hardy band of unlettered pioneers it was in the nature of a miracle. Coming from a babble of language backgrounds, they saw pictures on a screen which everyone could understand, Germans and French, rich and poor, old and young, those well educated and those completely unschooled. Pictures on a screen telling a story, moving. They never ceased to be amazed that motion pictures actually moved.

Despite the scoffers, the public hurried to movie theaters and devoured each new offering. The junk dealer and the clothes sponger and the furrier founded film empires called studios, which they ruled like medieval fiefdoms. The fledgling industry became highly competitive, but this hardy band survived because they were men of gargantuan energy who combined a striking variety of talents—gall, persistence, artistic impulse, imagination, showmanship, the gambling instinct.

Through the halcyon age of silent films they charted their course and on into a new miraculous development called talking pictures.

These men formed a kind of Our Crowd on the West Coast —but with a difference. Because they were conducting a Gentile art form, selling the blond hair and blue eyes of Mary Pickford, the movie moguls, as they were called, tended to divest themselves of their Jewishness. The coin they dealt in was talent, and it bore no tag of race or nationality. The moguls were keenly aware that films must not be limited to the American market, that they would have to appeal to their home countries in order to make the maximum in profits. As a result they imported actors, writers, and directors from every state of Europe and even from the Far East. The moguls were Jewish-born but very international, watching events abroad, sensing imminent wars, gauging the tide of the times and forming their product to meet changing challenges.

When Jesse Lasky of Paramount was taken to the hospital with a heart attack, he unhesitatingly replied "American" to a routine question about race.

"Now, now, Mr. Lasky," said the sweet little Hebrew lady behind the desk. "We're Jewish, aren't we?"

"Jewish? Oh, yes, yes, Jewish," said the surprised Lasky.

The movie moguls, that handful of refugees from foreign oppression, eventually became among the most powerful men in the land, sending out films which influenced style and morality in countries around the globe. By 1937 Louis B. Mayer of MGM was the highest-salaried man in the United States. Dictator Joseph Stalin's Russian regime declared that if it could control the world film industry it could control the world.

After World War II, television and a changing market were among the factors that led to the breakup of the old studio dynasties. Today, Louis B. Mayer is dead, along with Carl Laemmle, David Selznick, Jesse Lasky, B. P. Schulberg, Cecil B. DeMille, Harry Warner, and Jack and Harry Cohn. A few names remain, but an era has passed. With its going, it comes into a more revealing perspective.

This is the story of these unique and extraordinary motion picture pioneers, of their ascent to power, of the savage struggles that kept them on top while less resilient men were toppled from their perches. It is the story of their complex personalities, of their achievements and blunders, of their alternating generosity and cruelty, of their moments of laughter. It is an assessment of a vanishing breed of the men who created Hollywood's golden age.

1

The Selznick Saga

IF ONE FILM symbolizes Hollywood of the golden age, it is surely *Gone with the Wind*. Long years after its memorable Atlanta premiere, audiences were still flocking to see reruns of the epic love story of Scarlett O'Hara and Rhett Butler played out against the background of a bloody Civil War, but in Hollywood, producer David O. Selznick was supervising a melancholy task. Tara, the stately mansion built for the picture, was being dismembered, each section labeled and readied for shipment to the Georgia capital, where it was to serve as a municipal monument.

"Nothing in Hollywood is permanent," commented Selznick. "Once photographed, life here is ended. It is almost symbolic of Hollywood that Tara had no rooms inside. It was just a facade. So much of Hollywood is a facade."

Such traces of pessimism were indeed incongruous to many observers, especially those who recalled the fantastic energy and enthusiasm and daring with which Selznick had invested his days, qualities which reached their finest distillation in the making of *Gone with the Wind*.

Gone with the Wind was David O. Selznick at the zenith of his accomplishment, a brilliant reflection of the gambler, the showman, the artist. What few knew was that it was also an extraordinary act of revenge! It was the act of a son avenging a father, a story so crowded with remarkable incident and character that it, too, may one day become the scenario for an epic film.

Its beginnings lay in Russia, in the city of Kiev, and they can be told briefly since they form only a prelude to the larger action. Lewis J. Zeleznick was born there on May 2, 1870, one of a huge Jewish family of 18 children. At the age of twelve he ran away from home and worked his way to England, where he was a factory hand for five years before continuing on to the land of opportunity, the United States.

Pittsburgh was the scene of his first triumphs. He became a successful jeweler, his business philosophy dominated by two thoughts: first, that jewels were for suckers; second, that in consequence, jewelers would always be in demand. These buoyant, genially cynical views were to follow him later into a new field, the fledgling film industry.

His entrance into that arena is as adventuresome as an Arabian Nights tale. Grimy Pittsburgh was merely a stepping-stone for the lusty Russian refugee. As his earnings mounted up to a comfortable cache, he took them to the country's commercial capital, New York, and opened a flashy new jewelry store at Sixth Avenue near 14th Street. He brought along the wife he had acquired, Florence Sachs, the attractive daughter of a family of Orthodox Jews; and the three sons she had borne him, healthy squawlers named David, Myron, and Howard.

The New York jewelry store was a swift, splashy failure. Almost gaily, the proprietor, who had now shortened his name to Selznick, auctioned off most of the contents. A high-spirited, laughing dreamer with a tremendous zest for living, he looked about for new fields of action. Amassing money was a wild and crazy game, not to be taken too seriously.

His answer came in the form of Mark Dintenfass, literally translated Inkwell, one of those bizarre and colorful figures who dot the early history of films. Selznick had encountered Dintenfass in Pittsburgh. He was a salesman of salt herring, working for his father. A family quarrel drove him from the fish business and as far as Philadelphia, where he became the proprietor of one of the first motion picture theaters. Its failure only kicked him upstairs into production and all the financial gyrations that that encompassed.

It was 1912 when Dintenfass and Selznick met again in New York. The former herring salesman told a story that made the blond, bankrupt jeweler's eyes dance with delight. There was a film company called Universal Film Manufacturing, in which he had acquired a bundle of stock. He wanted to sell, but the question was to whom. Two rival factions were fighting for control of Universal. One was headed by a bright, bluff Irishman named Pat Powers; the other by a pint-sized but wily German called Carl Laemmle. A dozen deals were in the air—intrigue, shenanigans, conspiracy.

Dintenfass appointed Selznick his emissary to sell his stock. Powers was the first object of call. Selznick decided to match the latter's reputation for sartorial splendor with a dashing vested outfit of his own, complete with watch fob. He announced himself not as the purveyor of a stock offer but as a jeweler with something special to sell. This enabled him to get into Power's office rather than into the washroom, where the suspicious Irishman often held his appointments so that the rival faction would not get wind of his latest move. Selznick opened a small bag which contained the remnants of his failed affairs. Powers would not buy. He switched to the Dintenfass stock. Powers would not buy.

Undismayed, Selznick took his stones down the hall to the office of Laemmle, called Uncle Carl because he had brought so many nephews and other relatives over from his native Germany and given them jobs. Uncle Carl liked the sparklers. He liked Selznick. He smiled a bounteous, beaming smile when Selznick told him the Dintenfass stock was not only valuable in its own right but that he had ascertained its purchase would give Laemmle operative control of the company. Laemmle bought the stock.

As Selznick was leaving, he took a good look at the premises. Chaos seemed to prevail—offices with empty desks, papers and books scattered loosely about, employees apprehensive and demoralized by the struggle for control being waged around them. It was all wonderfully appealing. The next day the audacious Selznick returned to Universal at 1600 Broadway. He installed himself in an empty office, hung up his hat, and scouted the terrain.

From Laemmle he received a vague commission to make himself useful. Then that madcap tycoon left on one of his impulsive journeys to other parts of the forest. Selznick checked into first one phase of the business, then another, picking up good knowledge of its rudiments along the way. With his customary casualness, Laemmle had neglected to inform his lieutenants of the new man. As a result, everyone was wary of Selznick, the Laemmle forces suspecting him of being on the Powers team, the Powers group wondering if he was with the Laemmle team.

Selznick was with the Selznick team, a party of one. Working his way from rung to rung, he became aware that the company had no general manager. A sign painter put his name on the door with that title; he ordered stationery to match, and took over purchasing for Universal.

Meanwhile, the Powers forces were resurging, at one point calling in police to remove sets and props right in the middle of a Laemmle-sponsored picture, at another dropping the company's books and great seal out of a window during an annual stockholders' meeting. Back in town, Laemmle saw that the Pittsburgh appointee was aggrandizing power at an alarming rate. By letter he informed him that he accepted his "resignation."

The experience was nonetheless heady and stimulating for Selznick. With his newfound background he decided to continue in the mad world of motion pictures, where coup was followed by countercoup, a flop by sudden success and riches, where a quick raid could topple one company from the heights and replace it with another. He felt he now knew about as much as the next man about the industry. His likable persuasive manner, his energy and infectious enthusiasm, would be an asset, as would his presence, one that suggested that of a high-class lawyer.

He made his move in 1915, joining forces with Chicago mail order merchant Arthur Spiegel in the World Sales Corporation. His first move was to raid the rival Vitagraph Corporation of beautiful, dark-haired Clara Kimball Young. He put her into his first production, *The Common Law*. Bird in hand, he hurried to Wall Street for financing, and to film exhibitors across the country, asking for advance deposits against rental of films which were still only forming in his mind. He was one of the first to use this method of financing. Money was forthcoming, and the company quickly became a factor to reckon with.

Selznick's sharp, impulsive mind and his daring promotional escapades paved the way. "You can't keep a good idea down," was one of his favorite sayings. Among the best of his ideas was one he executed for bringing plays to the screen. With Broadway producer William A. Brady and the Schuberts he made arrangements for film use of their theatrical properties.

For World, comedian Lew Fields repeated his popular role in *Old Dutch*; Alice Brady and Holbrook Blinn appeared in *The Boss*; Wilton Lackaye and Clara Kimball Young made *Trilby*; Lillian Russell and Lionel Barrymore starred in *Wildfire*.

World advertised its films as "Features Made From Well Known Plays by Well Known Players." This brought newcomer Selznick up against Adolph Zukor, the tiny tycoon who ruled the destinies of a company which advertised "Famous Plays for Famous Players." Zukor and Lasky had gotten there first with the concept, but piracy of ideas was no more forbidden than the theft of leading players.

One of Selznick's directors, Allan Dwan, could humorously supply an illustration. When Dwan was employed by the American Film Company he used to watch each new film produced by that genuine genius D. W. Griffith. Dwan would immediately make the same film, varying the story line just enough to get away with it and using different actors, of course. When Griffith began using close-ups, Dwan began using close-ups. So hungry was the public for pictures that it was almost impossible to make a failure, no matter how slapdash the methods. Today Dwan, vigorous and crisp in his eighties, recalls how early stories would begin with a line written on the back of an envelope. The director would see a cliff, throw a dummy off, and film the scene. "There's the heavy," he would say. "Now why did we throw him off the cliff?" The end came first, and then the backtracking work would follow. Seeing an interesting house, Dwan would instruct his leading man to sit on the porch, hurrying the action in order to get away before the owner could come out to investigate. Techniques had advanced somewhat, but still it is not surprising that Selznick viewed the business of film making with sardonic good humor.

Adolph Zukor watched his new rival intently. Selznick gave him a show worth seeing. He built up a remarkable stable of stars in a short time. Clara Kimball Young became his top attraction, pushed along by a publicity buildup to such tremendous popularity that Selznick became apprehensive of losing her. One day he heard a great commotion in his outer office. When he rushed out to see what was the matter, he was told the steamship *Lusitania* had been sunk by the Germans, bringing closer America's entry into World War I. "Oh, is that all?" he gasped, visibly relieved. "I was afraid Clara Kimball Young was breaking her contract."

Alice Brady, the victim of mediocre stories, blossomed under Selznick's banner. Eugene O'Brien became an important leading man. Starlet Elaine Hammerstein, member of a famous family, became an important player. Owen Moore was a steady favorite. A stunning beauty named Olive Thomas, drifting after the decline of the Triangle studio, reached stardom. The famous Elsie Janis was lured to World by the dazzle of dollars.

Selznick asked the famed Russian actress Nazimova to appear in a picturization of her enormously successful vaudeville skit, *War Brides*. When she demanded $30,000 for the role, the equivalent of $1,000 a day, he agreed to the terms. He went further, accepting Nazimova's demand that she be paid in cash at the end of each day. He did not forget to have photographers present when the daily ceremony took place, knowing well that ensuing publicity would more than pay the high salary. *War Brides* grossed a cool $300,000. Playing a small role was a youngster whose mother had taught Nazimova English. His name was Richard Barthelmess.

Selznick the starmaker was once more in evidence in the case of the Talmadge sisters. He had tried several times to woo the upcoming Norma away from Triangle without success. His luck changed when Norma married Joe Schenck, good-natured booking manager for the Loew theater circuit. Schenck worked for and was a close friend of Marcus Loew, head of the circuit. Loew in turn was a friend of Selznick's, whose unorthodox and flamboyant methods amused him. Loew guided Schenck and Norma Talmadge to Selznick. Her first picture with the company was *Panthea,* brought home by Allan Dwan. Constance Talmadge, who had been featured in D. W. Griffith's *Intolerance,* also came to World, where she and Norma were soon reigning favorites.

Everyone was fair game for the enterprising Selznick. When he heard that the Czar of Russia had been overthrown in a revolution, he cabled the unfortunate Nicholas: "WHEN I WAS BOY IN RUSSIA YOUR POLICE TREATED MY PEOPLE VERY BADLY. HOWEVER NO HARD FEELINGS. HEAR YOU ARE NOW OUT OF WORK. IF YOU WILL COME TO NEW YORK CAN GIVE YOU FINE POSITION ACTING IN PICTURES. SALARY NO OBJECT. REPLY MY EXPENSE. REGARDS YOU AND FAMILY." There was no reply.

Rivals, especially the conservative, soft-spoken Adolph Zukor, appreciated Selznick's penchant for ballyhoo even less than his demonstrated ability to produce moneymaking pictures. For his first film, *The Common Law,* the brash producer had installed an electric sign at a theater on 46th Street and Broadway which boldly announced Lewis Selznick Enterprises as the picture's sponsor. As the pictures multiplied, so did the blazing lights, among the first so used for advertising. At one time, ten signs ricocheted the Selznick name across Broadway.

Along with his own, he publicized the name of his stars. Again his rivals were angry, for they were trying to minimize the contributions of their players in order to keep down their salaries. Selznick went further, setting up separate corporations for Clara Kimball Young, Norma Talmadge, and others, with himself as president and general manager. By this unorthodox procedure a theater owner could buy Clara Kimball Young pictures without being forced to take the rest of the World output. Selznick publicly denounced the block booking program of the other companies as well. "I consider myself a failure unless the exhibitor is a success," was one of his most widely quoted sayings. The tendency of his system was to force producers to make better pictures to gain exhibitors' acceptance. It endeared him to the latter, but not to his peers.

To them, he became known as Selznick the Jester. They watched him inaugurate special previews for his films, investing them with music, dancing girls, and all the florid flavor of a bacchanalia. They heard of his office, one of solid sumptuousness reached by long stone corridors manned by a phalanx of uniformed guards. Nearer the inner sanctum a tier of secretaries and assistants further protected the great panjandrum, who sat behind a magnificent desk in courtly seclusion. No Pittsburgh jeweler was going to sneak up on L.J., as he was called by the staff.

There was no end to his audacity. At one point he proposed the first profit-sharing system in the amusement field, 25 percent of the profits above a fixed minimum, distributed to his employees at Christmas. "Once profit sharing is generally accepted by employers throughout the United States the greatest problem which faces our civilization will be solved and the bogies of socialism and anarchy will disappear," he pronounced. "The whole future of our country and the salvation of our manufacturing industry and commerce depend upon employers recognizing the right of employees to share in the profits which they help to earn." He hastened to add: "I mean profits in excess of the average normal profits." The latter could be figured pretty high.

The ultimate derisive slap at his peers came when Selznick was among those called before a Senate committee investigating financial practices of film makers. "Less brains are necessary in the motion picture industry than in any other," he told the gaping Congressmen. As evidence he recalled that he had put $1,000 into the World Film Corporation and cleared $105,000 within ten weeks. His contempt was sincere. With a chuckle he harked back to the days when herring salesman Dintenfass had made a fortune in the business and to the crazy shenanigans at Universal Film Manufacturing.

Selznick ridiculed not only the men who made films but the films themselves. To him they represented a childish art form. He never went to a movie if he could help it, not even to those he himself produced. He liked to read good books, especially the classics of literature. He loved good art, and his cushiony 22-room apartment at 230 Park Avenue in New York was filled with priceless Ming vases from China. He loved good living, so choice food and vintage wines were always served by the half-dozen servants who attended to the family's needs. Four Rolls-Royces rested in the garage. He also loved women. By starlets whom he enticed to that ubiquitous item of studio furniture, the casting couch, he was nicknamed C.O.D., for cash on delivery.

What was one to do with such a man? If one was Adolph Zukor, one went to call on him. One offered him $5,000 a month for life if he would pack up and go to his beloved China where he could see all the celebrated vases in their native habitat. Selznick roared with laughter at the offer. Give up the boisterous, lusty, larcenous life of a film tycoon for exile at a piker's pittance? Never.

The crafty Zukor was prepared to go all the way. If you can't beat 'em, join 'em, he must have thought in his native Hungarian. He offered a dazzling million-dollar figure for a 50 percent interest in Selznick's enterprises. The offer to combine the two giants seemed irresistible. Selznick would remain as president; he would have access to all the other company's advanced facilities; and his son Myron, at seventeen edging into a precocious manhood, would go to work under such master producers as Jesse Lasky and Cecil B. DeMille.

Selznick was letting the fox into the chicken coop. Because the government was already concerned with monopolies in the industry, the move was not announced as a merger. Instead, a new company was formed, Select Pictures Corporation. That heading now replaced Selznick on Broadway's ribbon of light. It was only the first step in Zukor's gradual persistent obliteration of his partner's image.

The new company made almost $2 million in its first year. The only trouble for Selznick was that he was no longer in control. Bit by bit, power was slipping away. A much more orthodox businessman, Zukor was aware that Selznick was a buccaneer, a marauder, and he soon discovered that his accounts were a maze of mysterious alleys, a bookkeeper's prescription for migraine. To keep a check on matters, to act as buffer between himself and Selznick, he employed a relative as general manager. Morris Cohn was the uncle of Mrs. Zukor, a conservative man experienced in the film field. He tried for months to keep order in the house but eventually came to Zukor in despair. Selznick was too elusive for him to handle, too shifty in his methods to allow for a meaningful liaison.

Zukor was also unhappy over the earthy personal style of his partner. One day he was scheduled to take his teen-age son, Eugene, to boarding school in upstate New York. L.J. allowed as how he would like to go along for the ride. On the trip he asked the young boy whether he was making it with the girls. "My boys are getting plenty," he said proudly. Eugene blushed. Adolph flinched. L.J. lit a good cigar.

When word came from Hollywood that Constance Talmadge wanted the credit line "Lewis J. Selznick Presents" removed from her pictures, Selznick saw the guiding hand of Zukor. For his partner he prepared a glittering surprise. In 1919 his son

Myron announced the formation of the Selznick Pictures Corporation, with offices at 729 Seventh Avenue. Since Myron was only twenty, his mother was often called in to cosign papers. Soon, to Zukor's horror, the hated name of Selznick once more blazed away from electric signs on Broadway. L.J. was reportedly spending much of his time at 729. Zukor fumed for a time before deciding to throw in the sponge. He allowed Lewis Selznick to buy him out.

The parting did not come amicably, and the real battle was only beginning. Selznick won back most of his stars, and with his sense of showmanship spiraled back to the top. His annual advertising bill alone came to $2 million. Entrepreneur James Cox Brady offered him $5 million for a slice of his new empire. William Randolph Hearst made another topheavy offer of money but wanted at least partial control. L.J. would have none of it. He had had enough of partners. In the early twenties it is estimated that he could have liquidated his assets for $23 million.

Underneath the showy facade lurked trouble. In early September of 1920 a wire from the elegant Hotel Crillon in Paris brought disastrous news. One of Selznick's magnets, Olive Thomas, was found dead, her nude body still betraying the great beauty that once was hers, her fingers clutching a bottle of deadly bichloride of mercury tablets. It was a tormenting shock to the many fans of the twenty-year-old former Ziegfeld show girl, all of whom thought her happily married to Jack Pickford, the handsome brother of Mary, America's Sweetheart. When the whisper of extensive drug usage was heard, the scandal that ensued sadly belied Selznick's new slogan, "Selznick Pictures Create Happy Homes."

Hard upon the blow inflicted on the film industry by Olive Thomas' death came new disasters. Roly-poly comedian "Fatty" Arbuckle was accused of the rape-murder of starlet Virginia Rappe, and three sensational trials pointed a dirty finger at Hollywood. When distinguished director William Desmond Taylor was murdered and it was discovered that he had been leading a perplexing double life under another name, with a previously unknown wife and child residing in New York, the industry knew it was in trouble.

Selznick took the lead in finding an escape valve for the beleaguered film capital. Casting an eye at baseball, the nation's favorite pastime, he recalled that sport's bribery scandal and how it had cleansed itself by appointing Judge Kenesaw Mountain Landis as guardian of its morals. Selznick discussed the matter with Charles Pettijohn, an Indiana lawyer, who said Will Hays, just appointed Postmaster General by President Harding, might fulfill a similar role for the picture industry. With Pettijohn and his son Myron, Selznick went to see Hays. Hays was cool to the offer but gradually warmed up. Eventually he accepted the post of czar of the movies, receiving $100,000 a year to keep the industry's linen clean, or as the official word had it, to impose a "dictatorship of virtue" upon the screen. Among the founding fathers of the new organization which he headed, the Motion Picture Producers and Distributors of America, were such men as Winfield Sheehan, Carl Laemmle, Sam Goldwyn, William Fox, and Adolph Zukor. Hays guided Hollywood through perilous straits in the years ahead. He was one of Selznick's last bequests to the industry.

The industry was not notably grateful. Adolph Zukor had counterattacked some time earlier against the Selznick resurgence by founding another corporation, Realart Pictures, which made the same type of picture with young stars like Mary Miles Minter. Realart also made inroads on the Selznick sales organization. The most telling blow came when Zukor won over Clara Kimball Young, who broke her contract with Selznick and sued him for "making representations which he did not live up to."

The entire film business in 1923 was going through one of its periodic retrenchments, and Selznick had overextended himself. One by one, stars left his banner. To whom could he turn? Not to Adolph Zukor certainly. Not to his old friend Marcus Loew, who was cool to Zukor but who was now saddled with an illness that would bring death within the year. Not to Louis

B. Mayer, at the helm of fast-moving Metro Pictures. Mayer had quarreled with Selznick years before when Mayer was the New England distributor for the Select Film Corporation.

No one would come to the once powerful L.J.'s aid. Times were bad, and he was no great favorite of the other moguls. The creditors would not wait. The corporation slipped into bankruptcy on a trivial $3,000 debt. Overnight, Lewis J. Selznick fell from his throne and became prince of the paupers.

He took his losses philosophically. He knew the rules of the game. He had overplayed his hand and lost. From the swank $18,000-a-year apartment on Park Avenue he moved the family into a lowly three-room flat where the faithful Florence, who calmly sold her jewels, did the cooking. The servants were gone save for one Japanese retainer who asked to stay on without pay and continued to offer guests turkey or ham no matter what the hour of their arrival, midnight or sunrise. Friends were amazed to find L.J. enjoying himself almost as much in dire poverty as he had in opulence.

His sons, Myron and David, did not. They were convinced that their father had been toppled from his high perch by a conspiracy of the other movie moguls. Under ordinary circumstances this might have made them resentful. For Myron and David, however, the feeling went much deeper, for they loved their father intensely.

Lewis Selznick had given his boys undeniable gifts—love, lust for life, taste, and philosophical ploys that made them as daring and resilient as he himself was. One of his firmest maxims was that money was a tool, a toy, a plaything. As students in public school, the sons received allowances of several hundred dollars a week. At college age, entering Columbia University in New York, Myron got $1,000 a week, while David was given $750 with which to amuse himself. "Spend it all. Give it away. Throw it away," counseled the father. His theory was for them always to live beyond their means so that they would be forced to strive harder in order to keep up. He believed in work, in using the mind.

One should have fun with money, he felt, and so he gambled

with it like the wild Russian he was. Poker games were his great delight, and David later estimated that his father dropped a million dollars a year during the three or four years of his halcyon period. Producer William Brady recalled an evening where the elder Selznick won a single pot that rounded up to $300,-000.

It was an exceptional household, for that winning Jewish matriarch, Florence Selznick, would also sit down at the poker table and join the men. Years later, when Myron was hosting a party which included himself, Joe Schenck, and Darryl Zanuck, Myron asked Zanuck if it was all right if his mother played a hand or two. "I don't know about that," said Zanuck. "I've never played poker with a woman before."

"Don't let that bother you," said Florence, shuffling the cards. "Neither have I."

While they were still in their teens, Lewis Selznick sent his boys over to Europe on their own, fortified with cash and an introduction to the mother of English director Eddie Goulding in London. Goulding's sister, Ivis, and the mother shepherded the American visitors around the city, and even today Ivis Goulding recalls how young David stood in Westminster Abbey for what seemed like an hour before a ten-foot figure of Christ, admiring its poignant beauty. When he brought up his own sons, he later confided to her, he himself took them over the identical tour which had so impressed him. What impressed Ivis and her mother at the time was that sixteen-year-old David picked up the dinner tabs with the authority of a big-spending banker.

If it seems as though youngsters treated with such affection and indulgence might have turned into wastrels, the results were decidedly different. While taking courses at Columbia, Myron asked his father for a part-time job at the studio. It must have been a satisfying moment for Lewis Selznick, and he knew how to respond. He gave Myron an assignment in the film examining room at $15 a week, the going rate for the hours involved. He stopped the fat allowance—one should know how to live with pots of money, and how to make do with pennies. Soon Myron dropped out of Columbia. For two months he peered at film, looking for flaws and defects, his hands often raw with cuts. From the cutting room he went out on the road selling. Under his father's tutelage, he learned how film exchanges operate, the ins and outs of distribution and production. When he was ready, he was put in charge of the office of the Norma Talmadge Film Corporation, working there for Joe Schenck. Later he formed his own corporation, under his father's aegis. He was known as the "boy producer," helping to guide the destinies of Selznick studios spread out over Hollywood, the Bronx, and Fort Lee, New Jersey.

David lasted somewhat longer at Columbia than Myron, and he too was drawn at an early age into the field in which his father roved with such exuberance. While still in his teens, he was taken to business and story conferences at the studio. Lewis Selznick even drew his young son into the discussions, asking questions. For a time he edited *The Brain Exchange,* the house organ for Selznick employees. Step by step he learned the technique of making motion pictures.

One other boon came from his father. He dandled David on his knee and read him stories at an early age. Later, he read and discussed with him such favorites as *David Copperfield, Little Lord Fauntleroy,* and *A Tale of Two Cities.* To prepare for their talks about these books, David would try to prepare himself, painstakingly reading line by line, as beginners are inclined to do. Throughout life he remained an avid reader, albeit a slow one. The love of books and the storyteller's gift turned into splendid assets when David himself began making movies.

His first efforts were less impressive artistically than from the standpoint of enterprise and showmanship. It was 1922, and Luis Firpo, the Wild Bull of the Pampas, was training for his fight with heavyweight champion Jack Dempsey. The vast publicity surrounding the match was catnip to twenty-one-year-old David Selznick. He asked Firpo if he could make a short film of his training routine. The Argentine, usually un-

able to express himself in English, turned quite poetic when
it came to discussing terms. He demanded $1,000 a day. Selz-
nick accepted, rented a camera and props, and put the burly
boxer through a pace that left him limp. The entire short was
completed within twenty-four hours. Costs added up to $875,
plus the thousand to Firpo. Selznick sold *Will He Beat Dempsey?* the next day for $3,500.

A second venture led David to Madison Square Garden. There
Rudolph Valentino, waging a contract war with Paramount, was
picking up extra change by judging a beauty contest sponsored
by Mineralava, a face cream manufacturer. Selznick generously
offered to film the contest finals for nothing, and spoke in glow-
ing terms of the free publicity that would ensue. He made a
two-reeler, taking care to concentrate the camera on movie
idol Valentino rather than on the 87 long-stemmed girls on
parade. His only cost was the price of lighting the garden and
the actual film used; his sale price was $15,000. When he went
to his father and asked, "Dad, do you want to read this
contract?" the elder Selznick replied, "You're twenty-one now.
Read it yourself." It was the sort of remark that might well
make a young man feel ten feet tall.

There were not many more such gestures. It was at this junc-
ture, just as the road to princely power and pay dirt seemed
wide open, that Lewis Selznick went bankrupt. Now Myron
and David were doubly determined to succeed in their own
right and to vindicate their father. Conscientiously they set
about their appointed task.

The third brother, Howard, felt no such drive. Milder-man-
nered than his brothers, extremely likable, he quietly went his
own way, dabbling briefly in the film business before going on
to other ventures, none very successful. To Myron and David
he became an object of amused concern, referred to as "the
third brother." At one point they helped him buy a flower shop
in Hollywood called the "Forget Me Not." "That's what one
does for a third brother—one buys him a business," joked
David. The shop failed. People forgot.

For Myron and David, too, there were difficult days ahead, days eventually relieved, however, by a spectacular turnabout. The sequence began for Myron with job-seeking visits to other film studios. With Lewis Selznick out of power, the Selznick name was a distinct handicap. Many doors were closed altogether. Carl Laemmle granted an interview but only for the purpose of advising Myron to get out of the film business, a move probably dictated by memories of his encounter with the father.

Hat in hand, Myron at one point went to borrow money from an old friend, actor Owen Moore. He called on him at his dressing room at United Artists, where Moore was riding high. Both quiet men, the two old friends spoke little. Moore seemed distracted and said, "Come back in half an hour." Myron thought he was being gotten rid of but came back at the appointed time; he needed the money. Moore was not there, but pinned on the mirror in the bungalow was a check made out to Myron Selznick—blank, waiting only for Myron to fill in any amount he wanted.

A job working for Joe Schenck at United Artists finally came through, but Myron and his immediate superior, Johnny Considine, developed an instant loathing for one another, and Myron was sacked.

Myron stayed close at hand as his father formed a new company in 1926, the Associated Exhibitors. It folded quickly. Lewis Selznick could never find the road back. He and Myron went to Florida, attracted by the real estate boom. When the boom collapsed they returned within months to Hollywood. The father tried to set Myron up in the agency business, arranging an appointment with George Ullman, Valentino's former manager, who had gone into that field. Myron did not show up for the first meeting at all. At a second interview he appeared thoroughly soused. Nothing came of that encounter either. Seven years later, in 1933, Lewis Selznick died. By that time, however, he had lived to see his son become the most important agent in Hollywood, a man who could tweak the noses of the mighty moguls and make them like it.

The accomplishment was awesome; its beginnings were cartoon comic. In New York, the Selznicks had become acquainted with another boisterous, fast-living Russian émigré named Lewis Milestone. Milestone went to Hollywood, where he worked his way up at Warner Brothers, directing *The Cave Man* and an early version of *Seven Sinners* with Marie Prevost. Both were scripted by brash beginner Darryl Zanuck. When David and Myron came West, they used Milestone's house as a meeting place, he being a bachelor like themselves at the time.

Milestone's circumstances changed, however. Jack Warner liked his work and outlined a long-term deal to him. "Everyone here thinks you should be one of our regular directors. Here's the contract. You sign here."

"Can't I read it?" asked Milestone.

"What the hell for? It's a contract. Just sign it."

"I'll sign, but if there's something in it that doesn't sound right, I'll come back to you."

"If you delay us even one hour, the whole deal's off."

Milestone signed, read the contract, and found a number of objectionable passages. He refused to work, breaking the contract. Warners sued him for damages. Milestone pleaded bankruptcy and turned everything over to the courts.

By now, Myron and David had taken a house in Hollywood, where they lived with a young United Artists producer, Benny Seidman. The Selznick brothers invited Milestone to move in. David and Benny were both working, David picking up $100 a week on a trial basis at Metro-Goldwyn-Mayer. Accordingly, the two wage slaves slept in a room with comfortable twin beds. The unemployed Myron and Milestone slept in a big Murphy bed in another room. The living was casual, rich in wine and wenching. Occasionally a friend, youthful agent Leland Hayward, would stop by. Rolling up in a rug, he would sleep on the floor.

There were arguments, too, and one had a very happy issue. The bachelor household sallied out to catch *What Price Glory?*

in the 1926 silent version starring Dolores Del Rio, Victor Mc-
Laglen, and Edmund Lowe. Milestone had seen the stage
version in New York and didn't like the changes made for the
screen; he walked out and waited for his comrades. When they
came, they were annoyed with him. They all loved the picture
and began discussing it in rapturous terms. Mikestone told them
they were nudniks; he never wanted to talk to them again about
movies. Russian tempers flared. Milestone stomped off on his
own, hopped into a cab, and headed for the Plaza Hotel on
Sunset, a hostelry known to him from other escapades. From
the bellhop he ordered a bottle of nerve-calming spirits, drank
it, and slept late into the morning. He was awakened by a phone
call from Myron, who said he was coming right over; it was important.

Milestone received him with the *froideur* he thought the
situation demanded.

"Have you heard of Neil McCarthy?" asked Myron.

"No."

"He's a top attorney. He represents Howard Hughes."

"So?"

"You just got a call at the house from McCarthy. He says
Hughes is very interested in you. We've got to go down to RKO
and see them, and if you keep your mouth shut, we'll get a
deal."

"*We'll* get a deal. What in hell have you got to do with it?"

"I'm your agent—and don't you ever forget it."

Faced with this outlandishly assertive stand, the groggy
Milestone followed orders. Myron made the deal, getting him
$1,500 a week for the first year of a three-year contract, $2,000
a week for the second, and $2,500 for the third. Milestone figured
it was a pretty good deal, considering that he had been getting
$400 a week at Warner Brothers. Myron liked it too. He had put
it over on Hughes' negotiator, Johnny Considine, who had fired
him from a hundred-dollar-a-week job at United Artists. Now
with a 10 percent commision from his first client, he would get
$150 a week for just sitting.

Myron Selznick had tasted blood. The taste was sweet. Moreover, he was about to prove his father's contention that you can't keep a good idea down. Agents at this time were in low repute in Hollywood, middlemen considered basically the tools of the producers. Their social status was near the bottom. Myron Selznick swiftly introduced a new concept—he was on the side of the artist, whether actor, writer, or director. He did not call himself an "artist's representative" or any other euphonious title; he was an agent, working for his clients. Rather than charge arbitrary fees, he introduced a straight 10 percent commission.

His first aim was to increase his client list. Director William Wellman signed up. Myron, often a little high, wandered around the studio lots, explaining to prospects that he would not take a dime unless and until he got them a better deal. He found out that Pat O'Brien, making his first picture, *The Front Page,* was getting $75 a week from RKO, and that Irving Thalberg wanted him for the second lead in MGM's *Flying High.* Myron took him to Thalberg, asking $1,750 per week. Thalberg groaned; his lieutenant, Eddie Mannix, offered $1,250. Myron was firm. O'Brien got $1,750 per week, and *Flying High,* with Bert Lahr and Charlotte Greenwood, furthered his career. He became a satisfied client.

An unspoken rule among the moguls of this period said they would not raid one another's studio for talent. The gentlemen's agreement was the result of the bitter experiences of early days, when larceny was law. Now an actor dissatisfied with his roles or his salary had little recourse but to remain where he was. Myron Selznick put the quietus on this system with one of the boldest strokes of his young career. He was aware that Warner Brothers, having pioneered with sound pictures and come up with the revolutionary *The Jazz Singer,* was ready for a broad program of expansion. He was also aware that three of the brightest stars at Paramount had contracts coming up for renewal. They were Kay Francis, William Powell, and Ruth Chatterton. Paramount was, of course, ruled over by that old nemesis of Myron's father, Adolph Zukor. Myron persuaded all three to become his clients and overnight took them away from Zukor and into the arms of the waiting Warner brothers. The stroke left Hollywood gasping.

Myron followed by whisking Constance Bennett out from under Pathé and also taking her to Warner Brothers, which paid her an all-time high salary of $30,000 a week. She made an unimportant film which was, however, appropriately called *Bought*. Myron was selling; the moguls were buying.

At the end of Myron Selznick's first year as an agent, Zukor's production head, Ben Schulberg, was saying scornfully, "In a year people will be saying, 'Whatever happened to Myron Selznick?'" At the end of the second, Adolph Zukor himself said, "Myron, you have cost the industry five million dollars this year." At the end of the third, another producer phoned Myron and said, "We have raised a fund of three million dollars to drive you out of Hollywood."

"Give me two million and I'll quit," said Myron. "You'll save a million."

Success breeds success. Myron no longer scavenged on the lots for new clients; instead, they sought him out. He took in a partner, Frank Joyce, brother of silent star Alice Joyce. The agency signed its people to five-year contracts. It set up a business department that took care of investment and income tax problems for clients, guiding their financial affairs with professional acumen.

By the middle thirties Myron had lined up a client list that was awesome. His female stars included: Binnie Barnes, Edna Best, Billie Burke, Ruth Chatterton, Elisabeth Bergner, Mrs. Patrick Campbell, Constance Collier, Constance Cummings, Frances Dee, Kay Francis, Helen Hayes, Katharine Hepburn, Miriam Hopkins, Carole Lombard, Elsa Lanchester, Myrna Loy, Ida Lupino, Jean Muir, Merle Oberon, Maureen O'Sullivan, Princess Natalie Paley, Lily Pons, Zazu Pitts, Ginger Rogers, Dorothy Stickney, Margaret Sullavan, Verree Teasdale, Lupe Velez, and Fay Wray.

The men in the Selznick stable included: Walter Abel, Richard Arlen, Fred Astaire, Richard Barthelmess, Ben Bernie,

Charles Bickford, Gary Cooper, Jackie Cooper, Henry Fonda, Cedric Hardwicke, Boris Karloff, Charles Laughton, Victor McLaglen, Fredric March, Herbert Marshall, Raymond Massey, Thomas Meighan, Adolphe Menjou, Thomas Mitchell, Owen Moore, Pat O'Brien, Laurence Olivier, William Powell, George Raft, Lee Tracy, and Roland Young.

"Stars should get all the money they can while they can," said Myron. "They don't last long." Writers and directors often went without agents in the early days. Myron did pioneering work in these areas, giving them the same four-star treatment he gave his actors. Top directors Frank Capra, Gregory La Cava, John Cromwell, Ernst Lubitsch, Leo McCarey, and William Wellman came under his banner. Always, Myron showed a special loyalty to any writer, director, or actor who had stood by his father in the waning years of his life.

By 1937 the Selznick agency grossed a healthy 15 million dollars. In 1938 it moved into splashy new quarters in Beverly Hills, ultramodern in the interior, the circular patio an impressive riot of tropical blooms. More than 300 of Hollywood's top talents walked through the doors, giving Myron Selznick carte blanche to negotiate their contracts. Myron himself seldom appeared at the office, doing much of his work from a phone at home. Like his brother David he was liable to call up associates at two or three in the morning, his life irregular but obsessive, the goal always to be one up on the moguls.

Agency disputes with the studios could be savage. Twentieth Century-Fox accused Myron Selznick of undermining the morale of its players by telling them they were not getting either enough money or the right parts. The agency was banned from the lot. Myron bided his time for more than a year. Then he pulled one of his most valued clients, Loretta Young, off the lot and sued the studio, charging the equivalent of restraint of trade. Darryl Zanuck countered with a seven-year contract which would have netted the actress $3 million. Myron refused; he did not want her tied up that long. Zanuck raged, Myron waited. Twentieth Century-Fox capitulated. The Selznick agents once more roamed the lot, looking for new clubs with which to black-jack the studio.

"Remember what those bastards did to my father," Myron told writer Alva Johnston as they were riding home at the end of one happy day. "They paid more than a million dollars for it today."

Myron never made a secret of the fact that he was in business for revenge, to stick the moguls who had mocked his father. Whereas other agents went meekly into the lions' dens, Myron himself came in like a lion. If he had a ten-thirty appointment with Darryl Zanuck and was not immediately received, he would tip the door and say, "Do you want to see me or don't you?" There was no waiting in the outer office.

Myron would begin conferences by softening up the opposition with a diversionary attack. Once, riding with director Alfred Hitchcock, Myron explained that he was going to talk over some business with Eddie Mannix, the astute and expressive right hand of Louis B. Mayer at Metro-Goldwyn-Mayer. All during the ride, Myron kept saying, "What can I argue with Eddie Mannix about? What can I fight him on?" Suddenly he snapped his fingers and said, "I've got it. I'll fight with him over Bill Powell." Powell was then a leading MGM player, and a dispute involving him was bound to unnerve Mannix. Hitchcock later heard about the ensuing meeting, which Myron began brusquely by saying, "Bill Powell's upset."

Mannix looked bewildered. "Upset? What about?" he asked.

"He doesn't like the story material you've been giving him. He's very unhappy with the stories. I think he wants out."

"Is that so?" said Mannix. "I can hardly believe it. I had lunch with him yesterday, and he seemed happy and satisfied. As a matter of fact, he said he never wanted to work for any other outfit than this one."

"Well, he was crazy if he said that," said Selznick. "He didn't mean it."

"All right, Myron," said Mannix, revealing his own counter-bluff. "I didn't have lunch with Bill Powell, and you know he's not unhappy. Now what is it you want to talk about?"

The playful but tough Irishman was a match for the canny Jewish Selznick. The two then got down to business.

Myron's style varied with each opponent. One of his agents for a time, Dan Winkler, recalls how he would accompany Myron into the office of Louis B. Mayer. By then Mayer ruled over MGM, the Tiffany of the studios, and he was the untitled king of Hollywood. Myron was not awed; he called him a bastard and a sonofabitch. "Oh, Myron, don't start that again, please," Mayer would defend himself. At other times he would snap back, "Oh, Myron, shut up." It was a game between the two wheeler-dealers, an unpleasant game that neither could forgo. With archenemy Adolph Zukor, Myron would talk right off the shoulder, the way one would talk to a man trying to sell you insurance when you didn't want any. Myron would take lesser moguls like Harry Cohn in easy stride. When Cohn once barred agent Winkler from his Columbia lot, Myron called. "If you want anyone from me, leave Winkler alone," he said simply. Winkler went right back to Columbia. Harry Cohn needed Myron.

Everyone needed Myron Selznick—even his brother David. The word in Hollywood was that when David worked briefly for Paramount he let Myron know whose contracts were expiring so that he could move in for the kill. Myron could no doubt have gotten this information from other sources. In any event, when David set up his own producing company in 1935, Myron invested in it, a fact which never kept him from being a formidable negotiator when he dealt with his brother on the agent level. Indeed, many felt he drove harder bargains with David than with some of the other producers.

A case in point came when Myron sold Fredric March to his brother for a specified period at $15,000 a week. As the starting date approached, David phoned to ask for an extension; he couldn't get his script into shape. Myron gave him a week, at the end of which David called again to ask for still more time.

Myron angrily hung up. He told March to report for work and to collect his check. If the check was not forthcoming, they would sue. Still unable to whip his script into shooting condition, David pleaded. Myron chuckled. They compromised. David got the needed extension. March got $35,000 for sitting by his swimming pool while David and his writers labored. It was a hard bargain. The film turned out eventually to be the very successful *Nothing Sacred,* with March and Carole Lombard.

The relationship between the brothers was a boisterous, brawling, loving one. The two looked a good deal alike—big men, shaggy-haired—but whereas David was nervous and bounding, Myron tended toward the taciturn. David had a habit of taking a nap on the floor after dinner. Laid out in front of the fireplace, he was difficult to awaken. "I'll get him up," Myron would say, and give him a kick that might well have brought a horse to its feet.

David had something of the younger brother's worship of Myron and loved to tell of the elder brother's latest daring forays against the great powers of Hollywood.

The two could tangle about business but never for long. They could quarrel in like manner about their romances. Before either was married, David was interested in Jean Arthur when Myron made a pass at her. The result was a terrific fistfight— and a later reconciliation. Both were great womanizers like their father, incessant gamblers like their father. Myron's marathon poker parties were legendary and his racing stable another manifestation of the gambling mania. The day-to-day activity was at such a heightened pace that extraordinary stakes at poker, something extravagant, was needed to provide recreation.

Liquor was another way to lift the pressure. David liked to have a drink, but Myron liked to drink a lot. If his alcoholic intake was remarkable, so was his capacity to live with the bottle without becoming sleazy. At Haven Hill, his retreat up at Lake Arrowhead, a long weekend might begin on Thanksgiving Day and end after New Year's, with wine, women, and poker chips the binding ingredients. Draining life to the dregs, Myron had a favorite saying: "Tomorrow is a lovely day."

He made one venture into matrimony. He married the lovely, young, blond actress Marjorie Daw in 1929. Their daughter, Jean, was born in 1936. In 1939 the couple separated, and a divorce ensued in 1942.

Thereafter, Myron went his quietly intense way alone, hitting the columns with regularity, on one occasion when he lashed out with a right at John Barrymore on the lawn of the Ambassador Hotel, the argument and fight leading the Great Profile to a temporary unexpected fadeout.

Myron could have won a victory over a very special female species of Hollywood mogul, but he didn't. Louella Parsons, the queen of the film columnists, organized a radio program called *Hollywood Hotel,* on which the major stars appeared free for the publicity value. Myron did not like the idea of his clients appearing gratis and pulled them all off the program, which foundered. The resourceful Louella had an ace in the hole, however. When she was writing her first column out of Chicago, she had met Lewis Selznick and his wife. She now sent her husband to speak to Florence Selznick. That gentle lady told Myron that Louella had been a friend of his father. The word was enough for Myron to send his stars back to *Hollywood Hotel.* Perhaps, too, he remembered his father and the *Lusitania* episode. Louella had figured in a similar stance. The week that Mussolini began the rape of Albania, she solemnly spoke to her readers: "The deadly dullness of the past week was lifted today when Darryl Zanuck announced he had bought all rights to *The Blue Bird* for Shirley Temple." And then, too, Louella's husband, a physician known around town as Docky, could have figured in Myron's leniency. Docky got a great many calls from actors and actresses because they knew that Louella appreciated their using him. When a severe siege of a social disease hit town, he was frequently called upon. This led to an amusing incident. Docky was always in attendance at the boxing matches, with Louella at his side. One evening at the garden, a heavyweight challenger went crashing to the floor from a rain of blows. It looked like he had been hit below the belt. Docky hurried to his side and peered under the trunks to determine the injury. From high in the stands a voice shouted down: "Hey, Doc, he ain't got gonorrhea; he's just bushed."

Sometimes the laugh was on Myron. One of his clients was that inveterate practical joker Carole Lombard. As her contract came up for renewal, she induced agent Dan Winkler to take it and have it printed up in reverse. Assured that all was in order, Myron signed with a flourish, only to learn that it made Carole Lombard his agent, that she was to get 10 percent of everything he earned. The ruse revealed, Myron shared in the joke. Most of his clients adored him. Later, however, Carole felt that he was neglecting her and sued to break her contract.

Other of Myron's high-priced clients wanted more of his attention, and there were other ruptures.

Myron was dining at Chasen's one evening with his brother's sharp business brain, Daniel O'Shea. In the next booth were director Leo McCarey and his wife. McCarey had made a deal with David Selznick when Myron saw a better bet, the director's cap for *Ruggles of Red Gap* at Paramount. David released McCarey, and the film, with Charles Laughton, Mary Boland, and Charles Ruggles, established him as topflight. On this particular evening at Chasen's, Myron was concerned about something other than the rounds of whiskey doubles and his usual tartar steak. McCarey owed him $25,000. Over the back of the booth, he needled the director mercilessly. McCarey took the abuse as long as he could, then reached for his pen.

"Here's your Goddamn commission," he snapped, tossing a check over the back of the booth.

"Let's get the hell out of here," said Myron to O'Shea.

They crossed the street, where Myron called a friend, whom he instructed to take the check to the bank on which it was drawn at nine the next morning. He wanted to get it cashed before McCarey could change his mind and stop payment. For Myron, being an agent was no casual matter. He wanted his money and would hustle his clients for it if necessary. At the same time he was not money-hungry; he would lend it right back if a client needed it.

Myron must have felt keen satisfaction in 1936 when Carl Laemmle's Universal empire was sinking. Laemmle was forced to go to a bank for a loan, his collateral shaky. Myron, it seems, had become a director of the bank and one of its largest stockholders. "If you could just get Myron Selznick to put in a word for you," the bank president advised Laemmle. Laemmle preferred to borrow the money from former employee Irving Thalberg.

Myron weathered quarrels with clients and moguls, at one point bringing MGM to heel by threatening to set up independent companies for several of his stars. He dropped the plan when his terms were met. The idea later germinated again and burst into full flower in Hollywood after World War II. Late in his career he also thought up the package idea, selling star, story, and director as one big unit. It was one of the factors that increased costs and contributed to the breakup of the old studios.

"His work of vengeance changed the Hollywood climate," said writer Ben Hecht. "It doubled, tripled, and quadrupled the salaries of writers, actors and directors, myself among them. Myron making a deal with a studio head was a scene out of Robin Hood. He was not only dedicated to his task of bankrupting the studio but ready to back up his sales talk with fisticuffs, if the discussion was not to his liking."

Myron won most of his battles, but the cost was tremendous. Vengeance was a double-edged sword. It brought him great success, but in a sense it also destroyed him. David Selznick always kept a huge portrait of his father in his office; Myron kept it engraved in his heart. He played a tempestuous game and a compulsive one, in which reliance on the bottle was a necessity.

"One of the most colorful figures in the film industry died today," said *Variety* on March 23, 1944. At the early age of forty-five, Myron Selznick unexpectedly succumbed to portal thrombosis. He had prematurely burned himself out.

One measure of his extraordinary influence was the list of those attending the funeral services in Beverly Hills, officiated over by Rabbi Max Nussbaum. Louis B. Mayer was there with head bowed; and tall, erect Sam Goldwyn; and the mogul with the villain's moustache, Jack Warner; and Darryl Zanuck, with whom Myron had many times locked horns. They and others came to pay last respects to a man who had many times bruised their egos and ravaged their pocketbooks but whom they were forced to acknowledge as a peer.

The stars were there in numbers, from Ingrid Bergman to Myrna Loy to Loretta Young, from William Powell to Pat O'-Brien to Adolphe Menjou. Writers like Ben Hecht were there; directors like Ernst Lubitsch and Lewis Milestone and William Wellman.

They all listened to debonair William Powell read the eulogy Ben Hecht had written. Near the beginning it quoted Myron's mother, who was there to say good-bye: " 'He was a little boy who never grew up!' Oh, yes, we knew, admired, loved —sometimes quarreled with him, during the heat of battle— for we are volatile and impulsive in the arts. We loved him for his courage. We admired him for the quickest mind of anyone since the pioneer days of his great father, whose name he and his brother perpetuated with energy and honor. He was both brilliant and wise, as was his great and adventurous father before him. . . ."

Standing with the saddened Florence Selznick, her son David may well have thought back on his own career, on the path he chose to vindicate that bold fighter who was his father, to hit back at the men he was sure had ganged up on him. As a young man David decided very simply to make films so good that they would scare the wits out of them.

It was an audacious ambition for a twenty-one-year-old with only two modest efforts, the shorts on Firpo and Valentino, to his credit. For several years there was not even an opportunity to prove himself further, as door after door in Hollywood remained closed to the son of Lewis Selznick.

Persistence and self-confidence eventually paid off. In 1926 David Selznick walked through the gates of Metro-Goldwyn-Mayer in Culver City, hired on a two-week trial basis at $100 a week. Indirectly, his father was responsible. Years before in New York, L.J. had taken teen-age David along to a meeting with Nicholas Schenck of the Loew theater interests. At one point in the discussion when two divergent viewpoints were being presented, he asked his boy, "David, what do you think?" David's view coincided with Schenck's, much to the latter's amusement. If he could ever help him, he told the boy, he should feel free to call on him. The years passed, and David found Louis B. Mayer one of the people who opposed him in Hollywood, angrily determined that no son of a Selznick would enter his employ. Nick Schenck was now technically the boss of Mayer, for he was president of Loew's, MGM's parent company. When Schenck came to Hollywood on a visit, David reminded him of his long-ago offer of aid. Schenck came through.

David was put on as an assistant to Harry Rapf, the supervisor in charge of the B pictures at the studio. Rapf told Selznick that his job was to read scripts and make reports on them, that usually this job paid less than $100 a week.

"I'll do more for you than read scripts," said Selznick. "I'll help you fix them. I'll write titles. I'll do everything that has to be done on them."

So skilled was the new employee that within weeks Rapf doubled his salary and made the job permanent. Another month, and the salary jumped to $3,000 a week. Responsibilities likewise pyramided. Young David became Rapf's assistant on the Tim McCoy Westerns. Here he dazzled the management by making two pictures on the budget allotted for one. He explained to the puzzled Louis Mayer that he had gone on location with two scripts, two sets of stars, and one supporting cast. He had simply worked the supporting cast twice.

The cocksure Selznick was invited to sit in on meetings presided over by the brilliant young producer Irving Thalberg.

Soft-spoken Thalberg was about David's age, but his record already dazzled Hollywood. David spoke to him as a peer, and even went so far as to contradict him.

The occasion arose when Selznick was assigned to produce *White Shadows* on location in the South Seas. Thalberg gave him two directors, Robert Flaherty as a nature authority and W. S. Van Dyke to concentrate on human nature. At a commissary conference, Selznick argued that one director was enough; two would cause friction. When Thalberg quietly hewed to his decision, Selznick more loudly insisted on his viewpoint. Thalberg ended the discussion by walking out of the commissary as underlings in the vicinity held their breath.

"I want to talk to you, Irving," Selznick boldly accosted Thalberg in a corridor two days later. "I've got a great idea for Norma."

Thalberg was usually receptive to ideas for his wife, Norma Shearer, but not now. He told Selznick he was not accustomed to insubordination from his staff and asked for an apology. None was forthcoming. There was no way to reconcile the two young giants. Selznick was given his walking papers.

Incredibly, he now went to the lair of his father's nemesis, to Adolph Zukor at Paramount. He bearded the company's cultivated chief of production, Benjamin P. Schulberg, known to the trade as B.P. "You're the most arrogant young man I've ever known," said B.P., and promptly hired Selznick on a trial basis at $300 a week. The probation period was nearing its end when David realized he needed something spectacular in order to hang on. He found the company had set up contests to pick the titles of 17 projected films. He read the scripts, submitted titles under pseudonyms, and won all 17 contests.

Schulberg got the message. Over a period of three years he elevated Selznick in rank until he was second only to himself. For his part, David admired his superior, a man who loved good reading and all the extravagant pleasures of life even as he did. He was indeed somewhat in awe of him, saying, "Yes, B.P.," and, "Right away, B.P.," like the other lieutenants, rushing to hand the stylish Schulberg a sheaf of last-minute notes as he slipped into his cream-colored Rolls-Royce. Years later David gave Schulberg's son, Budd, his first film job as a junior writer at his own studio.

The experience with Paramount increasingly instilled in Selznick a desire to be first in command. He gambled and asked to get out of his contract.

The move infuriated Louis B. Mayer, a man whose furor seemed to reach higher levels than that of ordinary men, splattering everyone in the vicinity. Mayer's adrenalin had begun flowing four years earlier, when David had begun courting his youngest daughter, Irene. The son of a Selznick had met the darkly beautiful, aristocratic young lady at a New Year's party. Mayer was sorry that he had relaxed his strict rules and allowed her out until 1 A.M. He was even sorrier when the two began keeping company.

"Keep away from that schnook," he warned his daughter. "He'll be a bum just like his old man."

The advice went unheeded. Against Mayer's wishes, Irene married David Selznick in a quiet ceremony in April, 1930. Soon after, when David left Paramount, Mayer angrily demanded, "How dare you give up that contract, and you married to my daughter?"

Headstrong David left Paramount and within the year became a vice-president in charge of all production for RKO Radio. The years of apprenticeship and training were ending. The golden days were about to begin, the golden films to unreel.

Certainly there were still lessons to be learned. One of the most significant came from the picturization of *Our Betters*, from a play by Somerset Maugham. The British author's original story lashed out strongly against his homeland's reactionary aristocracy. As Selznick outlined his synopsis at a story conference, his director, George Cukor, appeared puzzled. The hard-hitting play had been turned into a comedy of manners, the insensitive heroine into a darling. Selznick had hired that bustling beldam, café society hostess Elsa Maxwell, as consultant on clothes for the film.

"Elsa, what do you think?" he asked.

"I think I'm going to be sick," said Elsa. "Why did you pay a lot of money for the play if you intended to cut the heart and guts out of Maugham's idea?"

"You can't have a big star like Connie Bennett play the part of a bitch," countered Selznick. "You've got to make her sympathetic."

The producer ruled the day but not the box office. The film flopped. Thereafter Selznick adhered as closely as possible to authors' originals when he transferred them to the screen.

The pressures of mounting a dozen films at once could make such fidelity a problem. Once Selznick handed director King Vidor, on loan from MGM, a copy of the stage play *Bird of Paradise* and told him he wanted him to do it. Vidor came back a week later and said he could not get beyond the first act. What did Selznick actually think of it? Selznick confessed he hadn't had time to read even the first act, let alone the second and third. He read scripts when he had to, often at the last minute.

Vidor lived across the street from Selznick at the time, and he noted with amusement the producer's unorthodox habits: breakfast in the afternoon, full-length films shown in the projection room after midnight, sleep while the rest of the world went to work.

Selznick threw out several properties already scheduled at RKO, including a Lili Damita film to be called *Chichi and Her People*. He chose Merian C. Cooper, whom he had known at Paramount, as his second in command. Cooper was the producer of the silent classics *Grass* and *Chang*. He had worked on a good many of director John Ford's films and had made an early color short, *La Cucaracha*, which won wide acclaim.

Among the Selznick regime's films for RKO were *The Animal Kingdom*, with Ann Harding, Leslie Howard, and Myrna Loy; the thriller *King Kong*, which Merian Cooper and Ernest B. Schoedsack guided home; an all-star-cast version of *Little Women*, again with Cooper as executive producer; Constance Bennett in *What Price Hollywood?* and *A Bill of Divorcement*, in which Katharine Hepburn made her movie debut fresh from a New York stage hit called *The Warrior's Husband*. One critic of that show took note of her clipped Philadelphia speech and manner and said her performance "ran the gamut of emotion from A to B." His sneer notwithstanding, young Miss Hepburn came West.

Hollywood memories are short and maddeningly muddled, to say nothing of downright contradictory. One often has several choices about episodes such as the arrival of the incomparable Kate. As writer Adela Rogers St. Johns recalls it, George Cukor wanted to do *A Bill of Divorcement*, which had made Katharine Cornell a great star on the New York stage. He wanted to make it with newcomer Hepburn, while Selznick was strongly in favor of Anita Louise. Late one night Cukor called Adela and insisted that she accompany him to the Selznick home in the beach community of Malibu, his purpose to soften him up to an acceptance of Hepburn.

"But I've never seen Katharine Hepburn. I don't know if she's such a splendid actress as you say," Adela protested.

"Don't you trust me?" asked the suave Cukor.

Adela capitulated. They drove to Malibu, woke Selznick out of a sound sleep, and walked him down the beach. Since he already knew Cukor's mood, he questioned Adela.

"Is this Hepburn really the best young actress around?"

"Oh, my, yes."

"Is she really terrific in *The Warrior's Husband?*"

"Oh, she is indeed."

After the groggy Selznick agreed to send for highly lauded Miss Hepburn, the conspirators returned home.

The scene switched to the studio, where Adela Rogers St. Johns, Selznick, and others sat at a commissary table waiting for Cukor to return from the railroad depot with his discovery. Cukor entered with a tall, gawky, plain-looking maid, all her clothes terrible and showing her to painful disadvantage.

"Mr. Selznick, this is Katharine Hepburn," said Cukor.

Selznick looked at the surprising apparition and turned to Cukor.

"You sonofabitch," he said, and stalked out of the room.

Still following the Adela Rogers St. Johns version, the producer fired Hepburn, Cukor, and everyone within earshot, though only verbally, for their contracts were binding.

As George Cukor remembers it, the arrival of Kate was a far different affair. For the female lead opposite John Barrymore in *A Bill of Divorcement,* two girls were tested: Jill Esmond, then married to Laurence Olivier, and Anita Louise. Both were good, but Cukor saw a test that someone had made of Hepburn. In it, she did a scene with Alan Campbell from *Holiday,* in which she had understudied. Cukor noticed her unique appeal, a blend of aristocratic and gamin qualities. She was strange. He'd never seen a girl quite like that.

He talked to Selznick about her and found him receptive. They made Hepburn an offer, which that shrewd bargainer negotiated until it was adjusted to her advantage. Since she was a rich society girl, she arrived in Hollywood in style, traveling in the company of her friends Flo Ziegfeld and Billie Burke. She had gone to much trouble to have a special dress made. If anything, she looked arty, with her auburn hair pulled tightly back over her head. A sliver had drifted into her eye on the train, however, causing it to tear, so that red-eyed Kate did not look at all like a movie type as she stepped onto the station platform.

She was a rather brash, garrulous, opinionated Bryn Mawr type, Cukor recalls, a far cry from today's extraordinary, warm, sensitive woman. As Cukor started remolding her, he cut her hair so that it fell, and immediately she looked like a movie queen, like the Hepburn audiences know. At first she objected strongly to the costumes designed for her.

"What makes you think you know anything about clothes?" Cukor demanded. "You're the Goddamnedest-looking girl I've ever seen. How would you possibly know anything about clothes?"

Cukor recalls that she was undeterred by any such attack. She had grown up one of a large family of children of highbrow parents. When the father was displeased with one at the dinner table, he gave the offender a healthy swat on the cheek, then calmly continued eating his dinner. The very first day on the set, John Barrymore winked at young Katharine. In him she saw the roguish Don Juan qualities of her father. She liked him instantly. Both were absolutely at home with each other.

Cukor and Selznick were enormously fond friends, with an almost chemical liking for one another. In fact, Cukor was often mistaken for the producer and the other way around. Cukor once told Florence Selznick that people were always saying he looked like David.

"I don't think so," David's mother said rather unhappily.

"Well, my mother doesn't like it either," Cukor comforted her.

Cukor's office at the studio was at the other end of a court from Selznick's. Thirty times a day during filming, he would send for the director, or trot to his office. Selznick's memo mania was still in its infancy. It was to grow to gargantuan proportions, sometimes productive, sometimes ill-advised, a form of self-indulgence. Later, too, there would be disagreements with Cukor and other directors.

For the moment there was dissatisfaction at RKO, where Selznick felt he did not have a free hand, that board chairman M. H. Aylesworth was encroaching on his terrain. Although he was offered financial inducements to remain, he resigned.

Amazingly, he returned to Metro-Goldwyn-Mayer at the strong urging of his father-in-law. Mayer was irresistibly attracted to talent in whatever form. Selznick's record was impressive. Furthermore, Mayer wanted someone to backstop Irving Thalberg, whose frail constitution tended to cause concern. This time Selznick was reluctant. He had become a good friend of Thalberg and wanted no friction. He was apprehensive of Mayer's looking over his shoulder. The father-in-law overrode these objections, telling Selznick he could choose his own stories and his own stars at $4,000 a week salary. Selznick accepted.

The immediate upshot was a violent argument between Thalberg and Mayer, and an initial coolness at the studio toward Selznick. Stars and studio personnel turned out not to be readily available. The big joke on the Culver City lot was: "The son-in-law also rises."

Selznick was forced to bring in some of his own staff to make his first picture. George Cukor directed a stunning cast—Marie Dressler, John Barrymore, Wallace Beery, Jean Harlow, Lionel Barrymore, Lee Tracy, Edmund Lowe, Billie Burke, Madge Evans, Jean Hersholt, Karen Morley, May Robson, Phillips Holmes, among others—in *Dinner at Eight,* adapted from the George Kaufman-Edna Ferber play.

The atmosphere changed rapidly after this auspicious beginning. Selznick took the book *Night Flight* and turned the rather grim aviation tale into an artistic success featuring Clark Gable, Robert Montgomery, and Helen Hayes. Wallace Beery scored a box office success in *Viva Villa.* Both Fred Astaire and Nelson Eddy made film debuts supporting Joan Crawford in *Dancing Lady.*

While looking for a youngster to play Clark Gable's kid brother in *Manhattan Melodrama,* Selznick spied twelve-year-old Mickey Rooney at a ping-pong tournament. The film launched the unemployed vaudevillian on his big-time career. It also teamed William Powell and Myrna Loy for the first time, turning the latter away from yellow peril roles and into a new career phase, giving Powell a new lease on his career at a time when he was considered washed up. *Manhattan Melodrama* became famous as the picture that caught John Dillinger. The notorious bandit quit his hiding place to see the film, in which a gangster goes to the chair. Dillinger was killed by police as he left the theater.

The Selznick treatment of important literary properties opened a new era. The usual process was to take a few key characters and situations and doctor them up with fresh material into a contemporary mix. In a memo the producer outlined his own point of view:

> The millions of people who have read the book and who worship it would very properly attack us violently for the desecrations which are indicated by this grafting but apart from

the feelings of these few million, I have never been able to understand why motion picture producers insist upon throwing away scenes of proven appeal to substitute things of their own creation. It is a form of ego which has drawn upon Hollywood the wrath of the world for many years. . . . Readers of a dearly loved book will forgive omissions if there is an obvious reason for them, but they will not forgive substitutions.

Selznick was also not afraid to make lengthy films. On this score he liked to cite Nick Schenck, who, when asked how long a film should be, replied, "How long is it good?"

After two highly successful years with MGM, Selznick determined to set up his own producing organization, in which he would have complete freedom, able at last to create pictures rather than supervise their making. This had been his idea on leaving RKO, but Louis Mayer had dissuaded him, well aware of the danger to the major studios if bright young men went off on their own. This time Mayer's cajolings were in vain.

Selznick International was formed in 1935 with David as president and millionaire John Hay ("Jock") Whitney as chairman of the board. David himself did not invest, but he owned a little more than half the company. Whitney put up one million dollars; other investors were David's brother Myron, Whitney's sister, Mrs. Jean Payson, bankers Robert Lehman and Dr. A. H. Giannini, Chicago taxicab magnate John Hertz, Irving and Norma Thalberg, and Cornelius V. Whitney. Space was rented in the old Pathé studio, where the main administration building with its white colonial front was often used as a set.

The new company's first picture was a version of Frances Hodgson Burnett's celebrated tale, *Little Lord Fauntleroy*. It starred Freddie Bartholomew, cost $560,000 to make, and swiftly grossed $1,700,000. Marlene Dietrich next starred in *The Garden of Allah,* an early Technicolor feature.

The use of color at this time was often somewhat gimmicky, a tacked-on attraction. One of the films that brought it to increased maturity was *A Star Is Born,* scripted in 1937 by

Dorothy Parker and Alan Campbell. The biggest moneymaker of the year, it gave double pleasure to the Whitneys, who were heavy investors in the Technicolor process. The film starred Fredric March and Janet Gaynor, whom it catapulted back to the top ranks after a period of decline at Twentieth Century-Fox—that studio's Darryl Zanuck had released her without a murmur and with a faint smile at Selznick's request.

A Star Is Born provided a vivid illustration of why David Selznick wanted to operate as an independent. The overhead on the film had been huge, so the tension was great the night of the studio preview. Dan O'Shea went to the preview with Selznick and was relieved to note that the audience was uniformly enthusiastic. Nonetheless, Selznick opened the picture up and did 70,000 dollars' worth of retakes, not for box office but due to his own sense of what was artistically fitting and proper. Only a rare studio head would have sat still for such extravagance.

A sad footnote to the film concerns John Barrymore. Selznick had a great reverence for the stage, reflected in his determination to capture on celluloid the great Maude Adams, then teaching at Stevens College; in his bringing stage directors like George Cukor to work for him in Hollywood; and in his friendship and admiration for Ethel, Lionel, and John Barrymore. He engaged John for *A Star Is Born,* only to hear that the failing matinee idol could no longer remember his lines.

"If we use him, we'll have to blackboard him," said the director, referring to a scheme whereby the actor reads his lines from a blackboard outside the camera's range.

"We can do it that way. Let's try it," said Selznick.

When even this method turned out to be hopeless, there was nothing left to do but to tell Barrymore.

"I can't tell him. You tell him," said Selznick to O'Shea.

O'Shea called the once great actor into his office and relayed the fateful news. For fully five minutes Barrymore sat in dazed silence; finally he rose and left without being able to utter a word.

An expensive production of Alexander Dumas' *The Prisoner of Zenda* starred Ronald Colman, David Niven, and Madeleine

Carroll. The first special preview, in Huntington Park, was un-
nerving. The audience, finding the action dull, sat on its hands.
Selznick devised a completely new opening, put Max Steiner,
whom he had met while at RKO, to working up an interesting
score, and made other changes. The revised film produced a
favorable response.

   The Adventures of Tom Sawyer introduced young Tommy
Kelly, the product of a nationwide talent search, as the hero.
Intermezzo introduced the American public to Swedish actress
Ingrid Bergman. The film also starred Leslie Howard. Like the
other Selznick pictures, it made money. Year after year, exhibi-
tors voted David the number one producer of box office successes.
No company dividends were paid, however; profits were turned
back into production.

   The path to success was frequently a frantic curlicue. After
Selznick hired Ben Hecht to prepare a script, the writer's agent
came shamefacedly to Dan O'Shea; he had thought Hecht was
to work exclusively for the studio, but he had learned he was
turning out material for others. Selznick was not dismayed.
He knew that Hecht filtered his writing chores through secretaries and assistants, but he thought his own demanding habits
would engulf the writer in spite of himself.

   After several weeks of presumed effort, Hecht turned up with
his results. All he had was an opening sentence—it seemed there
was a pleasure yacht entering one end of the Panama Canal.
All the urgent urging in the land could not seem to move the
boat any farther along. To get Hecht away from his other projects, Selznick coaxed him into going to New York to work on
the script. After a long interval, a hopeless first draft arrived. A
second version was worse.

   It was for this script that Selznick had hired two of his
brother Myron's clients, Carole Lombard and Fredric March,
and the crisis over the extensions had occurred.

   In desperation, Selznick sent Bobby Keon, his girl stenog-
rapher at story meetings, to New York to hustle Ben. Meanwhile, Val Lewton of the story department had come across a

magazine story by James Street. He told Selznick. Selznick liked the idea and ordered the story to be read to Bobby Keon on the telephone so that she could transcribe it for Hecht. Hecht liked it and wrote his first version of the screenplay while making the five-day journey back to Los Angeles on the Chief. The end product was that captivating comedy *Nothing Sacred,* with March and Lombard, directed by William Wellman.

The most ambitious project of all came, of course, with *Gone with the Wind.* The gambler's instinct prevailed at the very outset. In the Depression year of 1936, Selznick bought the as yet unpublished novel by Margaret Mitchell for $50,000, a sum that today seems trivial but which was at the time the highest price ever paid for a first novel. Friends and advisers warned against the purchase. Stories on the Old South, and particularly the Civil War, were considered taboo, box office bane. The author had labored over the original writing from 1926 to 1929, then had spent six more years in checking, rewriting, and developing scenes, so that the finished novel, as the Macmillan publishing company was bringing it to press, was a whopping 1,037 pages. The cost of producing a work of this scope would inevitably be staggering.

Selznick made the plunge. His Eastern story editor, Kay Brown, had set the wheels in motion. She read the book in proof, then fired off an exuberant telegram to her boss in Hollywood. His reading of the 150-page digest of the novel convinced him her judgment was sound. He made his offer. Other producers were in the running. At RKO, story editor Lillie Messinger recommended the novel to production chief Pandro Berman. The ever fragile economic fortunes of RKO could not countenance the ambitious project. A copy of the manuscript was spirited into the hands of studio star Katharine Hepburn, who developed an instant hunger to play Scarlett O'Hara, but still to no avail. For a time, Jack Warner had an option on the film rights. His tempestuous leading lady, Bette Davis, nosed out the property and felt in her bones that she must play Scarlett. Bette had fled to London, however, over a contract dispute.

Warner pursued her to the British capital and while there allowed his option to drop. At the last minute, director-producer Mervyn Le Roy entered the lists with a firm offer of $55,000.

Selznick was informed. Again he gambled, refusing to counterbid, hoping that the prestige of his past successes, *Dinner at Eight, Little Women, David Copperfield,* and others, would win him the prize. Macmillan tossed the decision into the lap of the author. Margaret Mitchell decided to take the Selznick offer. Contracts were signed on July 30, 1936.

A story that still makes the rounds in Hollywood adds an interesting footnote. It tells of a third producer, watching with dismay as the then high sums of $50,000 and $55,000 were sent out to snare an unpublished first novel. The producer asked his colleagues to meet with him. Around the conference table he voiced his concern. "If we keep bidding against each other, prices will go wild. Let's toss for it." As the story goes, David Selznick, who already had the inside track, won the toss. Gambler's luck.

Meanwhile, the book had taken off like a rocket. Fifty thousand copies were sold on publication day. Multiple printings rolled off the presses in the following months, spiraling the book onto the best-seller lists and into a babble of foreign editions.

The gambler had taken a hand; perhaps two; the showman was dealing the next. The very weekend of his closing for the rights, Selznick put publicist extraordinaire Russell Birdwell, a former crack Hearst reporter, into orbit, his first assignment to plant a rumor that Clark Gable was to play Rhett Butler. Gable, "the King," was in fact his instinctive and immediate first choice. As the book built up its mammoth audience, the public made it unanimous. A flood of mail descended on the production office, demanding that Gable play Rhett; in poll after poll he led all the rest. The only problem now was getting him, a problem accentuated by the fact that the box office favorite was under long-term contract to Metro-Goldwyn-Mayer, a fiefdom ruled by Louis B. Mayer. Selznick had married Mayer's daughter, Irene, against Mayer's wishes. He had also worked for Mayer's studio, against his wishes, and left to produce independently, once again against Mayer's wishes.

Gable, moreover, was at the height of his game. Born in Cadiz, Ohio, Gable, a solid youth with obtrusive cauliflower ears, was a stock trouper before descending on Hollywood in 1924. Tests, rejections, and bit parts were his lot until Lionel Barrymore got him a key role in *A Free Soul,* with Norma Shearer, in 1930. His progress thereafter was rapid. In 1934, on loan-out to Columbia, he won an Academy Award for *It Happened One Night,* which also garnered an Oscar for Claudette Colbert. In 1935 he scored a great success in *Mutiny on the Bounty.*

It was predictable that Mayer would drive a hard bargain with his son-in-law for the services of this hottest of properties. He did. Gable would be made available—but not for two years, a costly delay. MGM would cosponsor the entire production, contributing $1,250,000 to the film's cost, budgeted at $2,500,000. In return, exclusive distribution rights would go to MGM's parent corporation, Loew's, and MGM would get 50 percent ownership of the picture for seven years, and a quarter thereafter.

Of course, if Selznick made the picture at MGM, said Mayer, under his aegis, he could offer him far more favorable terms. Selznick chose to make it completely independently. As the film racked up its record grosses, it was estimated that the move cost Selznick at least $25 million. He never regretted it. His father had taught him a thing or two about money. It was a toy, a tool, a plaything, an instrument to do things with.

Still one hitch remained—Gable did not want to play the role. He felt that millions of readers would have a preconceived image of the dashing Civil War profiteer and he could never live up to their ideal. No great judge of story, Gable had similarly protested against his roles in *It Happened One Night* and *Mutiny on the Bounty.* Mayer convinced him that he must play Rhett Butler. He gave him a bonus of $100,000 on signing, but thereafter maintained his regular salary despite the immensely favorable terms MGM was able to get because of Gable.

At one point, while bargaining with Mayer, Selznick had a wayward thought. He went to Jack Warner and asked him to loan him Bette Davis and Errol Flynn as a costarring package for the film. Warner was willing. Bette Davis was not. Fond as she was of Flynn, she was appalled at the thought of someone with his limited acting ability in the exacting role of Rhett Butler. With her refusal went her last chance to play Scarlett.

The negotiations with Warner did bear other fruit. For supporting roles, Selznick wanted to borrow Leslie Howard and Olivia de Havilland. Warner came across with the wistful, sensitive-faced Howard, but he was reluctant to give up de Havilland. He had made the doe-eyed Livvy into a star, and her presence on the lot reminded him of that accomplishment. Behind Livvy's soft brown eyes, however, was a steel-trap determination. She wanted the role of Melanie and went out to get it. Using her friendship with Warner's wife as a wedge, she induced her to win Jack over to the deal. Leslie Howard and Olivia de Havilland were in due course added to the cast.

The extraordinary sale of the novel and the skillful Birdwell publicity binge made Selznick's every move a news story. The public itself seemed to turn producer, assuming responsibility for the creation of the film. Letters poured in with suggestions for casting various roles. Warnings were issued that the book must not be tampered with. Greatest concern of all focused on the Selznick choice for the female lead—who would play the fiery, rebellious Scarlett O'Hara?

As word spread that Bette Davis was up for the part, or Tallulah Bankhead, or Norma Shearer, or Katharine Hepburn, the public divided into armed camps. When another series of news leaks talked of Selznick's interest in Paulette Goddard, and Frances Dee, and the lesser-known Margaret Tallichet, a thousand pens began furiously scribbling their reactions. For a time, Miriam Hopkins followers were leading the pack. If they nodded for a moment, the Margaret Sullavan camp took the reins. Carole Lombard came into contention. Even Lucille Ball was asked to test for the role. "Me play Scarlett O'Hara? Are you kidding?" she said in bowing out. Newspapers conducted polls;

clubs had violent arguments and sent in rival sheets of nominating signatures. So engrossed was the nation in the choice that when Norma Shearer declared her noncandidacy the august New York *Times* ran an editorial regretting her decision.

Selznick took his cue from the heat of the contending camps. Rather than offend one large segment of the public, he would cast an unknown in the role. And to find her, he would use one of Hollywood's tried and true inventions, a nationwide talent search. Across the land, from under haystacks and from behind department store counters, he would seek out his Scarlett. The ensuing campaign was dished up to the public with a hoopla that would have made even Phineas T. Barnum envious.

Russell Birdwell organized his army. He deployed talent developers Oscar Serlin, Maxwell Arnow, and Charles Morrison to contact 150 far-flung talent scouts. Their job was to search for girls, girls, girls. Each time they found one that seemed a likely prospect to play Scarlett, there were interviews, sometimes screen tests, and always news stories, local or national. A New York hat model named Edythe Marriner was flown out to Hollywood and tested. She did not get the part but decided to stay on and try her luck. She gained fame as Susan Hayward. Others failed to get the coveted role but used the experience as a stepping-stone to film careers. The number of girls interviewed grew and grew. Among them all, David Selznick could not find his Scarlett.

He was making progress on the other fronts, displaying at once his fierce attention to detail and his extravagant passion for excellence. There were constant conferences with Lyle Wheeler, head of his art department, and with production designer William Cameron Menzies, with Walter Plunkett, costume designer, and with Joseph Platt, one of the nation's foremost industrial designers, whom he called in to create the film's interiors. With a flare for color and costume, Selznick supervised each facet, keenly aware of just how a particular silk or velvet would shoot.

For more than a year he worked with writer Sidney Howard on the script. Other writers were brought in at different stages, among them Jo Swerling, Oliver H. P. Garrett, Ben Hecht, John Van Druten, Michael Foster, and John Balderston; even F. Scott Fitzgerald embarked on his troubled flirtation with Hollywood. Everyone had a hand at bringing the unwieldy novel into manageable focus, at balancing the love story and the epic historical passages. Concessions also had to be made to the National Association for the Advancement of Colored People, which objected to the novel's depiction of the Negro and threatened to picket the film.

As his director, Selznick chose George Cukor, who had triumphed on the Broadway stage and with his own stock company in Rochester before coming to films. The two had worked well together on *A Bill of Divorcement, Dinner at Eight,* and other pictures.

Casting proceeded apace. Hattie MacDaniel won the role of the Negro mammy, Butterfly McQueen that of the Negro maid. Thomas Mitchell and Jane Darwell were signed, along with Victor Jory, Laura Hope Crews, Harry Davenport, Lillian Kemble Cooper, Ward Bond, Ona Munson, Evelyn Keyes, and Ann Rutherford.

Only Scarlett O'Hara was still missing. Over a two-year period an astonishing 1,400 girls were interviewed. Close to 400 were given readings. Sixty were extensively tested, in color and in black and white. None qualified for the role.

"Only 74 more days, until *Gone with the Wind* goes before the cameras," wrote New York *Times'* film critic Bosley Crowther in late October, 1938. "On or before December 7, 1938, the world will know Scarlett."

"I still hope to give the American public a new girl," said Selznick, "a girl whom they won't identify with a lot of other roles."

Actually, he was despairing of finding an unknown. The current wisecrack was that Shirley Temple would play Scarlett from a wheelchair if there were many more delays.

An offer of a million dollars for the film rights gave Selznick a chance to get off the hook. He refused it. To gain time, he set up a three-week shooting schedule of scenes that did not involve Scarlett. The role was still not cast when George Cukor set the cameras rolling on December 15, 1938. The scene was the burning of Atlanta, which occurred well along in the book. Acres of old sets were put to the flame to simulate that holocaust—facades and props that had served for such films as *King Kong* and *The Garden of Allah*. The press was not alerted, but reporters drawn to the scene found 40 telephones set up to let them contact their city editors.

David Selznick was concerned because his mother, Florence, and his agent brother, Myron, had not arrived for the spectacle. As the flames rose in the night sky, he felt a tug at his arm. It was Myron. His mother was with him, along with one of his clients, Laurence Olivier, and a young girl.

"I want you to meet Scarlett O'Hara," he said, presenting the girl. Her name, he said, was Vivien Leigh, and she was fast becoming known in her native England. More interested in explaining the action to his mother, David paid scant attention.

"She has the sixteen-inch waist, the green eyes, and the experience to play Scarlett," Myron continued. "She isn't even a client of mine, but I know she's the right one for the picture."

David Selznick asked George Cukor to test the pert-nosed Vivien. When he saw the result, he knew his long search was over. At a cost of $92,000 the studio had shot 149,000 feet of black and white film, and $13,000 in Technicolor, the most extensive testing in the records. It was worth it to find the right Scarlett.

Born in Darjeeling, India, of a French father and an Irish mother, Vivien Leigh had attended London's public schools, a French convent in Italy, and finishing schools in Bavaria and Paris. She had studied drama in London, won stage roles, and then appeared in films. Her reputation in England was beginning to grow, but now it was to take an almighty worldwide leap.

"That it was a great role for any actress was obvious, yet I can truthfully say that I looked on Mr. Selznick's request that I take a test for Scarlett as something of a joke," she explained after being chosen. "There were dozens of girls tested, and I did not seriously consider that I might play the part."

The selection was no joke to Selznick and his publicist. Their campaign was designed to exploit to the full the finding of an unknown for Scarlett and at the same time to retain an element of mystery. While the name of Vivien Leigh was trumpeted to all corners, photos were deliberately withheld. By special arrangement, one important editor was allowed to pirate the first prints of the fledgling star, and in consequence these were given the widest circulation. Meanwhile, even as shooting began, on January 26, 1939, Selznick engaged Willa Price, an expert on Southern dialects, and Susan Myrick, known as the Emily Post of the South, to coach his Scarlett. Her role was to be extremely demanding, 22 weeks of shooting with only four days off; a splendid wardrobe involved 40 costume changes.

During those weeks, the work habits of David Selznick became legendary, his artistic acumen a byword. His pace was so mercurial and demanding that the Hollywood saying was Selznick eats directors, writers, and secretaries. Energy was a keynote. Although he engaged topflight talent in every area, he himself supervised every facet, often going for two and three days without sleeping at all. He approved each line of script. His usual word to a writer after a conference was that he liked what was there but felt that the man could do even better. When one writer pinned him down and asked for specifics, he confessed he had not read the passage at all. Usually writers who argued with him later saw method in his apparent madness. For madcap madness would appear at times, much in the manner of the moguls of old, men like Carl Laemmle or his own father. Under great pressure, David was capable of postponing an important story conference to grant an interview to a persistent but obscure reporter.

A large broad-shouldered man—six feet one and close to 200 pounds—Selznick moved quickly, acted impulsively, and spoke with a rapid, staccato beat. He supplemented an ever proliferating series of conferences on *Gone with the Wind* with another technique which he made his specialty—the written memorandum. To two secretaries who operated in relays he dictated short memos and long memos and medium-sized memos. Before the end of the film, the exhausted amanuenses had transcribed a staggering one and a half million words. Messengers would deliver these droppings from the restless mind of the producer at whatever hour they were produced, often in the middle of the night. A rebellion by the cast finally produced a nine o'clock curfew on delivery. One single memo to Vivien Leigh was so lengthy it weighed close to a pound. The peppery actress took ten days to reply to it point by point, much to Selznick's chagrin. He hated to *read* memos!

A crucial decision was taken after only three weeks of filming when Selznick removed his director, George Cukor. Various accounts exist of the reasoning behind the move. One version has it that Selznick was deeply impressed with Cukor's handling of interior scenes but felt the director was not grasping the epic magnitude of the picture, and the action was not as sweeping as he thought it should be. Sources close to the situation recalled a specific instance which seemed to cause friction. Selznick apparently believed that in the scene in which Leslie Howard walked down the mansion staircase to meet the infatuated Scarlett, Howard should give some indication of fear and apprehension. Cukor did not share this interpretation. Most current was the view that Clark Gable provoked the actual break, that from the beginning he felt Cukor was a woman's director who would throw key scenes to Scarlett and that actual filming confirmed his suspicions. One Hollywood source recalls a certain antagonism that developed between Cukor and Gable even before they were both engaged for the film. At a truth game, Cukor was asked to give his evaluation of a certain figure about town. Backed into a corner, he expressed his honest opinion, which was unfavorable. He was unaware that the person in question was one of Gable's closest friends. Today, Cukor says he does not recall the precise circumstances of his dismissal from *Gone with the Wind*. He only remembers being summoned to the Selznick home in Malibu, where the producer's wife, Irene, greeted him with tears in her eyes. Selznick spoke to him alone, telling him that he must make the picture his own way, for better or worse, and that he was out. There was no rancor on either side. In retrospect, Cukor believes that for Selznick the film marked an important change in his method, that he was at this time entering fully upon his capacities as a triple-threat man, a writer-director-producer. He wanted to be there even during rehearsals, an unorthodox procedure for a producer, who habitually does not come into the picture until he sees the rushes. Cukor hated it, felt as if he were being clocked. He was used to working with Selznick as a producer, but not in this expanded role.

Gable's favorite director, Victor Fleming, took the helm. He was fresh from such triumphs as *Captains Courageous,* whose male cast was headed by Lionel Barrymore, Spencer Tracy, Mickey Rooney, and Freddie Bartholomew, and *Test Pilot,* starring Tracy and Gable. It was now Vivien Leigh's turn to be upset. Her quarrels with Fleming often left him in a rage and her in tears. When Selznick offered the new director a percentage of the profits if he would waive part of his salary, Fleming laughed a bitter laugh.

"Do you think I'm a damn fool, David?" he asked. "This picture is going to be the big white elephant of all time."

More than one observer agreed with Fleming. Delays, arguments, and revisions plagued *Gone with the Wind.* One evening a weary Vivien Leigh called George Cukor and said, "I was a bitch today. The scene wasn't going well at all, and finally I said, 'For Christ's sake, let's go down and see the tests George made.'" For a time Fleming took to his bed. Director Sam Wood temporarily took his place.

Together the three directors shot 474,538 feet of film, enough to run for 88 hours. To reconstruct the city of Atlanta, Selznick had ordered the largest set ever built in Hollywood, with more than 50 full-size buildings and 7,000 feet of streets. He used 1,100 horses, nearly 400 other animals, and 2,400 extras. The film's costs soared far over the budgeted figure, winding up just under 4 million. Only *Ben Hur* and the Howard Hughes production of *Hell's Angels* ran higher. To gain added financing from MGM, that studio's share of profits was escalated.

Victor Fleming made the last shot on November 11, 1939. Of the mammoth footage, 16,000 feet were printed. At the end of his colossal editing chore, Selznick wound up with 20,300 feet of film with a running time of 3 hours and 45 minutes. Only a man with his superb storyteller's sense could have done as well. To break up the lengthy epic, Selznick decided on a ten-minute intermission.

One last bit of salesmanship was necessary before the tireless producer could unveil his product to the public. From the Hays office came word that the final scene—Clark Gable's telling farewell speech to Scarlett, "Frankly, my dear, I don't give a damn"—would have to be censored. Selznick flew to New York. In a four-hour session he convinced Will Hays that the speech was completely in character and that diluting it to "I don't give a darn" would destroy its impact.

Finally, on December 15, 1939, *Gone with the Wind* had its world premiere at the Grand Theatre in Atlanta. The city had experienced no such excitement since Sherman marched into the city in 1864. Governor Rivers declared the day an official holiday. Mayor Hartsfield proclaimed a three-day festival, decking Atlanta in bunting, calling on the city's men to sport sideburns or goatees and to wear beaver hats and tight-fitting pants, and asking the women to forgo rouge and parade in hoop skirts and pantaloons.

Southern society sponsored the premiere, deciding whom to invite, presiding over a mad scramble for tickets to the theater —which seated only 2,500—and the gala *Gone with the Wind* ball afterward. Eight governors attended the ceremonies, but the crowds which lined the city's streets for seven miles had eyes only for the film's cast, headed by Vivien Leigh and Clark Gable. As the band blasted out "Dixie," the radiant Vivien remarked, "How sweet of them to play the theme song of our picture."

Everyone paid $10 for tickets, including the governors and

the critics. Perhaps the move had its psychological effect, for the critics proceeded to shower accolade after accolade on the picture, giving it a momentum which made it certain that the costly investment would pay off sooner than even the optimistic had expected.

At the Academy Awards ceremonies the following spring, the film walked off with extraordinary honors, winning a record ten, including those for best picture, art direction, film editing, and color cinematography. An award went to the director of credit, Victor Fleming, and to the only writer given credit for the script, Sidney Howard, who died in a tragic accident without ever seeing the film. Vivien Leigh won an Oscar for best actress, as did Hattie MacDaniel for best supporting actress. It was the first such award ever to go to a Negro.

The guessing game in Hollywood was what Selznick would do to follow up his prodigious success. The answer came when Kay Brown told him to buy Daphne Du Maurier's romantic novel *Rebecca*. Others cautioned him against the purchase, viewing the theme as too subjective for his particular sweeping talent. Selznick was forced to a decision when Kay Brown told him he would lose out to Walter Wanger if he did not act. With the impulsive speed he inherited from Lewis Selznick, David told her to close for the novel.

Myron Selznick had found Scarlett O'Hara for David in the person of Vivien Leigh. For *Rebecca* he provided her fiancé, the mesmerically gifted Laurence Olivier. He also brought Alfred Hitchcock over from England, where he was well known for his work as a writer, art director, and director. Myron had made his acquaintance in the 1920's when he bought several films involving Hitchcock for the Select company.

The cherub-faced, potbellied director worked very carefully from a minutely detailed shooting script. The method puzzled Selznick, who was used to a vastly different method of operation. He would have the picture shot completely by the director, with no retakes, since he never knew which scenes would be telescoped or dropped completely if the film ran too long. Why retake a scene which was possibly not to be in the final cut at all? Why retake a scene which might have to be vastly elaborated later? Selznick once said of a certain MGM producer: "He's very good with a finished picture." He meant he was good at elaborating the director's product. That was Selznick's forte, to go over the finished film and open it up, having scenes completely rewritten and reshot, expanding, cutting, editing with a vengeance.

Selznick liked to come down to the set while Hitchcock was shooting and whisper suggestions into his ear like an *eminence grise*. But so elaborate was the Hitchcock preparation that little could be changed. When he showed Selznick the final version for editing, that frustrated man said, "I don't know what to make of this damn jigsaw puzzle." In actuality, all the editing involved was clipping the numbers off the various takes and letting the film run as made. *Rebecca* won an Academy Award as the best picture of 1940, the second successive winner for Selznick. It greatly furthered Olivier's career and made an important star of Joan Fontaine.

Today Alfred Hitchcock says that Selznick never sent him a memo during *Rebecca*. The temptation to capitalize on legend is very strong, however, and on occasion Hitchcock has succumbed to it. When Selznick received the Milestone Award of the Screen Producers Guild, Hitchcock spoke briefly. He said, "When I came to America twenty-five years ago to direct *Rebecca*, David Selznick sent me a memorandum." Pause. "I've just finished reading it." Laughter and another pause. "I think I may make it into a motion picture." More laughter. "I plan to call it *The Longest Story Ever Told*." Even at the time of *Rebecca*, stories circulated that the Selznick memos about the film were so long that Hitchcock planned to film the memos rather than the script. The old rumor thus came home to roost —still false.

Hitchcock went on to make other films for Selznick. He received memos in ample numbers and feels that David used them to clear his own mind as much as to communicate with others.

While many of the moguls floundered financially during the

depressed thirties, Selznick never failed to make money and to do so while winning critical acclaim as well. It was what he had set out to do in tribute to his father. At the end of the decade, with the foreign market withering away under the impact of war, Selznick International voted to liquidate.

David Selznick's life style was in many ways patterned after that of his father, another form of tribute. He was one of the mainstays of the Clover Club, a favorite Hollywood gambling hideaway. One evening he lost $50,000 and calmly wrote out a check. When the manager demanded cash, David phoned his wife, Irene. She in turn called her father. Mayer was drawing closer to David as the years went by. He awakened the managers of all the theaters in the environs who rented MGM pictures, prevailing upon them to bring their night's receipts to the Clover Club. By the time they had made their deposits, the restless David had lost an additional $10,000 at the roulette table.

On one occasion, Adela Rogers St. Johns found herself sitting between David and Irene as they returned from the Dunes, a gambling house across the Mexican border run by a crony of mobster Bugs Moran. David had dropped $27,000 at the crap table, at a time when his personal finances were already in a perilous position. His studio at the time was RKO, also on the thin edge. Irene brought it to his attention.

"We haven't got a dime. We're broke," she began. "The studio hasn't got a dime. The studio is broke. We haven't got enough money to buy a cup of coffee, and you drop twenty-seven thousand dollars at the gambling table."

The challenge aroused David's ire.

"Never talk to me like that. When you married me you knew that I was a gambler," he countered. "I'm gambling right now as a film maker, and it's my gambling instinct that's going to help me make some of the greatest pictures this country will ever see. I'm a gambler; it's part of me. It's part of my work at the studio, and I can't turn it off at the end of the day. We'll have to take the twenty-seven-thousand-dollar losses and lump them."

For the rest of the trip there was silence, for Irene and David had said all they had to say on the subject. Adela Rogers St. Johns looked straight ahead at the road.

Dan O'Shea feels that David was not really a good gambler when it came to poker. In a poker game, one should never let the odds get higher against him than they are inherently in the game; he should try to minimize the odds against himself. David would not do this. He was a reckless gambler. In the year that Harry Truman ran against Tom Dewey, the latter looked like a sure winner. One of Selznick's publicity men, however, told him he had this odd feeling that Truman was going to win.

"I'll give you a thousand to one," said the astonished Selznick.

"I'll take ten dollars of it," said the publicity man.

Truman won.

"You owe me ten grand," said the hireling the next morning.

"I know it," said Selznick as he wrote out a check for $10,000 on the spot.

Irene Selznick came to understand her husband's complex explosive nature and to play a great stabilizing role in his life. For a time, these two expansive natures grew together. Irene, the daughter of a very domineering man, was at first quiet and self-effacing. If they saw a play together and David asked her if she liked it, she would say yes or no and leave it at that, deferring to his opinion.

"For Christ's sake," he demanded one day after they had viewed the daily rushes of a film, "don't you have any mind of your own?"

She was startled by the question and began to express herself. He began to rely on her keen mind, on her theatrical instinct, to draw her into his world. When he despaired of ever bringing *Gone with the Wind* to fruition, she reinforced his flagging drive.

Home movies cast a revealing light on the marriage. David is seen bringing Irene out of herself, and the films show an increasing flood of love as these two strong natures devoured one another with affection.

Two children were born to the pair. The first, a boy, was named Lewis Jeffrey after David's father. The second, again a boy, was called Daniel Mayer in recognition of Irene's father. Mayer had always wanted sons himself, and he became very fond of his grandsons. Irene watched his moods, the pressures at the studio, and brought the boys to him when things were relatively calm.

She protected the boys from their father as well as the grandfather, bringing them up in normal fashion, with no limousines and no $1,000-a-week allowance. Indeed, when their allowance was determined, she asked each one to itemize his needs, down to the penny. The weekly figures that resulted were specific and odd. Both went to El Rodeo, a public grammar school in Beverly Hills. Jeff went on to the progressive Cambridge School in Weston, Massachusetts, then to Deerfield, and to Yale, where he became a dropout at the end of his freshman year. Danny went on to Dalton School in New York, then the Putney School in Vermont, before transferring to the Quaker George School in Bucks County, being graduated from that institution.

Irene's role in their upbringing was partly to play the role of the devil's advocate, to force them to clarify and test their ideas. When Danny was debating which college to attend, she would say, "You tell me what the advantages of Harvard are, and I'll take the negative." David communicated his tremendous energy and vicarious enjoyment of life. When Danny did register at Harvard, the father looked over the catalog and checked the courses he thought Danny should be interested in for his first term. Danny was dumbfounded to see check marks next to 65 courses, for many of which he did not even have the prerequisites. School regulations permitted him to register for four.

The family experienced its troubles. As Irene felt her own strength, she inevitably became more assertive; she was after all the daughter of Louis B. Mayer. At times David would come home tired from the studio and begin shedding clothes to make himself comfortable. Irene would tell him to pick them up and prepare himself for the guests who were due to arrive.

Certainly a man as obsessive as David Selznick could not have been easy to live with. There were his erratic work habits, his day which might extend from three or five in the afternoon to the middle of the night, or go on for 72 hours without stopping. Once when he said he was tired, Dan O'Shea said that was only normal after such a stretch. "That's the trouble. I don't want to be normal," said Selznick. "Who wants to be normal?"

David had a temper and could be violent. He could scream and yell, and his lips could turn white with compressed anger. And he could fight when the spirit or the spirits moved him. Once he and Myron got into a drunken fistfight with their friends writers Ben Hecht and Charles MacArthur. The brawl broke up when the nearsighted David took off his heavy-lensed glasses and in the resulting myopia charged brother Myron.

David could be quickly generous. When his studio vice-president, Henry Ginsberg, lopped people off the payroll, David would hire them back one by one. When he heard that his friend Charley Koerner was dying of leukemia, he studied the disease and checked doctors around the world for their opinions. When another friend was dying of pneumonia, he ordered a rare serum flown in from halfway around the world. The circumstance later was incorporated into an emotional scene in a film called *Made for Each Other*.

Like many people used to money, Selznick seldom carried any on his person, and he was often reduced to borrowing 15 cents from an employee so he could buy cigarettes. One evening he was one of a party of four having cocktails in a hotel room in New York. As they prepared to go to dinner, they found no one was carrying cash or a credit card. Selznick called to ask the management for $1,000 in cash. When it arrived, the four well-to-do people gleefully counted and fingered it. They were not used to actually handling bills.

Selznick's demanding ways with associates sometimes drew retorts. One set of players was so exasperated by him that they decided on a practical joke. They were aware that a ritual at the Selznick household was David's awakening ceremony. He would push open the great glass doors that led out to the swimming pool, lumber out to the water, and dive in as his first activity of the day. The conspirators bought case after case of Knox Gelatin, insinuated themselves into the grounds, and during the night poured the colorless gelatin into the pool. The next day they hid behind shrubs and bushes and waited to see the result of the maneuver. They were disappointed. The night had been warm, and the gelatin did not really jell, turning instead to a stringy mass which slowed the unsuspicious Selznick down considerably but not totally. A gardener was at hand to help pull him out of the goo.

The most inveterate jokester of them all, Carole Lombard, exempted no one from her pranks. While working for Selznick on *Nothing Sacred,* she and her costar, Fredric March, found a red fire engine on the lot and spent their lunch hour racing it around the studio, siren screaming. One day an exasperated Carole induced studio technicians to put director William Wellman into a straightjacket while she tried to win a point. To another director, Norman Taurog, she sent a 200-pound bear as a birthday present, seeing to it that the animal was delivered at seven in the morning. Taurog sent the bear to a local zoo with instructions to forward feeding bills to the actress. At a social gathering where the hostess decreed all-white dress, the comely Carole arrived swathed in white bandages and brought in on a white-sheeted stretcher carried by white-uniformed attendants. When Russell Birdwell coaxed city councilmen into making Carole mayor for the day, she launched her reign by declaring an official holiday. David Selznick arrived at his studio to find a lone watchman guarding the empty streets.

Another practical joke amused David not at all. In the forties he made a film of Robert Nathan's novel, *A Portrait of Jennie,* starring Jennifer Jones. He commissioned an artist to paint an oil of Jennifer, then became so fond of the portrait that he would not use it in the film. Instead he had it copied. The original went into his dining room, where it hung facing him and where he often praised its merits to guests. At the conclusion of *Portrait of Jennie,* several of his associates took the copy, painted a beard on it, and smuggled it into the house, replacing the original with it. At the elaborate dinner celebrating the picture's end, Selznick entered the dining room. He saw the defaced portrait, was horrified, and talked of firing everyone who had anything to do with it. Only then was the substitution explained to him. He made sure by peering closely at it before relaxing somewhat.

Jennifer Jones was never a laughing matter to David Selznick. He was rumored to have carried on romances with a number of women, with Nancy Kelly and Joan Fontaine among others, but his passionate involvement with the shy, sensitive Jennifer became the final obsession of his obsessive life. It was, however, only one of the factors that contributed to the breakup of his marriage to Irene. They separated in 1944, with Irene heading for New York and a brilliant career of her own as the producer of Tennessee Williams' *A Streetcar Named Desire* and other plays. They were not divorced until 1949 when Irene confided to a friend, "The confusion that has gone out of my life is immense." Shortly after, David and Jennifer Jones were married, he at the age of forty-seven, she a considerably younger thirty.

Earlier, in 1942, David had set up a new company, Vanguard, which turned out such Hitchcock-directed films as *The Paradine Case,* with Gregory Peck, Ethel Barrymore, and Ann Todd, and *Spellbound,* with Peck and Ingrid Bergman, but which also placed a heavy focus on the talents of Jennifer Jones. Selznick supervised her work in *Since You Went Away, Duel in the Sun,* and *A Portrait of Jennie,* the latter a 1948 release. Thereafter, he took a long leave of absence from producing, returning in 1958 to make *A Farewell to Arms* with Jennifer and Rock Hudson.

David Selznick had added the middle initial O. to his name for euphony, and he fell in love with a girl who changed hers more drastically. Phyllis Isley was born in Oklahoma to two old-time vaudeville troupers. She came to New York to study at the American Academy of Dramatic Arts in 1937 and the following year married another aspiring youngster, Robert Walker. Both tried Hollywood without much success, then returned to a cheap Greenwich Village flat where they raised their two children, Robert, Jr., and Michael, on the proceeds of her modeling jobs and his work in radio.

The break in both their lives occurred in the early forties. Walker was offered a part in *Bataan,* which brought him swift recognition. The former Phyllis Isley, rechristened Jennifer Jones, tested for David Selznick and landed a contract. Selznick was sponsoring a season of stock in Santa Barbara, with Alfred de Liagre producing. One evening was devoted to one-act plays, including a short entry entitled *Hello, Out There.* Ava Gardner was pretty well set for the lead when a call came in from Selznick to the general manager.

"I'm sending a young lady over," he announced. "She'll be the lead in *Hello, Out There.*"

"De Liagre has already cast it," said the manager.

"I'm afraid you didn't hear me. I'm sending over a young lady and she'll be the star of *Hello, Out There.*"

The message was clear. Conveyed to de Liagre, it did not agree with him at all.

"I don't want her," he stormed.

"I do," replied Selznick.

Jennifer Jones played the part and was excellent. She was noticed and tested by Fox for the lead in *The Song of Bernadette.* In this first major outing, she won an Academy Award for best actress. The roles with the Selznick company followed, as did a divorce from Robert Walker, whose career was also spiraling.

Long before the advent of the Maharishi Mahesh Yogi, intense, soft-brown-eyed Jennifer Jones was traveling to India to meditate. She also made two trips to Switzerland to see psychologist Carl Jung. It was said that her decision to marry the arduously pursuing David Selznick came only after the most extensive soul-searching. Perhaps Jennifer was aware that whereas David had leaned on his first wife, Irene, in this relationship she, Jennifer, would lean on him.

Many observers of the Hollywood scene felt that the great producer was no longer at the top of his game in the films which starred his wife. Andrew ("Bundy") Solt, a writer who worked for Selznick on *Little Women,* was once awakened at 2 A.M. by a phone call. Would he come over to the Selznick house and watch a film? His opinion was needed. Solt went, and the two sat alone as *Portrait of Jennie* unreeled.

"What do you think?" Selznick asked apprehensively as it came to an end.

"Well, I don't want to hurt you, or be in any way offensive, but—"

"But what?"

"Well, I'm afraid I think it's simply dreadful."

"Really that bad?"

"I really think so. I'm so sorry to have to say it."

"All right," Selznick said sorrowfully. "If it's that bad, you've got to help me. You've got to rewrite it for me."

"I can't. It's so far removed from my range of comprehension. It's so foreign to the sort of thing I can offer that I don't think I can do a thing. Usually when I see something I have an instant reaction—ideas come right away on how to improve or condense or touch a certain chord that's called for. In this case, absolutely nothing comes to mind."

"All right, all right," said Selznick. "I'll rewrite it myself and you produce."

It was indeed a desperate, almost pathetic, last resort for the producer of *Gone with the Wind* and *Rebecca* to ask a writer to reverse roles with him and take over the production. It was perhaps an admission of how far he was from the immense creative capacity which had once been his.

At another time, Selznick asked Solt to see another private screening, this one of *Duel in the Sun.* Asked his opinion at the conclusion, Solt said he found the film colorful, beautifully photographed, with some powerful passages—but interminable. He remarked on the Tristan and Isolde love-death at the end, a scene which went on and on with Jennifer Jones dragging herself across the desert on her belly.

"It could be a powerful scene," he said, "but how much crawling along on the ground can any audience take?"

"You should have seen Jennifer's belly after that scene was made," Selznick said plaintively. "It was scratched and bruised, livid with the marks of that beautiful and terrible trial. I don't see how that scene could be cut. She put so much into it."

The reaction, thought Solt, was highly personal, and he wondered if the audience, not having had the producer's first-hand inspection, could appreciate the scene from the same angle.

Others asked themselves if the producer's infatuation was impairing his judgment as a film maker. Was he not casting his young wife in roles meant for an even younger actress? The question came up pressingly when he chose her to play the young heroine of Ernest Hemingway's *A Farewell to Arms* in 1958. The girl of the novel was supposed to be in her early twenties; Jennifer was now forty.

If there was a slowing of the creative process in Selznick, there was certainly no letup in the flood of memoranda that issued from his teeming brain, and in his duels with directors. Some, however, viewed these too as manifestations of increasing insecurity.

In early days at MGM, the famous blue memos were still in manageable proportions. For *A Tale of Two Cities*, Selznick put on French-born Jacques Tourneur as a special unit director to film the Bastille sequences. In one scene actor Donald Woods was supposed to approach on horseback, riding down a lane of poplars. Selznick's quest for authenticity led him to seek out terrain which approximated the French countryside depicted in the novel. The unit was sent to Bakersfield, where there was a row of poplars second to none. There was also rain when the unit arrived, heavy rain, day after day. Technicians and actors holed up in a hotel and waited for the rain to cease. The first day a series of blue memos arrived with instructions for filming the scene. The second day the memos demanded the unit's return with the completed film. The third day veiled threats appeared. The fourth day the threats were no longer veiled. The memos piled up, each signed with the familiar capitals, *DOS*. When finally a distinctly abusive missive arrived, Tourneur replied with one of his own saying that he was aware that the scene needed to be shot, of the manner in which it was to be shot, and that he was eager to begin. He ended by saying, "Unfortunately for five long days it has been raining and I cannot control this for it is an act of *GOD*." The *GOD* ended the memo as *DOS* ended the master's. The next memo from the home office was also signed *DOS;* it said Tourneur was fired. As so often happens in Hollywood, however, the director was rehired shortly after: he was needed to film the sequence, for which he had prepared by steeping himself for months in works on the French Revolution. He later received a call from Selznick saying he was being given screen credit as director of the Bastille sequences. Tourneur wondered if he would have been so honored if his name had been Smith.

The memos grew as Selznick's personal supervision of each detail of production grew. He would choose capable men to work for him, then look over their shoulders, over both shoulders, peppering them with memos of incredible prolixity, some of which explained in 40 different ways what he wanted to say. One of his first memos to the man he chose to direct *A Farewell to Arms* tried to clarify his position: "TO JOHN HUSTON . . . because of the extent to which I personally produce in every sense of the word, I am perhaps not unnaturally worried lest unquestioned eminence of your present position would cause you to resist and resent functioning as director rather than director producer. . . ." The memo was signed: *"Affectionate regards, David."*

His apprehensions were well founded. He and Huston came to a parting of the ways, and Huston was relieved. "It was a case of one Alp and two Hannibals," said Huston. Selznick replied: "I asked for a violinist and instead I got a soloist . . . as the producer, mine must be the final word. I have signed Charles Vidor to direct my film." Vidor, in a tense moment, later said, "What he wanted was a piccolo player."

The memos kept coming, dictated at the studio, at home, in autos, while walking with secretaries to catch a plane. By the time *A Farewell to Arms* was in the can, no less than 10,000 memos had flooded the production staff. It was no great surprise that along with Huston, several writers and art directors, a film editor, a photo chief, a special effects editor, four chauffeurs, and the complete staff of Selznick's rented villa in Italy walked out or in turn got their walking papers.

The range of these communications was almost as vast as creation itself. A minimum sampling follows:

TO CHARLOTTE GILBERT (casting): "What do you think about Bertrand Russell for Greffi? Regards. *DOS.*"

TO ARTHUR FELLOWS (production executive): "Regarding the selection of a hairdresser, the appearance of the woman star in this picture, as in any picture, is far more important to its success than the difference between one Alp and another. This is not to minimize the difference between one Alp and another. Rather it is to stress the importance of Jennifer's hairdresser. . . . *DOS.*"

TO PRODUCTION STAFF: "That idiotic number of umbrellas in the exodus from Orsine—which, thank goodness, I personally cut down at least partially in number—is going to haunt us in the retreat. . . . *DOS.*"

TO CHARLES VIDOR: "I don't believe I've ever used such terms with you as idiotic. I may have *thought* your excessive takes and angles were idiotic, but the most I've *said* was that they were a waste of my personal money. . . . *DOS.*"

TO JAMES NEWCOMB (editing): "We must add some moans of the wounded, at the Milano Nord station, and a few cries of pain to get more agony than is there visually. . . . *DOS.*"

TO CHARLES VIDOR: "I am bothered by the stirring of the

gruel for such a long period of time in the kitchen scene. I think it is going to be a bore. Couldn't the nurse be fiddling with an Italian coffee machine or preparing *Italian* bacon, etc., since we make a point of Henry not being so fussy about the bacon? *DOS.*"

TO CHARLES VIDOR: "It is my personal opinion that you have done a magnificent job of direction, and it is my fervent hope that upon the release of the film you will be universally recognized as one of the finest directors in the world. *DOS.*"

A Farewell to Arms was a dull film, poorly received by the critics and the public. Again, Selznick went into retirement. Still the memos continued, to the production staffs of other studios where Jennifer Jones made an occasional film.

There were those who seemed to know how to handle the situation. To a memo the size of a novelette MGM exploitation chief Howard Dietz replied by wire: "In reply to your epigram, the answer is no."

Writer-producer Nunnally Johnson worked with Jennifer on *The Man in the Gray Flannel Suit,* with which Selznick was not officially involved. Years before, he had made a job offer to Johnson, who had replied: "I would certainly like to work for you, although my understanding of it is that an assignment from you consists of three months work and six months of recuperation." Now on the Sloan Wilson story, he received memos from Selznick relating to Jennifer's hairdo, the camera angles which showed her to best advantage, the clothes that accented her skin. Johnson discreetly passed them on to the film's director and each time sent Selznick a note to that effect. Then one day Johnson saw the daily rushes of a scene with Jennifer. They were so splendid that he could not resist a memo of his own to Selznick.

"I don't think that Jennifer is aware of it, and in any event I think she would be too modest to tell you, which is why I'm doing it," he wrote. "The scene we shot today is one of the finest things she's ever done. She was really splendid."

Johnson looked at his little epistle, then remembering that he was dealing with the master memoist of all time, he added, "P.S. Don't answer this."

Like so much of the Selznick style, even the memoranda derived from the father. Lewis Selznick gave his sons early responsibility, calling on their minds to grow. When he let David work in his studio after school, the young boy was often present at conferences with men of experience who were much older than he. Somewhat self-conscious in their presence, he would later type out his thoughts and send them along. How the little habit grew! Near the end of his life, David Selznick estimated that he had composed a total of 250,000 memoranda. As the executor of his papers, his son Danny ordered an inventory, and four fat notebooks were produced. He next ordered an index to the inventory, and even this came to 90 crowded pages.

One of the Selznick memos on *A Farewell to Arms* was to Ben Hecht. "Let's really try to do a job that will be remembered as long as *Gone with the Wind,* something that we can be proud of for years to come," it read. But there could be only one *Gone with the Wind.* That culmination carried its own curse, many felt, and they sensed in David a sense of anticlimax in his later efforts.

After *A Farewell to Arms,* the once prolific producer rested on his laurels. He became involved in some European film distribution, negotiated the sale of Selznick films to television, toyed with several stage and film properties but never brought them to fruition. In the mornings he would occasionally rise with the idea of making another movie, but after a phone call or two and a few pages of reading he would take a nap and forget the whole thing.

"Very few people have mastered the art of enjoying their wealth," he said. "I have mastered the art, and therefore I spend my time enjoying myself."

Alternating between his Tower Drive home overlooking Beverly Hills and his suite at New York's Waldorf-Astoria, he watched his two sons grow up, along with his young daughter by Jennifer, named Mary Jennifer. Jeffrey had worked with him on *A Farewell to Arms,* and found his father a tough task-master. He had gone on to do editorial work, then banking, before sailing off to self-exile in Paris. Here he began producing films, both his shaggy appearance and his restless, searching, penetrating mind strangely reminiscent of the father. Danny, too, seemed to have some of these characteristics, studying acting in New York simultaneously at Lee Strasberg's Actors Studio and with Stella Adler, writing and editing, directing in summer stock, heading toward the production of films.

Both Irene and David Selznick had tried to dissuade their sons from film careers, content to see Jeffrey in banking, Danny in legitimate stage activities, but the attraction of the field furrowed by their father and by both grandfathers was proving irresistible.

While in New York, David had occasion to see another Selznick who was surfacing. He offered a job to Joyce Selznick, a young woman with an interesting background. Her father was Phil Selznick, one of the numerous brothers of Lewis. Phil spent years on the road selling L.J.'s films before quitting and going into the nightclub field. This brought him into disfavor with the film Selznicks, who consequently saw little of Phil or Joyce. Myron was the exception, sometimes sleeping off a hangover in the club when he didn't want to go home. On the maternal side, Joyce was related to the Warners. The Warner clan also disapproved of Phil Selznick.

Related to two great dynasties, Joyce took little help from either. She found her way to Nate Spingold, a top executive at Columbia Pictures, and from him and his associate, Lee Jaffe, she learned the business, becoming expert at exploitation and promotion. Early in her career she wanted to change her name, but Nate Spingold told her not to be self-conscious, that she would get into an office five minutes earlier through the name but thereafter she would have to prove herself in order to hang on. To add to her dilemma and drama, young Joyce learned at twenty-one that she was an adopted child, therefore neither a Selznick nor a Warner. Her record as a talent developer has been considerable, from past protégés like Tony Curtis to her current success, Faye Dunaway. Joyce did not accept David Selznick's offer of a position, remaining at Columbia until Paramount brought her to Hollywood.

On his visits to New York, David also established a warm friendship with his former wife, Irene. Whatever antagonisms had once existed were apparently gone, and a brother-sister bond of intimacy grew. After her success with *A Streetcar Named Desire,* which launched Marlon Brando and Kim Hunter, Irene produced other Broadway triumphs, including John Van Druten's *Bell, Book, and Candle,* with Rex Harrison and Lilli Palmer; and Graham Green's *The Complaisant Lover.*

In one interview she talked a bit of the roles Louis B. Mayer and David Selznick played in her life. "Where there are men like that around, a woman either withdraws completely into her own shell and thickens it as fast as she can," she said, "or she sticks her neck out and develops muscle she never knew she had before." The forceful, magnetic Irene chose to stick her neck out, with good results.

After David had been inactive for almost a decade, his former publicist, Russell Birdwell, wrote a long article for the *Hollywood Reporter,* which told of the more stirring moments that occurred during filming of *Gone with the Wind* and *Rebecca.* He concluded his piece, "Come home, DOS, the industry needs you."

David Selznick never came home to Hollywood. In 1964 he was producing a play with Jennifer Jones, a summer stock try-out in Florida, when he suffered two small heart attacks. Knowing that David and his son Danny had a tremendously close personal relationship, Irene had always counseled her son not to work for David. She knew the professional liaison could be dangerous. Now, however, she urged him to step in and relieve the strain on David. Danny changed the play's title from *The Goddess on the Couch* to *The Man with the Perfect Wife* and took over many of the producing chores. For the compulsive David it was a supreme act of self-control to abdicate. He went to New York to rest but returned to see the play's opening. Immediately thereafter, he dictated a 30-page memo to his son which was phrased in his usual tone of outrage. It was insulting and abusive. Danny read it with astonishment, hurried to his father, and asked how he could speak to another human being in those terms. David seemed not quite aware of the situation, was puzzled that his son was upset, and reassured him that he had the highest regard for him in every respect. Danny was grateful for this somewhat painful but also revealing glance at his father in action. It made him aware of his dimensions, his tensions, rounding out a figure who could be compassionate and generous, demanding and difficult, alternately wise and foolish, but always desperately human.

On June 22, 1965, David Selznick died of a coronary occlusion at the age of sixty-four.

His life's accomplishment was remarkable. No other producer functioned on so many levels. Looking over the much belabored script for *Gone with the Wind*, director Victor Fleming felt the two writers whose contributions were foremost were Margaret Mitchell and David Selznick. When William Wellman received an Oscar for *A Star Is Born*, he carried it over to Selznick's table and gave it to him with the words, "You deserve this more than I do."

Selznick's contributions to films lay in the meaning and importance he gave to the role of the creative producer, wrote Bosley Crowther of the New York *Times*, dean of the country's film critics: "Whereas in Europe the director ruled the roost, Selznick was among the finest examples of the Hollywood system, with the producer reasoning with bankers, picking stories, overseeing the script's preparation, hiring the cast, selecting the director and designer, birddogging the filming, even masterminding the selling campaign."

The task required the maximum in know-how, intelligence, and taste, said Crowther, and David Selznick had helped establish and endow it with standards and traditions and ideals.

For the memorial service at Forest Lawn Cemetery, there was of course a Selznick covering memo; it directed that the services should be simple and brief. They were. Rabbi Max Nussbaum of Temple Israel read a short prayer. George Cukor read a eulogy written by Truman Capote. "His fantastic vitality was matched only by the profoundness of his sense of integrity, responsibility, honor and loyalty, his good taste by his originality," concluded the Capote tribute. Her brown hair tied back simply with a black bow, Katharine Hepburn gave an emotional reading of Kipling's poem "If." Silver-haired Cary Grant peered through his spectacles to read a tribute which said, "The one word that fits David Selznick better than any other is extravagance. He was extravagant in every way, in his generosity, friendship, attention to those who sought him out for advice and guidance, and his love for those he loved."

The portrait of Lewis Selznick could now be taken down. David had served him well, as had his brother Myron in his way. Myron had changed the financial structure of Hollywood, leaving behind a good deal of love, some rancor, any number of legends. One said that agents eager to gather up his clients actually made several appointments during his funeral. David left behind his mountains of memos, of course, and love and legend, too, and one more thing. "Nothing in Hollywood is permanent," he had said. "Once photographed, life here is ended." He had photographed it—in *A Tale of Two Cities*, *David Copperfield*, *Dinner at Eight*, *Rebecca*, *Gone with the Wind*. . . . David Selznick left behind the films.

2

"Uncle Carl" Laemmle

ON MARCH 15, 1915, the better part of Hollywood's 13,000 denizens made a mass hegira and headed for the Cahuenga Pass and the open lands to the north. On horseback, in buggies, and in newfangled automobiles they crowded the rutted dusty road through the pass and into the valley below. They traveled until they came to an imposing triumphal arch of brightly painted stucco and plaster. Through the arch they filed, gathering inside around a huge open-air stage 400 feet long by 150 feet wide. Starlets were there and famous stars of the silent screen, cowboys and Indians, soldiers and clowns, extras of every variety, along with studio dignitaries, officials of municipal and state governments, and visitors from far-off states, including those who had arrived on a special train from the East.

When some 10,000 festive spectators had gathered in the sunny spot shadowed by surrounding mountains, an American flag was unfurled and three lusty cheers rent the air to greet a tiny cherub of a man. The little five-footer who ambled across the stage was Carl Laemmle, "Uncle Carl," the round-faced president of the Universal Film Manufacturing Company, on hand to officiate at the opening of Universal City, a new municipality founded for the sole purpose of producing motion pictures.

From Miss Laura Oakley, first chief of the newly founded police force, Laemmle accepted an incongruously large gold key
to the city. For a moment he seemed overwhelmed. The audience waited attentively for the mini-magnate's welcoming
words. They finally came.

"I hope I didn't make a mistake in coming out here," said
Laemmle.

The colorful occasion and the unexpected remarks were perfectly in character with the man who produced them. Carl
Laemmle was the prototype of the more than slightly mad
movie mogul, impulsive, quixotic, intrepid, unorthodox, and
unpredictable. Only the gossip columnists could consider him
otherwise, for to them he was always dependably good copy.

Uncle Carl himself called Universal City the Bottomless Pit
as he signed voucher after voucher authorizing the ever increasing expenditures. The dedication ceremonies over, the attending crowd took to the streets to see where the money went. They
were on a 230-acre tract in San Fernando Valley, ten miles out of
Los Angeles on the Camino Real, the old road which connected
Spanish missions from San Diego to San Francisco. The spot was
a historic site; in 1847 Mexican General Andrés Pico and U.S.
Army Colonel John C. Frémont had here signed the treaty
which ceded California to the United States. Laemmle bought
the acreage in March, 1914, for $165,000, and the first ground
was broken in October.

The area provided a wide range of natural scenery for filming—hills and flatlands, wooded areas and open stretches. To
supplement these, there was the large main stage and a smaller
one for minor productions. In a sense, the entire city was a set.
The main street ran along for six miles, the width constantly
changing, the path winding and then turning straight, the ele-
vation varying, passing over streams and gullies, by bridges each
of which was in a different style. Some unity was provided by a
core of service buildings which were Spanish bungalow-type
houses with red tiled roofs, but along other streets the archi-
tecture was deliberate hodgepodge, English colonial giving

way to French provincial, log cabins to Japanese teahouses, teahouses to Italian villas, villas to structures of classic antiquity.

There were company offices and 80 dressing rooms and such
standard municipal features as a police department and fire bri-
gade, together with a bus system and education facilities both
for children of employees and for little actors and actresses still
of school age. Two restaurants were ready to serve more than
1,000 customers a day as well as the possible needs of cameramen. Blacksmith shops and garages, mills and apothecaries,
tailor shops and leathercraft shops dotted the streets. Wild and
dangerous animals from the far corners of the globe were
housed and kept in readiness for a director's needs, while such
manageable creatures as goats and cats and dogs were given the
freedom to roam.

Visitors enjoyed the opening day ceremonies. They were impressed by the wide range of resources at the disposal of Universal's film makers, and no less by the studio cowboys who rode
down the macadamized streets firing their pistols and giving
exuberant yells. A fitting climax came when one broncobuster
blew up a ranch reservoir, flooding most of the outbuildings.

The days that followed often gave cause for further apprehension. When the rains came, the only road to the new city
became a muddy morass. Old Charlie, dean of the studio's elephants, was then to be seen in Cahuenga Pass nudging trucks
and other vehicles along in the mire. A grandstand which
Laemmle built opposite the main stage was also a cause of occasional aggravation. Spectators came there to watch the film
makers at work, a treat for which Uncle Carl charged them 25
cents. Inevitably they began to cheer their favorites and hiss
the villains, tossing peanuts—on sale for still added revenue—
at the latter. For crowd scenes the audience might be invited to
join the action on the big stage.

No visitor to Universal City could miss the presence of a
swiftly proliferating species of white chickens. They were a pet
project of Laemmle, who was exceedingly proud of the smooth,
white eggs laid by the sleek, white hens in his clean, white-

washed hatchery. So pleased was he that he made them available to employees—at a reasonable rate. It took a courageous employee indeed to turn down his boss's offer of eggs. Many a Universal star sent his chef out to buy an omelette cookbook, for the hardy hens kept laying and laying and laying.

More important than the peanuts and eggs, however, were the films that flowed out of Universal City. A steady stream of program pictures kept the open-air stages occupied and soon increased their number from two to six and beyond. The confines billowed out from 230 to 410 acres. The head of the successful studio added to his other nicknames that of Little Champ.

Carl Laemmle was forty-eight years old in 1915. When he entered the film industry in 1906 he was already thirty-nine. The first four decades of his life gave little clue to the destiny that lay ahead. Born in the South German kingdom of Württemberg in 1867, Carl was the tenth of thirteen children, eight of whom died during a cruel epidemic of scarlet fever. His father was a middle-class Jewish businessman in Laupheim, a pleasant little town of 3,000 inhabitants. Here Carl lived in the family's three-story house, attended public and Latin school, and grew up with the friendly easygoing disposition of the locale. At thirteen, the age of Jewish manhood, he was apprenticed to a family friend in a nearby town. He learned the stationery business and became the firm's bookkeeper and office manager.

The unexpected death of his mother interrupted the pattern of his life, loosening the ties to his homeland. One other brother, Siegfried, had already gone to Munich, where he dealt in antiques. Another was in America, sending back intriguing accounts of life in New York and Chicago. Carl persuaded his father to let him buy passage in steerage to the United States; the cost was $22.50. The S.S. *Neckar* sailed from Bremerhaven on February 14, 1884, and arrived 13 days later at Castle Garden with its cargo of mail, merchandise, and 509 passengers, including the groggy, seasick, and homesick seventeen-year-old boy.

New York was then edging up to a million and a quarter in population. Across the East River, Brooklyn was known as the City of Churches. Harlem was a small village to the north. The settled area of Manhattan did not yet extend beyond 57th Street. For a time, young Laemmle worked as an errand boy in a drugstore on East 38th Street.

Through his brother Joseph, the secretary to a midwestern businessman, he made his way to the country's interior. First he lived in Chicago, working as an office boy, as errand boy for a silk agent, as deliverer of wholesale bundles of newspapers via a cart route, as bookkeeper to a jeweler. A brief excursion with a friend took him to South Dakota and life on a farm. Ten years after his arrival in America he was back in Chicago working for a department store and earning $18 a week.

His next move took him to Oshkosh, Wisconsin, a city of 25,000 named for a Menominee Indian chief, and the center of a lumber and woodworking industry. The magnet that drew him was a job with the Continental Clothing Company. Young Laemmle, a good bookkeeper and a better salesman, rose to the position of store manager, spurring business with mail promotions and such incentive devices as free turkeys for volume purchases. He also married the boss's niece, Recha Stern, a native of Flieden, Germany, and fathered a son, Carl, Jr., and a daughter, Rosabelle.

It seemed like a propitious time to ask for a raise. To the prospering store manager's surprise, the request was turned down. The ensuing discussion led him to sever his connections with Continental, by mutual consent. The Laemmles returned to Chicago, looking for an enterprise that might multiply their savings. Robert H. Cochrane, a young advertising man, suggested the five-and-dime store business which was then in ascendancy. To his astonishment, Laemmle announced his intention of entering the film field, generally considered a fly-by-night, lunatic adventure.

What prompted him to this move was a chance entry into a nickelodeon. Films had already progressed from such early entries as Edison's recording of a sneeze, in 1893, the famous kissing scene between May Irwin and John Rice from their stage success, *The Widow Jones,* three years later, and Sigmund Lubin's *Horse Eating Hay* in 1897. In 1903 Edison presented the first narrative film, *The Great Train Robbery,* an 800-footer directed by Edwin S. Porter. Laemmle saw a story told through moving pictures, and he was impressed.

Cannily he noted two aspects of the situation which fired his interest as keenly as the actual presentation. The customers who filed in left at the end of the performance without carrying anything out with them, no bundles containing suits or sweaters or jackets, no boxes with shoes. They had come to see a film, and when they left, they left the film behind, where it could be shown again and again. Furthermore, they paid cash. In the haberdashery business one was often forced to give credit, and sometimes the customer subsequently disappeared. Here, there was no entrance without the clinking sound of the coin of the realm.

In January, 1906, Laemmle rented a vacant building on Milwaukee Avenue and converted it into a nickelodeon. To give an impression of cleanliness and respectability, the facade was painted white; appropriately, the theater was named the White Front. So successful was the enterprise that a scant two months later Laemmle bought a second, which he called the Family Theatre. When the local film exchanges, middlemen between producers and theater owners, gave him poor service and inferior films, he set up his own exchange, the Laemmle Film Service, in which Robert Cochrane bought a tenth interest for $2,500. Three years later its efficient, progressive, courteous procedures made it the largest film distributor in the country.

From the first, Carl Laemmle was immensely successful in the film field, and from the first he encountered men—or boys —of great fascination. Sam Katz was a rosy-cheeked thirteen when he walked into the Family Theatre and asked for a job as piano player. Laemmle hired him at $8 a week, much to the dismay of the boy's Russian refugee parents, who dreamed of his becoming a concert pianist. Sammy tinkled away during the film and the intermissions, competing with another youngster down the street, Abe Balaban, who was escaping from his father's grocery store and fish market to vocalize the illustrated songs at another nickelodeon. Both boys were ambitious and bright. They saved their small salaries and began buying theaters, which could be had then for a few hundred dollars and a promissory note. Combining forces, they began to experiment with a new type of operation, tying together vaudeville acts and motion pictures. In 1917 they opened Chicago's Central Park Theatre, the first of the huge Picture Palaces, where the snappily uniformed ushers were trained by graduates of West Point. "The patron is our guest" became their rule in their superbly run houses, riotous with rococo ornamentation, gleaming with giant crystal chandeliers, the lobbies a show in themselves, with fortune-tellers to beguile the waiting crowds, fashion models on parade, and sketch artists ready to do a free rendering. Daring innovators in the field of motion picture exhibition, the partners later became top-rung executives, Abe and his brother Barney with Paramount, Sam Katz first with Paramount and later with Metro-Goldwyn-Mayer.

In 1909 Carl Laemmle collided head-on with an entire array of formidable men, giving them a sample of that spirited pugnacity which earned him his position of industry leadership. At a January luncheon in New York's Imperial Hotel, executives of the leading producing companies—Edison, Vitagraph, Essanay, Selig, Kalem, Biograph, Lubin, and Kleine—joined two French firms, Pathé and Méliès, to form the Motion Picture Patents Company. Declaring a moratorium on competition, the new organization announced that only its members would be allowed to exercise the patents used in the photographing, developing, and printing of motion pictures.

The men involved included founding father Thomas Alva Edison, now almost deaf; the English triumvirate at Vitagraph, creative J. Stuart Blackton, organization-minded Albert Smith, and their third and much older partner, rotund, loud-laughing "Pop" Rock; colorful "Colonel" William Selig of the spurious title; the easygoing Sigmund Lubin of Philadelphia; Essanay's

George K. Spoor, a former Chicago theatrical agent and brother-in-law of evangelist Billy Sunday; hearty-living George Kleine; jaunty delegates from the French firms; and last but far from least, Jeremiah J. Kennedy. The long-jawed Kennedy came to the industry from the banking field when the Empire Trust Company, of which he was a director, began to exercise increasing control over financially troubled Biograph. Quick-thinking and ruthless in the execution of his ideas, he became the leader and spokesman of the Patents Company.

So happy were the lucky ten with their monopoly of film production that they greedily aimed to extend it into distribution and exhibition. The same members speedily formed the General Film Company, which proceeded to buy up film exchanges at prices determined by the monopoly. Those that refused to sell were told they would no longer be supplied with products. The most audacious stroke of all followed—exhibitors were informed they would henceforth need a license in order to show the motion pictures of the General Film Company and that that license would cost them $2 a week for each week of the year. With more than 10,000 theaters operating across the land, the extortionate fee would bring in well over a million dollars annually.

Faced with the awesome power of the Trust, as it was increasingly called, many exchanges sold out or were forced out of business. There were only two notable exceptions, two loners who refused either to sell or to quit. One was the metallically hard-eyed William Fox of New York. The other was owl-faced, deceptively amiable Carl Laemmle of Chicago. The latter was more than annoyed and angered. He was outraged and decided to do battle with the giants.

His first move was to announce that he would go into independent production, supplying films to his own customers and to exhibitors everywhere. In a trade paper he advertised: "I MAKE YOU A PROMISE. No matter what happens during the crisis or afterwards, I will take care of you through thick and thin! I will see that my customers get the best of films and the best service on God's green earth and at the very best price that can be made."

His second was to broadcast to the entire film world the facts of the matter, in the process heaping ridicule on the Trust. With the aid of Robert Cochrane, increasingly his trusted right hand, he created a cartoon character called General Flimco. The fat and greedy general appeared regularly in full-page advertisements in *Show World* and *Moving Picture News,* always contrasted with the honest but downtrodden small exhibitor. "Good morrow!" the copy often began. "Have you paid $2 for a license to pick your teeth this week?" After a folksy presentation of the latest developments in the fight, it would end, "By the way, have you paid $2 for a license to kiss your wife?" or "Have you paid your $1 for a license to breathe this week?"

The Trust fought back, buying space in *Film Index,* where Jeremiah Kennedy influenced editorials which spoke of "the passing of Laemmle," referring to him as "the little man with the big noise" who had gone independent. Thugs hired by the Trust beat up employees and tried to destroy Laemmle's equipment, wily negotiators sought to lure away his staff, and finally a series of almost 300 court actions were brought against him, an attempt at legal strangulation. For three years the savage battle raged.

When victory came it was complete. In 1912, Judge Learned Hand of the United States District Court decided an important patent suit brought by the Trust against Laemmle in the latter's favor. Next, the government itself filed suit against the Trust, charging it with violating the Sherman Act. In October, 1915, a landmark decision forced the Kennedy combine to discontinue all unlawful practices, an order which in effect destroyed its monopolistic power by dissolving it back into separate units. On their own, many of the constituent companies floundered.

Even while the legal battle raged, the Laemmle company started making films. It was called the Independent Moving Pictures Company of America, aptly shortened to IMP by the trade. The first studio was situated on 11th Avenue and 53d

Street in New York City. Since the Trust was hoarding the East-
man film, Laemmle went to a French firm called Lumière for
his celluloid.

"My motto will be: The best films that man's ingenuity
can devise and the best films man's skills can execute, and no
cheating on measurements," Laemmle trumpeted as he entered
active production. His success was phenomenal even for that
wildly extravagant era of industry development, and much of
it was due to his ability to ballyhoo the box office. "You can
bet it is classy or I wouldn't make it my first release," he said
of his initial offering, a 988-foot interpretation of Longfellow's
poem "Hiawatha." Flamboyant publicity using bold caps, italics
and every variation of typography greeted such subsequent efforts as *The Death of Minnehaha, Ivanhoe,* and *The Scarlet
Letter.* IMP made a dozen films in 1909 and more than 100 the
following year.

Laemmle's first major publicity stunt proved to be of extraordinary and far-ranging significance. One of the IMP players
was Florence Lawrence, who had earned $15 a week with Vita-
graph before decamping for Biograph and $25 weekly. Her
pictures became so popular that fans demanded to know her
name. When this was withheld by Biograph, which along with
other Trust companies tried to keep the players anonymous in
order to keep their salaries down, the public began referring
to her as the Biograph Girl.

Shortly after the foundation of the IMP company, filmgoers
were shocked by a news report that the Biograph Girl was dead,
killed in a streetcar accident in St. Louis. Great was their relief,
however, when Carl Laemmle ran an advertisement in *Moving
Picture World* which showed a soulful photo of their favorite
under the heading "We Nail a Lie." The copy read:

> The blackest and at the same time the silliest lie yet circu-
> lated by enemies of the "Imp" was the story foisted on the
> public of St. Louis last week to the effect that Miss Lawrence,
> the "Imp" girl, formerly known as the "Biograph" girl had
> been killed by a street car. It was a black lie because so

cowardly. It was a silly lie because so easily disproved. Miss Lawrence was not even in a street car accident, is in the best of health, will continue to appear in "Imp" films, and very shortly some of the best work in her career is to be released.

To prove that his newly acquired star was still very much of this world, Laemmle announced that his top male player, King Baggott, would personally accompany her by train to the city of her supposed demise. Newspapers picked up the pace of the drama so that when the two players arrived at the St. Louis railroad terminal they were greeted by an emotional crowd larger than that which had welcomed President Taft the week before.

Florence Lawrence was frightened by the fans who tore at her hat and clothes, snatching buttons for souvenirs. Her subsequent fame did not sit well on her either, and for a time she left the screen to tend to her roses and petunias. Before that moment came, however, she appeared in a swirl of one-reelers for IMP and effectively launched the star system. Thereafter, players began to be known by their names and salaries started to spiral. In England, the phenomenon made its appearance somewhat earlier, as theater managers satisfied their customers by simply making up names for American favorites—Mabel Normand, for example, being blithely billed as Muriel Fortescue.

At the time of Florence Lawrence's temporary retirement, Laemmle lured another young player away from his enemy, Biograph, by raising her weekly wage from $100 to $175 and promising to make her name known to the public. At Biograph she was known only as Little Mary; but now her idolaters could call the blond, blue-eyed favorite, a Canadian who had played child parts in stock companies since the age of five, by the name she had chosen for the stage, Mary Pickford. Actually she was born Gladys Smith. With her came a young actor who was covertly courting her, handsome black-Irish Owen Moore. Together with the rest of the company they went to Cuba to get out of range of the Trust's henchmen, and here they made a quick series of pictures which popularized the name of Mary Pickford. After a time, however, the climate caused discomfort, and bickerings began to unsettle the company. The final annoyance came when the chef mistook a tin of cold cream, placed in storage because of the heat, for lard, and proceeded to cook a sequence of truly horrendous meals. After the company returned home, Mary wanted to go back to her old mentor at Biograph, D. W. Griffith, and Laemmle released her.

King Baggott was the studio's foremost male star, a triple-threat player who acted, wrote, and directed, at times turning out a complete picture in a day. As his popularity grew, he advanced in salary from $75 a week to $100 and on to $150. Mary Pickford's young brother, the smoothly attractive Jack, performed in IMP pictures, along with Tom Ince, who later became a producer and was known as the Ace of the Westerns. Tony Gaudio was the gifted man behind the camera and one-time actor George Loan Tucker the most prominent director.

It was Tucker who helped Laemmle to another motion picture milestone, one which contributed to a growing Laemmle legend. The year was 1912. The company was prospering, but on one- and two-reelers which Tucker found limiting. He approached Laemmle with the idea of shooting a longer feature dealing with the white slave trade, then in the news as the result of a sensational newspaper report. The project would call for a record budget, possibly as high as $5,000. The cost did not ruffle the Little Champ, but his battle with the Trust was preoccupying his thoughts and his energies. No go-ahead was forthcoming. Tucker therefore turned to fellow employees of the company for support, obtaining guarantees of $1,000 from each of four—Bob Daley, director Herbert Brenon, King Baggott, and a broad-shouldered young man named Jack Cohn, who had worked his way from department to department and now functioned as a film cutter and editor.

Almost unbelievably, Tucker shot ten reels of his film on the lot without Laemmle's learning about it. Luck was with him, for the studio manager was off on a trip to Europe. Cohn proceeded to trim the footage to six reels, and wrote titles. When all was ready, Laemmle was again approached. With easy good humor, he agreed to view the renegade film at 1600 Broadway, his New York office. He liked it. Now there remained only one hurdle. Laemmle had taken on partners over the years, and his directors would also have to approve the venture. When they balked at the then heavy expenditure, terming the film Tucker's Folly, Laemmle offered to buy it outright for $10,000 and market it on his own. The directors gave in.

The public reception accorded *Traffic in Souls* was an industry eye-opener. The Shuberts agreed to show it simultaneously in their 28 New York houses and bought a third interest for $33,-000. Although the film was made in four weeks at a total cost of $5,700, the advertising for it spoke of "a $200,000 spectacle in 700 scenes with 800 players and showing the traps cunningly laid for young girls by vice agents." At Joe Weber's and other theaters four daily showings carried a 25-cent admission charge. Receipts swiftly mounted to more than half a million dollars.

The lessons were multiple. Feature films, which everyone feared would bore the audience, could mean box office. Sex could be a commercial bonanza. Skillful exploitation was a vital ingredient in a good movie mix.

Only at the studio of Carl Laemmle could a pirate film be made right on the lot and go on to such sensational success. The impulsive, erratic, accepting nature of Uncle Carl allowed it all to happen. From the beginning he was able to attract talent as black serge attracts lint, men like Robert Cochrane, now his vice-president, dapper Jules Brulatour of Lumière, investors like Charles Baumann, who later founded a film company of his own.

As his production company expanded, Laemmle sold his film exchange, which had meanwhile expanded into nine cities. By 1912 he had acquired additional partners, including the sporty Irishman Pat Powers, with whom he early waged a battle for control of the company, and the one-time herring sales-

man Mark Dintenfass, who sold his stock to Laemmle, enabling
him to maintain his mastery of the firm's destinies. It will be
remembered that the Dintenfass intermediary who actually
spoke to Laemmle about the stock was the Pittsburgh jeweler
who had gone bankrupt in New York, Lewis J. Selznick, and
that along with the stock, Selznick sold Laemmle a few left-
over stones and a bill of goods, setting himself up in the company's office and promoting himself until he became the general manager. It could only have happened at the studio of
Carl Laemmle.

As the operation expanded, the IMP imprint gave way to
another. At a directors' meeting, Uncle Carl was asked to come
up with a new name. He glanced out the window and caught
sight of a passing truck which heralded Universal Pipe Fit-
tings. "I have it, gentlemen," said Laemmle. "Universal." The
Universal Film Manufacturing Company was born, christened
with a name appropriate to a medium which aimed to supply
entertainment for everyone.

The New York studio was reinforced by a large new branch
at Fort Lee, New Jersey, then by the purchase of one of the first
California studios, that of the Nester Company at Sunset and
Gower. A second West Coast studio opened at Edendale, outside of Los Angeles. And finally came the giant step to Universal City.

Through the gates of Universal passed an endless parade of
colorful characters drawn to the valley studio by the impish
Uncle Carl. Jack Cohn left for other ventures, but his brother
Harry arrived to serve as a Laemmle secretary. The two
brothers later founded Columbia Pictures, with Harry its president, Jack the vice-president and treasurer.

Young Harold Lloyd served a Universal apprenticeship as
an extra before finding his unique and great gift as a comic.
Lon Chaney played routine character roles at $35 a week for
years before finding his sinister signature. A sleek Italian named
Rudolph Valentino played bits and then went elsewhere, as
did Mae Murray of the bee-stung lips.

The traffic was heavy. Uncle Carl was able to get good people to work for him, but then he did not always want to pay them top salaries, so they left. As a result he would get a poorer species, whom he would fire. Half the great names of Hollywood stopped in at Universal on their way up the ladder. Some stayed for a sojourn. Often the manner of their coming was as interesting as what they did once there, for it was revealing of the personality of the studio's proprietor and reflective of the period.

Allan Dwan, whose long directing career began in pioneering days, stretched through Douglas Fairbanks silent features, and extends into the present, originally trained at Notre Dame to be an electrical engineer. When George Spoor of the American Film Manufacturing Company became interested in one of his ideas, a mercury vapor arc, Dwan took the occasion to present him with stories he had written for the Notre Dame *Scholastic*, the school's literary magazine. Spoor bought all 15 stories at $25 a throw, and then, to Dwan's surprise, said, "How would you like to be our scenario editor?"

"What's that?" asked Dwan.

Spoor explained. When Dwan inquired about the pay, Spoor quoted a figure three times higher than a young engineer could ever hope to earn. Spoor even told him to keep his engineering job, to take on scenario work as a moonlighter. Dwan accepted and soon found his salary doubled.

In 1909 Spoor sent him to California. One of his units had disappeared; the last word from its director complained that they had no stories. Dwan wrote half a dozen on the train trip west and located the company. Actors, technicians, and director were holed up in a hotel in San Juan Capistrano. They were not filming because the director turned out to be hopelessly addicted to the bottle. Dwan wired his management, located in Chicago, "You have no director." The reply came back immediately: "You direct."

"What does the director do?" Dwan asked his company. The actors and cameramen explained their craft. Dwan cooked up a little story about a cowboy and followed their instructions. They all concluded he was the very best director around.

Dwan was a prolific film maker, and other companies sought his services. Soon he was in a position to accept. His leading man, J. Warren Kerrigan, became angry because he set up a second unit with a second leading man, graciously handsome Wallace Reid, a property man turned actor. Kerrigan complained to the company president, and Dwan was fired from a job which was now paying $500 a week.

He sought out an old friend, Marshall Neilan, known as Mickey to his intimates. Neilan was a red-haired Irishman who had been a chauffeur. One day, after taking someone in a touring car to a movie set, he simply stayed on, eventually talking himself into a director's chair. Neilan took Dwan to Universal, where two officials offered him $1,000 a week.

"I didn't bring you together with Allan so you could insult him," Neilan charged them.

The officials apologized and asked what he would consider a fair salary. Neilan said $1,500 a week. Everyone agreed on this comfortable compromise.

Dwan was now summoned to New York to meet the man who would be signing his check, Uncle Carl Laemmle. Laemmle invited him to luncheon. There was good food and cheery conversation on many subjects.

"Well, well," Uncle Carl said casually over coffee. "What are you going to do?"

"I'm going to work for you," said the puzzled Dwan. "I'm going to make pictures for you."

"What kind of pictures?" asked the equally puzzled Laemmle.

Here indeed was a howdy-do. The two talked of the sort of thing Dwan had done in the past, and Uncle Carl's eyes twinkled.

"Can you get the American Film Company people to work with you?" he asked. "I liked your work with Kerrigan and Wally Reid."

David Selznick with a portrait of his father, Lewis J. Selznick

Myron Selznick *(inset)*

David Selznick and his wife, Jennifer Jones

Uncle Carl Laemmle *(right)* with Jan Paderewski, immortal of the piano and wartime president of Poland

Carl Laemmle, his Imperial Highness Archduke Leopold of Austria, and Erich von Stroheim *(right)*

Laemmle with son-in-law Stanley Bergerman and son, Junior Laemmle

Carl Laemmle receiving Elliott Roosevelt, son of the President, and his bride

A Hollywood party. Among the guests: Groucho
Marx, Jesse Lasky, Jimmy Durante, Maurice
Chevalier, Leslie Howard, and Fredric March

Eddie Cantor, Josephine Hunt, and Sam Goldwyn

Director George Fitzmaurice, scenarist Frances Marion, and Sam
Goldwyn with the doll used in a 1924 film, *Cytherea*

Lieutenant Eddy Duchin, USNR, Mrs. Samuel Goldwyn, Orson Welles, Mrs. Averell Harriman, Samuel Goldwyn, and Elsa Maxwell

Adolph Zukor in 1936 with Roscoe Karns, Bob Burns, Shirley Ross, William Frawley, Eleanore Whitney, Robert Cummings, Sir Guy Standing, Mary Carlisle, Marsha Hunt, Ray Milland, Dorothy Lamour, and Lynne Overman

se Lasky visits Cecil B.
Mille on the set of *The
n Commandments*

B. P. Schulberg

William Perlberg, Bob Hope, Gloria Swanson, Bessie and Jesse Lasky, George Jessel, Cecil B. DeMille, Sam Goldwyn, Mary Pickford, and Jack Benny at the 1951 Milestone Award ceremony

"I think I can bring them over. What offer can I make them?"

"Double everybody."

Dwan conveyed the terms to his old associates, who all swarmed to his side. It was the end of the American Film Manufacturing Company.

The slapdash little Laemmle was always flitting between New York, California, and Europe, his comings and goings unscheduled, turmoil in his wake. He could be waspish. After one long trip, employees gathered at the Los Angeles train terminal to meet him. He was furious to find them away from their work. The next time, no one met him. He was irate at their neglect.

Everywhere he collected people. In 1917 he was vacationing at a Long Island summer resort when he met a well-mannered young boy of eighteen and offered him a job. Irving Thalberg at first turned him down. He was, after all, already on the road to a comfortable life in commerce. During a delicate boyhood complicated by a heart ailment, Thalberg's mother, Henrietta, had helped him to keep pace with his schoolmates by bringing him books, reading to him, urging him to develop his mind. This enabled him to get through public school number 85 in Brooklyn, and high school in the same borough. Even while working in a small department store, he studied shorthand, typing, and Spanish at night. An ad in the New York *Journal of Commerce* landed him a job at $15 a week with an export firm. At the end of the year he was promoted to assistant manager.

The Laemmle offer left its impression nonetheless. Several months passed, and then Thalberg went to the Universal office at 1600 Broadway. Without even mentioning his contact, he obtained a position as secretary to a Laemmle assistant. The salary was $35 a week. A year later he became Laemmle's secretary. Diligent, thoughtful, fascinated by film making, he became a valuable employee, offering suggestions on both commercial matters and production.

He was nineteen when Uncle Carl asked him to come with him on a trip to California, presumably to handle his correspondence. In the cavalier manner so characteristic of him, Laemmle headed for another part of the forest, leaving his secretary behind, his duties undefined.

Under the modest, disarming facade of Irving Thalberg waited an ambitious, resourceful nature. The young man began taking charge of the studio, where chaos reigned. Laemmle liked to fire people as well as hire them. General managers came and went so rapidly that the incumbent was jokingly referred to as the Officer of the Day. Soon Thalberg settled into the post and held firm.

He brought new talent into the company and new ideas. Films such as *Outside the Law, Merry-Go-Round,* and *The Hunchback of Notre Dame* won wide acclaim. When Uncle Carl returned from the baths at Carlsbad, he was confronted by a general manager the industry referred to as the boy wizard, the boy Napoleon. At first he was not even able to sign checks because he was less than twenty-one.

Uncle Carl was at first pleased with his protégé's progress, but gradually the enthusiasm waned. Laemmle was never happy to see too much power or glory concentrating in one employee. His displeasure grew when Thalberg began courting his daughter, the dark-haired Rosabelle. The two made a handsome couple, but Laemmle was aware of the boy Napoleon's weak heart and did not consider him a good match.

Thalberg was no longer happy at Universal either. He was working too hard. Battles at the studio strained his nerves. There was too little encouragement. When a friend, lawyer Erwin Loeb, offered to steer him elsewhere, he did not demur. Loeb took him to Joe Schenck, who failed to make a firm proposal. The next step was a Loeb client, Metro president Louis B. Mayer. Mayer needed a production chief. He hired Thalberg at a liberal $600 a week, winning away from Uncle Carl one of the brightest geniuses ever to enter the industry. In later years, Laemmle always acknowledged his loss as the biggest blunder of his career. Perhaps the second biggest was Bette Davis. Uncle Carl looked quizzically at her when she came to his office wearing no makeup, her hair tied in a simple knot in back. "She has as much sex appeal as Slim Summerville," he told an associate. "What audience would ever believe the hero wanted to get *her* at the fadeout?" After a few films, Universal let Bette depart.

One of the men with whom Irving Thalberg tilted swords during his tenure was the singularly gifted Erich von Stroheim, a thick-necked Austrian who gained fame during the First World War by playing Prussian officers. To filmgoers he became known as "the man you love to hate." With the end of the war, racial prejudice worked against him. The extravagant von Stroheim was penniless the day he walked out to the home of Carl Laemmle, hoping to interest him in a script he had written, *Blind Husbands*. Laemmle, at dinner, heard a servant refusing entry to the visitor; he interrupted to say he would give him a short audience. At midnight the two men were still talking, switching from English to their native German and back.

The result was a characteristic Laemmle gamble—he assigned von Stroheim to direct and also star in *Blind Husbands,* on the promise that it could be brought in for $70,000. The final figure was $90,000. The film was a prestige success for Universal, demonstrating the new director's inventive camera placement and cutting, aptly expressing his intimate view of European decadence. *Blind Husbands* was an expensive production, however, as was its sequel, *Foolish Wives,* for von Stroheim spent lavishly and insisted on authenticity in every scene. When the script called for it, his players were served real capon, real caviar, real champagne. If there was a bordello scene, the set was closed, even to studio officials, and the action was remarkably real. On one occasion, von Stroheim entered so gaily into the sport of things that he passed out even as he was directing his cameraman.

Thalberg was on hand as von Stroheim began his third film, *Merry-Go-Round,* and he watched the mounting costs with uneasy emotions. He learned that the director often delayed shooting for what seemed to him quite bizarre reasons. In a scene requiring a bell-pull he demanded that the pull be wired to a real bell, even though the silent film would never record the ring. For three days he trained a group of extras playing guardsmen to salute properly, although the saluting scene lasted only a few seconds. Thalberg himself saw the voucher which ordered silk underdrawers for the guardsmen, each garment embossed with the monogram of the Austrian Imperial Guard, even though the players were to appear on screen in full uniform. The prodigal Von, as he was known to his admirers, was going too far. Thalberg fired him and put another director in his place.

Years later von Stroheim was induced to come back to Universal by Laemmle's roving European ambassador, Paul Kohner, who suggested he remake *Foolish Wives* as a talking picture. Von had not changed. He arrived and immediately headed for Lake Arrowhead to prepare the script. Although Kohner begged him not to come back with the sort of outlandishly long document which had caused his banishment from other studios, von Stroheim produced a script which was as fat as a metropolitan phone book. Kohner's agonized groans induced him to cut it somewhat. When all was in readiness, the company prepared to go back up to Arrowhead to film the wedding scene, which involved boats on the lake, soft music, and church bells. At the last moment the assistant director rushed up to Kohner. Von Stroheim had been spending long hours listening to all the bells in the studio repertoire, and he now wanted the bells transported to Arrowhead.

"What is this with the bells?" asked Kohner.

"I have selected bells, and we must take them along. They will ring over the water during the wedding scene."

"There's no need to take them along, Von. We can record the bells right here at the studio and coordinate the different sound tracks later on."

"You mean my people will not be talking while they dance?" von Stroheim demanded in a fury. "Music will not be playing while the scene takes place over the lake?"

"That's right."

"But don't you realize that bells sound different over the water than over the land?"

The newly inaugurated methods of filming aroused such ire in the director that he brought his heavy cane down over his knee, breaking it into two parts and almost maiming himself in the process.

Von Stroheim drove his employees through long hours of shooting. Later, when he appeared as an actor again in a Garbo picture, he took a decidedly different tack. "Isn't that sonofabitch ever going to quit?" he demanded one evening when director George Fitzmaurice held the company a few minutes past five o'clock.

Paul Kohner, today a top Hollywood agent, arrived in the Laemmle camp via a characteristic route. It was 1920 when his father, publisher of a film trade paper in Prague, sent young Paul to Carlsbad to interview Laemmle. Kohner made the three-hour journey, left his card as was customary, only to be told the American film magnate had no time. Kohner persisted, leaving another card which said he had taken three hours to get there and surely Laemmle could find three minutes to spend with him.

He was thereupon invited to breakfast the next day, an occasion he still recalls vividly. He was ushered in while Uncle Carl was having his pedicure. For this ceremony, he was surrounded by his chauffeur, his valet, and a giant seven-foot Russian who was his secretary at the time. At six thirty in the morning, the sound of Strauss waltzes filled the air. After the pedicure, Kohner and Laemmle drank half a dozen glasses of hot mineral water, then walked through the handsome gardens before going to the breakfast table. Here they were joined by other members of the Laemmle entourage, two brothers, their wives, friends—fourteen people in all. Pretty girls in local costumes came with trays heaped with fruit, sausages, eggs, and rolls. Kohner ate heartily, and Laemmle was amused by his capacity. When the check came, Uncle Carl signaled *"Alle"* and paid for everyone.

The meeting concluded with Laemmle putting the seventeen-year-old journalist into his temporary employ, sending him on various missions to European cities. Back in Prague, Kohner received a letter saying Laemmle would like to see him once more before leaving. This time he offered him a job in America. Kohner accordingly debarked with young William Wyler, a Laemmle relative, who was also going to work for him.

In the United States Kohner learned English and was made an assistant director, one of a vast army of that species. When Laemmle's secretary called to ask if he knew shorthand, he said yes, neglecting to add that he took it in German only. For a time, Laemmle's dictation was all in that language, but on a train trip out of New York he switched to English. "You get off in Albany," he told Kohner when he discovered his limitation. However, he liked the way Kohner had handled the German and gradually turned that segment of his correspondence over to him. The volume was great, for Uncle Carl kept in touch with countless relatives, with nunneries and convents near his brithplace at Laupheim, with charitable institutions all over the world. Kohner came to know his style so well that he started composing the letters, even to close relatives. It amused Laemmle to read what he had written for him.

Kohner took on the duties of casting director for a time, then directed a few small Westerns before turning producer. In 1929 he went to Europe as roving ambassador for the studio and ran into several situations which gave him an amusing insight into the character of Uncle Carl.

Laemmle loved to see his name in print, no matter where. All about the studio were signs such as: TURN OFF LIGHTS BEFORE LEAVING. CARL LAEMMLE; KEEP OFF THE GRASS. CARL LAEMMLE. He commissioned John Drinkwater, the noted biographer of Lincoln, Robert E. Lee, and Byron, to write his biography. Drinkwater earned his huge fee with such statements as: "Laemmle, a man without whom modern civilization would have been a very different story," and "In the early organization of the medium, Laemmle must always be remembered as the ablest, the wisest, and the most intrepid of pioneers."

While Uncle Carl loved personal publicity, he was not keen on associates who took the limelight. Kohner ran afoul of the master when he arrived in Vienna to take up his new duties. He had produced a film called *The Man Who Laughs,* with Conrad Veidt, well known in Europe, and as a consequence his visit was headlined, "American Film King in Vienna," in the city's leading paper. A photo showed Kohner with Laemmle.

Predictably, as soon as the paper reached Laemmle he sent Kohner a cable saying he was not pleased with his self-promotion and should return to the United States where they would decide what his future would be with the company. Kohner knew the publisher and persuaded him to run off several editions of the paper with a revised headline, "Representative of American Film King in Vienna." He sent them to Laemmle, but all to no avail. He was on the train platform preparing to go to Berlin, his European headquarters, and then on to New York, when a friend tapped him on the shoulder. The papal nuncio to Berlin was on the train, he said. He introduced Kohner to Cardinal Pacelli, who was later to become Pope Pius XII. Pacelli spoke with such feeling of the current Pope, of his progressive tendencies, that Kohner had an inspiration.

"Your Excellency, are you familiar with that new invention called talking pictures?" he asked.

"Yes," said Pacelli.

"Do you think you might possibly induce His Holiness to speak to the world through this new invention? He could give any message that he wants to convey, whatever is most meaningful to him. We could show the Vatican and it glories, and this could be a very splendid film indeed."

The idea appealed to the cardinal; in Berlin there were further discussions. The proposal was made to Rome, where the Pope accepted. Kohner now wired Laemmle that he had the greatest scoop of the century, the Pope before the Univer-

sal cameras. Laemmle was enthusiastic and kept the trans-
atlantic cable humming with messages not to let the competition know, and to make all arrangements speedily, a thousand
details. Most important for Kohner were the words, "Stay in
Europe."

Final plans were laid. Kohner was about to go to Rome when
Pacelli's secretary called. There was one little point they had
not yet discussed.

"What is that?" asked Kohner.

"The matter of a donation to some charitable institution in
recognition of the service rendered."

"What sum did you have in mind?"

"One hundred thousand dollars."

Kohner wired Laemmle of this latest development, saying the
Vatican at the last moment had brought up the matter of a
donation, that the sum mentioned was $100,000, that in view
of the tremendous value of such a unique scoop, he felt it was
worth it. Usually the Laemmle cables were a lengthy maze of
detail. This time the message was a model of brevity.

"Kohner," it said. "Forget Pope. Laemmle."

Kohner was often thought to be a Laemmle nephew, a mistake he did nothing to dispel. The Universal lot was known to
contain a veritable riot of relatives. Uncle Carl at first brought
over everyone in his family who wanted to see America. Then,
during both the First and the Second World Wars he sponsored
scores of refugees, some very distantly related, others not at
all. They were given jobs at the studio as third assistant director, fourth assistant director, fifth assistant director. Many
did very little assisting, for they could speak only German. The
whole group was known as Laemmle's Foreign Legion. Producers were careful to say "sir" even to the janitor because he
was likely to be the second cousin of Laemmle's wife's brother-
in-law. One of the "nephews" was for a time the studio manager, where he was particularly disliked because of his economizing tendencies. When a producer came to him with a plan
to shoot a film on location he told him, "A rock is a rock. A

tree is a tree. Shoot it in Griffith Park." The comment was later much quoted, for it seemed aptly to characterize the bread and butter "program" pictures which were the studio staple. Most of the Laemmle relatives remained anonymous and obscure. The exception was dark-haired, volatile, young William Wyler, who came over on the same boat with Kohner and developed into one of Hollywood's foremost directors.

Uncle Carl found employees at every turn. Waiting for a train in Kansas City, he was interviewed by a reporter—whom he promptly hired. By the time the young newsman got to Hollywood, Laemmle had completely forgotten him. He was put on the payroll nonetheless and told to make himself useful. Another young man sent in a promotion idea from far-off Terre Haute. Laemmle replied with a check and the words, "Be sure and see me if you come out here." The young man, Grover Jones, took up the offer. Soon he was painting in the studio's back lot, then editing the house organ, before departing for Vitagraph as a gagman.

As a form of advertising, Laemmle ran a regular letter column in the *Saturday Evening Post*. Robert Cochran wrote the column, but Uncle Carl signed it and read the correspondence which it invited. Here, too, he would pick up employees. From Cedar Rapids, an aspiring actor named Robert Downing engaged his attention and came out to the studio. A film bit or two came his way, but his main job was meeting Laemmle relatives at the railroad station and getting them settled. Downing later became a protégé of the Lunts, and one of the most prominent of legitimate stage managers.

A characteristic Laemmle caper involved author George Oppenheimer, who on one occasion received a summons to the Universal offices, where Uncle Carl launched into an impressive eulogy of his great abilities. Oppenheimer then made the mistake of asking what his assignment was to be. The question floored Laemmle. "Whatever the job is," he finally concluded, "you fit it like a glove."

A new writer came from Australia. Laemmle asked him how

long he had been in America and was told two weeks. "It's amazing how well you talk English after only two weeks," said Uncle Carl.

Canadian authoress Winifred Eaton first came to Laemmle with a letter of introduction. Great was her surprise when he plunked her into an office as the head of his scenario department. Since the salary was more than generous, she later thought of repaying him by dedicating her new novel to him. Laemmle loved the idea. She was again surprised when his secretary called to ask if black jacket and gray striped trousers would be appropriate garb for the dedication ceremony. She thought this was probably a joke, but friends told her it was nothing of the sort. She thereafter held a ceremony at which she formally announced the tribute she was paying to the Little Champ.

The task of the Laemmle secretaries was not always an easy one. Uncle Carl was somewhat of a hypochondriac, with frequent recourse to the medicine chest. Even on the hottest days, his office windows were closed to guard against germs. As the years passed, he became increasingly deaf, so that one secretarial requirement was strong vocal cords. He also had a habit which could be troublesome. At all hours he would scratch his thoughts on a pad, later turning the scribblings over to his secretary to decipher. "Fair: 10:30," was the sketchy message he left on one such sheet.

"Did you want to go to a circus?" the secretary asked him in an effort to give the message meaning.

"No," said Laemmle.

"Maybe you were driving last night and maybe you saw a poster that announced some fair or circus?"

"No."

"Would it have something to do with a picture about a fair or a circus?"

"No."

There were further questions with further negative responses until suddenly little Laemmle remembered.

"I've got it," he said. "I had a bowel movement last night at ten thirty—and it was only fair."

The health-conscious Uncle Carl watched himself with precision, checking every movement!

The Laemmle legend took full account of his eccentricities, of the extravagant elements in his nature—Uncle Carl went from faro, a card game dating to his Chicago days, to gambling for high stakes with old pros like Joe Schenck and Sid Grauman; he went from the raising of blooded chickens to breeding racehorses, winning and dropping grand sums on the giddy-ups; from a modest home to the purchase of Tom Ince's Spanish hacienda on Benedict Canyon Drive, 25 rooms of baronial splendor called Dias Dorados—Golden Days.

Less was said of his more orthodox qualities. Uncle Carl cared little for the glamorous life of Hollywood, for the gay whirl in crowded night spots. Loneliness was a part of his nature, and like other lonely men, he was a joiner—a Mason and an Elk, a member of the Harmonie Club of New York, the Breakers, the Gables, the Hillcrest Country Club, and the Breakfast Club of Los Angeles. Actually, he preferred to sit around and chat with a small group of old cronies, many of them relatives or friends from his homeland.

He married only once. When his wife died in 1919 he kept her picture in a locket which he wore next to his heart. He did not go off in pursuit of sexy starlets.

Laupheim, his hometown in Germany, was never far from his mind. On his frequent trips there, he made bequests for public baths, a gymnasium, and an agreeable little park; his reward was a Carl Laemmle Strasse. His generosity extended to Jewish and Catholic and Protestant institutions alike.

On one occasion, a beauty contest conducted by Universal had come down to the finale when Laemmle was brought in to select the winner from a group of five entries. The winner was to receive a six-month contract and the opportunity to become a star. Universal employee Lou Greenspan, a former editor of *Daily Variety,* watched as Uncle Carl walked by each of the five a number of times, then selected the one with the least glamour, by all odds the least obvious beauty.

"Uncle Carl, why did you pick this girl among all the others?" asked the intrigued Greenspan. "Was there any particular reason that made you favor her?"

"Yes," said Laemmle. "When I was a young boy in school in Laupheim, there was a little girl who sat across from me. She looked just like this girl. The face reminded me so much of that girl from my childhood."

To paraphrase an old saw, you could take Carl Laemmle out of Laupheim, but you could never take Laupheim out of Uncle Carl.

Laemmle loved his daughter, Rosabelle, who grew up to marry an agent, Stanley Bergerman, who went to work for Uncle Carl. He was extremely devoted to his only son, Carl, Jr., who looked like him and whom everyone called simply Junior. He tended to indulge the boy, on one occasion handing him $1,500 in cash with the injunction to run along and not interrupt Daddy's card game. He also gave Junior an education at New York's Ethical Culture School and the now extinct Clark School and a chance to learn the film business. At the tender age of twenty-one he was put in charge of the studio as a birthday present.

Junior's reign at Universal was an interesting and controversial one. During the twenties the studio made money by making mostly low-budget Westerns and inoffensive little comedies. While most of the great players paused briefly at Universal, players who spent longer sojourns there included Margaret Sullavan, William Powell, Edmund Lowe, Sally Eilers, Chester Morris, Paul Lukas, Russ Columbo, Boris Karloff, Buck Jones, Binnie Barnes, Slim Summerville, Zazu Pitts, Henry Hull, Victor Moore, and June Knight. The list was substantial if not overly impressive.

In his most active days, Uncle Carl was always closer to the exhibitor and distributor than to the production people. In response to their needs, his aim was to provide family entertainment.

Junior announced a drastic change in policy. He would make big-budget features with challenging themes. While many executives of the company groaned, Uncle Carl stood completely behind his son. He was perhaps just as happy to let the reins slip from his hands. As long ago as 1908 Uncle Carl had installed a device called Greenbaum's Synchroscope in the Majestic Theatre in Evansville, Indiana, announcing, "I tell you that talking pictures are the coming craze in all America." The invention was not refined enough as yet, however, and won no audience. Later when talkies did come in, Laemmle was not pleased. He never fully appreciated sound, preferring the silent pictures which he felt were better made and better understood by an international audience. He hoped and half expected the silent days would return.

Junior plunged into production with the purchase of Erich Maria Remarque's antiwar novel *All Quiet on the Western Front*. Since the current antiwar play in New York was called *Journey's End,* the project became known at the studio as Junior's End. Every executive except Uncle Carl voted against it. The first choice for a director was Herbert Brenon, who wanted $125,000, a sum the thrifty Uncle Carl thought excessive. Agent Myron Selznick thereupon presented his client, Lewis Milestone, offering him at $5,000 a week with a ten-week guarantee, and a pro rata follow-up. Myron was aware that this type of picture would take time. He was wise enough not to frighten off Laemmle by demanding a lump guarantee. Since it took ten weeks to prepare the script plus seventeen weeks of shooting, Milestone earned a total of $135,000.

Junior's first word to Milestone was that he had engaged playwright Maxwell Anderson to do the script and had given him his initial briefings. Milestone contacted Anderson, who was already half finished. He took his script home, read it, and could not believe the great writer had done something so horrible, so pedestrian and sentimental, so far removed from the spirit of the novel. He said nothing critical, however, only that the project was difficult, the novel's theme such an unusual one to translate into a picture that he wanted to saturate himself with the story, to get a point of reference. He suggested Anderson finish his script, and by then he would know the book from every angle and find his orientation.

Milestone contacted a friend, Del Andrews, the man who had taught him cutting, and together they holed up in a house in Catalina, next door to director John Ford. Ford chastised Milestone for taking on the project, suggesting he follow his lead and stick to Westerns, which were cheap and easy to make, which always made money, which no one could on consequence criticize. Milestone replied there was no adventure to such a pattern. With Andrews he read and reread *All Quiet on the Western Front,* marking up pages with comments, literally tearing books apart and making galley sheets of the pages. No form developed.

The reading, the marking of pages, continued. Finally Milestone saw the spine of the story. The picture must start in school, show the young boys being recruited for the army, then go to the first experience in military school, then the first experience at the front, and so on. In half an hour, Milestone wrote out the complete story line.

He called Anderson, who arrived on Catalina with a completed script in a briefcase. Milestone handed him two sheets of yellow paper with his one-line continuity of the entire story. Max read it very slowly. When he had finished, he went to his briefcase, took out his own completed script, and tore it in two.

"When do you want to go to work?" he asked.

Anderson had come to Hollywood a playwright inexperienced in picture ways. He had tried to please Junior with a version he thought would be commercial, but seeing the structure of Milestone's effort put him back on the right track.

Together the two craftsmen worked in harmony, continually impressed by the scope of the book. Whenever they thought they had come up with an original idea, a swift check showed it to be in that remarkable novel. Since talkies had just come in, the modus operandi was experimental. Milestone would give Anderson an episode, a segment that he had set up

just as for a silent film. Max would then breathe life into it by
supplying dialogue.

Milestone wanted unknowns for most of the roles, especially for the lead, the young soldier named Paul. They
tested many actors but could not come up with the right lead.
Producer Paul Bern, later the ill-fated husband of Jean Harlow,
said he knew a boy who would be perfect, a young player who
had been in only one film.

"Have him call me," said Milestone.

Several days later, Bern saw him and said, "I didn't know
you could be such a mean fellow. That boy called you, and you
were rude and hung up on him."

"What time did he call?" asked Milestone.

"Early. Early in the morning."

"Tell him not to be a jerk. I work late, and in the morning
I don't function. Have him call me at a reasonable hour."

"You did it again," said Bern on seeing Milestone several
days later. "He called you and the same thing happened. I'm
going to give up."

Milestone was beginning to despair of finding an unknown.
He called David Selznick, at the time Ben Schulberg's right
hand at Paramount, to see about testing Phillips Holmes for
the lead. David was cool to the idea but gave him a valuable
tip in another direction.

"You're doing too much, working on the script with Anderson, preparing the production, casting the picture," said Selznick. "I have a man who can help you. He had a stock company in Rochester. Before that he worked with Gilbert Miller
in New York. You should hire him as dialogue director."

"Send him to see me."

The man was thoughtful, dark-haired George Cukor, who
got along immediately and famously with Milestone, taking
much of the load off his shoulders. Milestone would set up
scenes, and then Cukor would make tests of various actors and
actresses. Most of the roles were cast, but still there was no Paul.
With production scheduled to start the next day, still no Paul.

"Anything today, George?" Milestone asked wearily.

"No."

"Well, you took the trouble to shoot a test this afternoon, so I might as well see it."

The two men went into the projection room. The scene that unreeled showed boys, young soldiers, lined up in front of a field kitchen, their first respite after two weeks of solid bombardment at the front. The field cook served regular portions, and the boys began to riot. Their unit, once comprising 150 men, had been decimated, cut to half, and they insisted on double portions. The cook said when he cooked for 150 people he fed 150 people, not 75 with double portions. As the riot developed, a young lieutenant stopped by and a man stepped out of the group to explain what the soldiers' complaint was about. Milestone watched as the young lieutenant spoke. The scene was not a close-up but only a knee-figure shot, yet the stance, the self-possession, the interesting manner caught him.

"I thought that was interesting," he told Cukor. "How did you get him to do that?"

"I worked like hell."

"Good. That's what we're here for. We don't want ready-canned goods."

Cukor was not keen on the young actor. He felt that dialogue was the least important element in the scene, and he worried that the boy would not be adequate at the pantomime. Milestone asked to meet the actor.

That evening at nine he drove up in an old dilapidated jalopy. Cukor and Milestone tried to break him down, to find out what kind of a man he was. They asked him impertinent questions, including off-color inquiries into his sex life. The boy stood on his dignity, like a young king, at once sensitive and like steel.

Milestone was impressed, and Cukor was increasingly positive. Together they decided to take the boy to a back office to meet George Abbott. Abbott had a great reputation as a Broadway director and an equally fine one as a play doctor. Milestone had hired him to look over the script. Now he wanted his opinion of the young actor.

"So you would like to play Paul?" said the great Abbott somewhat patronizingly.

"Yes, very much."

"Do you think you can handle the role?"

"I've read the book over and over again. I was born to play it."

Abbott was becoming annoyed because there was no trace of humility in the young actor, only self-assurance.

"Are you familiar with the shell hole scene, where you, the hero, kill a Frenchman and are then forced to spend forty-eight hours with his dead body in a shell hole? Do you think you know how to play that scene?"

"That to me is the easiest scene of all to play."

"Throw him out of the office," shouted Abbott. "He's nothing but a fresh kid."

Milestone and Cukor smiled as they left with the young actor, who was told the part was his. Cukor said he could guarantee the boy would speak well, but he still worried about the pantomime. Milestone reassured him.

The next day Milestone ran into Paul Bern and told him he had finally cast the role.

"Who'd you get?" asked Bern.

"Lew Ayres."

"That's the boy I told you about."

After discouraging calls to Milestone, Ayres had dropped his reliance on Bern as a liaison and had lined up with other young hopefuls to test for the part. To Milestone there seemed a touch of destiny about that.

His next step was to take Ayres to meet Junior Laemmle. Junior, twenty years old, as was Ayres, got up from behind his desk and walked completely around the actor on a tour of inspection before asking, "What's your name?"

"Lew Ayres."

"We'll have to change that."

"You're not going to change my name. I was born Lew Ayres, and I'm going to die Lew Ayres. Nobody's going to change my name."

"If you want to work here, you'll have to learn a little something about taking orders."

"He's under twenty-one," interrupted Milestone. "His mother's coming in tomorrow. We'll talk to her."

Milestone convinced Junior that Ayres was a perfectly good euphonious name, that Agnes Ayres had done well with it. Junior was not difficult. He allowed Milestone and his other people considerable rein.

During the filming of *All Quiet on the Western Front* the seven principal boys became inseparable friends, welded into a unit. For them it was a real war experience: they were always together except for Ayres. All noted that Lew would do things by himself. When they wanted to go for a walk, he would read; when they wanted to play cards, he went for a walk. He seemed always to be looking for something, something he couldn't put into words, searching. When finally he became a conscientious objector in World War II, it was clearly a matter of deeply felt principal. Miraculously, he came out of that troubling situation a national hero.

Lew Ayres came out of *All Quiet on the Western Front* a star, and Junior Laemmle was hailed as the boy wonder of Hollywood when the film won an Academy Award for best picture of the year.

For a time Junior's policy seemed to be paying off. He lured John Murray Anderson from Broadway to direct Paul Whiteman in a superproduction called *The King of Jazz.* He started a whole new trend of horror films, beginning with Bela Lugosi playing Bram Stoker's *Dracula,* and following up with Mrs. Mary Shelley's *Frankenstein,* which catapulted English actor Boris Karloff to eerie fame. The distinguished pioneer director James Whale was at the director's helm for *Frankenstein.* Junior courageously bought George Kaufman's comedy *Once in a Lifetime,* despite the fact that it poked fun at Hollywood.

The Depression was at hand, however, and Junior had embarked on a policy of features which pitted him against the powerful major studios. MGM, Paramount, and Warner Brothers all had great galaxies of stars and stories and directors, tough competition indeed. A number of clinkers, like *East Is West,* could not meet it. When the Universal sales staff asked for less expensive pictures to peddle, Uncle Carl swung into action. He hired young exhibitor-producer Sol Lesser, founder of West Coast Theatres, and assigned him to an office.

"What am I supposed to do?" asked Lesser.

"We'll find something for you," said Uncle Carl.

Lesser expected to be involved in some capacity with film making, but all that crossed his desk were sales reports. They were not encouraging. The thought behind Laemmle's actions soon became apparent.

"I want you to go to New York and fire Phil Reisner," he told Lesser.

"How can I do that?" asked the latter. "He's one of my best friends."

"Good. That should make it easier."

Lesser agreed to go to New York to look into the situation. Reisner explained that the trouble was the big-budget features made under Junior's regime. There was a glut on a falling market, and he could not sell them; they were not so superior to other studios' products to win out; the oldtime cheaper Universal program pictures would be easier to sell. Lesser confirmed this with various sales representatives and reported to his boss.

"Cannot sell expensive features. Change policy," he wired.

"Junior will not change policy," Laemmle wired back.

"Speak to Junior; convince him to change policy," countered Lesser.

"Do not persist," said Uncle Carl's reply. "You will give Junior a breakdown."

"Junior will break down Universal if policy is not changed," was Lesser's last word.

Reisner was fired. The next day he went to RKO, becoming the foreign sales manager for his old friend, Joseph Kennedy. Lesser continued to draw his $1,000-a-week salary while Uncle Carl took to the baths at Carlsbad. Eventually Laemmle, with great reluctance, relieved Junior, putting his son-in-law, Stanley Bergerman, in charge of the studio for a time. One Hollywood

rumor said Junior's spirit was somewhat broken when his father, a Conservative, if nondisciplinarian, Jew, disapproved of
his plans to marry actress Constance Cummings, because she
was not of the same faith. Junior later went into independent
production but without notable success.

IT CAN BE DONE, said the motto over the enormous paneled
desk behind which tiny Carl Laemmle sat, a pink carnation
neatly placed in a buttonhole. In March, 1935, the motto came
down. The financially troubled film empire was sold to a group
of financiers for 5½ million dollars. In September, 1939, Uncle
Carl died at home at the age of seventy-two, and was praised by
Rabbi Magnin as "the little man who was a big man." His will
provided generously for all who had been close to him, containing countless provisions for charities he had established and for
the support of his foreign legion of refugees.

The new regime at Universal struggled back into solvency by
making inexpensive action pictures, horror films, farces, and
cheap musicals. Their biggest asset was singer Deanna Durbin,
who made millions for the studio under the aegis of German
director Henry Koster and Hungarian producer Joseph Pasternak. Both were leftovers from the Laemmle era.

The executives who now guided the studio also turned up
some astonishing facts about the past. On the payroll they found
the names of two men who were dead. Other employees came to
the studio only to get checks. In tiny offices scattered over the
lot were more conscientious "workers," who at least came in
to be counted. All in all, more than 70 relatives, friends of relatives, and other pensioners of Uncle Carl were uncovered and
ousted. Uncle Carl Laemmle was an original.

3

"Samuel Goldwyn Presents"

SAMUEL GOLDWYN, producer of some of the best pictures of Hollywood's golden age, has gained a parallel popularity for coining many of the most amusing non sequiturs of the era, his celebrated Goldwynisms. One does not become a male Mrs. Malaprop without the ingredients, in this case the producer's background, a gift for garbling his acquired tongue, and the cooperation of accomplices able to help create or embellish a legend.

Goldwynisms cover a wide range. Some are largely verbal, an often quite slight tilting away from the normal that draws a smile without further explanation. Others stem from a situation or the personality of the perpetrator and need clarifying circumstances in order to be fully appreciated. The credited catalog includes the following:

> Let's bring it up-to-date with some snappy nineteenth-century dialogue.
>
> In this business it's dog eat dog, and nobody's going to eat me.
>
> Our comedies are not to be laughed at.
>
> I've been laid up with intentional flu.
>
> You've got to take the bull between your teeth.

There is a statue of limitation.

I can answer you in two words—im possible.

I would be sticking my head in a moose.

I love the ground I walk on.

Any man who goes to a psychiatrist should have his head examined.

The trouble with these directors is they're always biting the hand that lays the golden egg.

The publicity for this picture is sweeping the country like wildflowers.

I'll write you a blanket check.

I never put on a pair of shoes until I've worn them at least five years.

I read part of it all the way through.

He treats me like the dirt under my feet.

For this part I want a lady, somebody that's couth.

My horse was in the lead, coming down the homestretch, when the caddy had to fall off.

I want to make a picture about the Russian secret police— the G.O.P.

I had a monumental idea this morning, but I didn't like it.

Certainly the most famous of all Goldwynisms is the classic "You can include me out." This was uttered before members of the Motion Picture Producers and Distributors of America, the so-called Hays Office, as they were discussing their labor troubles shortly before the notorious Bioff scandal shook Hollywood. Goldwyn disagreed with the prevailing viewpoint and gave his notice of withdrawal. In another dispute with the organization years later, when Goldwyn again threatened to secede, the new head, Eric Johnston, said he was relieved. "He has demonstrated a unique and singular flair for saying one thing and doing another . . . he has a penchant for getting into violent disagreement with himself on all sides of a question," said Johnston. A fine sequence of stories illustrates the lovely illogic of Sam Goldwyn, his unique ability to manhandle syntax, to mix metaphors, to misapply and misconstrue, to snarl, twist, and tangle words and thoughts.

In the early days of the talkies, Goldwyn was working with Florenz Ziegfeld on the film version of Eddie Cantor's Broadway success *Whoopee*. Ziegfeld wanted the picture made on Long Island. Goldwyn held out for the West Coast, and as a final inducement he insisted, "Ziggy, the facilities are so good in Hollywood. For instance, you have that Indian scene. We can get our Indians right from the reservoir."

When Goldwyn made plans to film another Broadway play, *The Captive,* his associates warned him he might have trouble because the leading character was a Lesbian. "We'll get around that," said Sam. "We'll make her an American."

Advisers once tried to steer him away from a certain property with the admonition that the story was too caustic. "To hell with the cost," said Goldwyn. "If it's a sound story, we'll make a picture of it."

During the filming of *The Wedding Night,* Goldwyn had ample cause for alarm. Young Gary Cooper's mumbling monotone was barely audible, while Russian actress Anna Sten was giving out with an accent as thick as glue. Their love scenes were particularly horrible. Goldwyn turned to director King Vidor and asked to speak to his stars. He made an emotional plea for cooperation, outlining what was lacking, what was needed, begging them to come through for his sake and for their own. He thought they had understood his instructions, which concluded with this sweeping flourish: "And I tell you if this isn't the greatest love scene ever put on film, the whole Goddamned picture will go right up out of the sewer."

Later an adman wrote copy for a forthcoming Anna Sten feature which read: "The directing skill of Mamoulian, the radiance of Anna Sten, and the genius of Goldwyn have united to make the world's greatest entertainment." "That is the kind of ad I like," said Goldwyn. "Facts. No exaggeration."

To another actress, Helen Hayes, he waxed eloquent on the splendid picture he intended to make from Elmer Rice's *Street Scene.* "If you don't believe me," he concluded, "come up to my office and I'll read you the letter I wrote to New York only this morning."

Once, recuperating from an illness, Goldwyn was depressed. The generous-spirited Marion Davies invited him to come to the baronial Hearst mansion, San Simeon, of which she was the mistress. Goldwyn rested in his room for several days before appearing at the main house. "Marion," he said to his hostess, "you just don't realize what life is all about until you have found yourself lying on the brink of a great abscess."

One season it seemed all the long-awaited Hollywood weekends were rotten after a week of fair weather. Producer William Goetz encountered Goldwyn on an exceptionally sunny Thursday afternoon. "Hello," said Sam cheerily. "What a beautiful day to spend Sunday."

On the golf course, after slicing a half-dozen balls, he finally made a stunning drive. "What did I do right?" he asked the wide-eyed caddy.

Walking in a garden with friends, Goldwyn came upon a sundial. The instrument intrigued him, and he asked the host what it was, learning that one could use it to tell the time of day by observing where the sun was hitting the dial. "Marvelous!" exclaimed Goldwyn. "What will they think of next?"

A member of his staff became embroiled in an argument which angered Goldwyn. Back and forth went the retorts until the producer had had enough. "This is it. You're fired," he shouted. "You're fired. Definitely." The associate started to walk out. "Wait a minute," commanded Goldwyn, a quick cover man. "I didn't say positively."

After a European trip, Goldwyn assembled his promotion staff. With great enthusiasm he told of a new slogan he had devised: "Goldwyn pictures griddle the earth."

Dining at the Stork with his young star Joan Evans and her equally young escort, Goldwyn watched as the waiter brought the boy his first course, a bowl of cold vichyssoise centered in a giant bed of ice. "Eat your soup before it gets cold," said solicitous Sam.

When film writer and educator Robert Gessner suggested to Goldwyn that he compose his autobiography, a look of horror crossed Sam's pixyish face. "I write my autobiography?" he asked incredulously. "Oh, no. I can't do that—not until long after I'm dead."

"Will you give your word of honor that you'll work for me when you finish your present assignment?" Goldwyn asked a writer. The writer said he could not. "If you can't give me your word of honor," persisted Sam, "will you give me your promise?"

"What beautiful hands your wife has," a friend told Sam, who replied, "Yes, I'm going to have a bust made of them."

"David, you and I are in terrible trouble," Goldwyn excitedly exclaimed to David Selznick in a midnight phone call. "What's the matter, Sam?" asked Selznick. Goldwyn replied, "You've got Gable and I want him." This story, in the way of Hollywood lore, is often told with Darryl Zanuck on the other end of the line and another actor the objective.

The midnight and later calls were, however, an authentic Goldwyn habit, for whenever an idea struck, he would begin dialing. When N. Richard Nash was engaged to write the screenplay for *Porgy and Bess,* he retreated to his farm in Bucks County, Pennsylvania, to begin work. At 3 A.M. the sleepy Nash heard the phone ringing. It was Goldwyn. "Do you know what time it is?" Nash asked indignantly. There was a moment of silence. Then at the other end of the line, Nash could hear Goldwyn speaking to his wife. "Frances," he said, "Mr. Nash wants to know what time it is."

Just before the opening of *The Best Years of Our Lives,* studio executives voiced the hope that the film would recoup its large investment. "I don't care if it doesn't make a nickel," said Sam. "I just want every man, woman, and child in America to see it."

As Goldwyn was preparing his version of *Guys and Dolls*, columnist Hedda Hopper learned that Frank Sinatra was to play Nathan Detroit, a role which Sam Levene had interpreted so brilliantly on Broadway. "Why not get Levene?" suggested Hedda. Goldwyn looked at her in amazement. "You can't have a Jew playing a Jew," he exclaimed. "It wouldn't work on the screen."

Director William Wyler was discussing a scene at the home of Goldwyn, who said he could not understand its meaning. Wyler said it was perfectly clear to him. "Do you understand it, Sammy?" he asked Sam Goldwyn, Jr., then fifteen years old. "Sure," said the boy. Senior turned scornfully to Wyler. "Since when are we making pictures for kids?" he demanded.

Wyler directed a film version of Lillian Hellman's *The Children's Hour* for Goldwyn, who ran into censorship problems with the Lesbian theme. To star Joel McCrea he complained, "Can't you straighten those girls out? I'm having more trouble with those people than Mussolini with Utopia."

Early in his career, Goldwyn came to Edward Chodorov with a property, asking him to work on the scenario. "Don't do it, Sam," said Chodorov. "It's not a good story. It's a dog." Goldwyn insisted on following through, hired other writers, and ended up with a resounding flop. Years passed, and Chodorov heard that Goldwyn was planning to make *Gentlemen's Agreement,* a story he really cared about. He told an associate, who called Goldwyn with the news that Chodorov was interested in working for him on the film's scenario. "Never," Sam exploded. "I couldn't even let him in the house. He was involved in one of the worst flops I ever had."

"Take a letter," Goldwyn once commanded his secretary. He began dictating: "James Mulvey, 729 Seventh Avenue, New York City, New York. Dear Jim." He stopped pacing and hesitated. "Read that back," he said.

The producer for a time had a mania for saving every bit of paper relating to film production, every memo, every letter, every script, every report. The material kept piling up and became the bane of secretaries, one of whom came to Goldwyn to ask if she could throw some of it out. "Absolutely not," said Sam. The secretary persisted, pointing out how desperately they needed the space. "Some of the material goes so far back that it's unlikely we'll have use for it," she added. "Can't I just throw out all the letters that go back before the year 1935?" "All right," said her acquiescing chief. "Throw out all the letters before 1935—but before you do, be sure and make a copy of everything."

In 1942 Goldwyn made a contract with International Pictures by which they were to share equally the facilities of his lot. After their third film, however, the renters noticed that each time they started a picture, Sam had started one two weeks before, preempting trucks, cameras, sound equipment, technicians. They complained. To pacify them, Sam called a meeting of some 25 department heads, wardrobe, construction, makeup, and others. He graciously introduced International's top executives, calling Lee Spitz an old friend, saying nice things about William Goetz, admitting that he did not know general manager John Beck well but nonetheless admired him. "I want everything here to be fifty-fifty," Goldwyn then explained to his people. "It's like a partnership—although it isn't. It's an arrangement where I want everything to be fifty-fifty. Is that clear?" Heads nodded as everyone left the genial conciliatory meeting. Later the International people learned that less than half an hour had passed before Goldwyn reassembled his department heads. "Now everything I told you about these people I meant," he said. "I want this to be fifty-fifty like I said." He paused. "But," he said firmly, "I want you to see that I get the best of it."

For a segment of television's *I Love Lucy,* Lucille Ball found her script, in which she was getting up an entertainment program for the PTA, running short. Her husband, Desi Arnaz, decided to call up Goldwyn to try and borrow Frank Sinatra, just finishing *Guys and Dolls* for Sam. Sinatra would sing for the PTA benefit, filling the allotted time. A definite language problem developed over the telephone between the heavy accent of the producer and the no less limping English of Cuban Desi. In halting terms they seemed to come to an understanding. Desi excitedly told Lucy. Lucy, wary, couldn't believe the good news. She was ready to have her secretary confirm when the phone rang. "This is Mr. Goldwyn's office," said the girl. "Mr. Goldwyn gave Mr. Arnaz something. Could you tell us what it is so we can send it over to you?"

At parties in Hollywood, a heavy international flavor is often in evidence. On one occasion, guests were richly amused to see Sam Goldwyn engaged in a 50-mile-an-hour conversation with author Brendan Behan. Behan's Irish brogue was heavier than the densest smog, and further blurred by bonded liquor. He would launch into a long mumbo jumbo, while Goldwyn listened attentively. As soon as an opening occurred, Sam would counter with a long sally of his own. It was doubtful that either understood much of what the other said, yet they were strangely drawn.

Goldwyn's splendid production of *Wuthering Heights* was transformed by Goldwynese into *Withering Heights*. Louis Bromfield became Louis Bloomfield; Arthur Hornblow became Arthur Hornbloom and Author Hornblower; Joel McCrea was Joel McCrail; King Vidor became Henry King; Shirley Temple became Ann Shirley. The confusion was compounded when Anne Shirley then turned into Olivia de Havilland, the former often receiving Goldwyn's warm congratulations for the latter's performance in films. Goldwyn was not unaware of some of his eccentric pronunciations, but he saw them in perspective. Joel McCrea came to him and said he thought they had worked together long enough for Goldwyn to pronounce his name correctly. "Come here," said Sam. From the window he pointed to his block-long car. "That's a Rolls-Royce," he told McCrea. "What do you drive?"

At times a Goldwynism might result from a reverse of order, as when Sam, leaving on a trip, would rush to the boat railing and shout, *"Bon voyage! Bon voyage!"* to his friends on shore.

Samuel Goldwyn is an extraordinary man and an amusing one, but he is not the originator of all the sayings attributed to him. Once a reputation for malapropisms is developed, stories from other times and places begin to attach themselves to its owner.

Adman Arthur Mayer was present when Goldwyn said: "First you have a good story, then a good treatment, and next a first-rate director. After that you hire a competent cast, and even then you have only the nucleus of a good picture." Reporters picked this up and converted it into "only the mucus of a good picture." The concocted version was widely reproduced, the correct one forgotten.

When Mayer was handling publicity for New York's Rialto Theatre, he became known as the Merchant of Menace because the Rialto specialized in horror films, its phone operator answering calls with the words, "Help, murder, police, this is the Rialto, now playing. . . ." Director Michael Curtiz, a Hungarian, no mean mangler of language, exclaimed to Mayer, "When I see the pictures you play in that theater it makes the hair stand on the edge of my seat." The expression gravitated to Goldwyn.

Author publicist Alva Johnston maintains that the line, "Our comedies are not to be laughed at," derives from two brothers of pioneer days in Hollywood; that, "I can answer you in two words—im possible," came from a humor magazine of late 1925; that the sundial story originated with a gardener from far climes and took long years to travel to California.

George Oppenheimer recalls consciously working up a Goldwynism. While he and three other writers were working for Goldwyn, they were aware that he was less and less pleased by his reputation for word-whirling. They also found him difficult and demanding, however, and decided to add one more nail to his cross. Each contributed $10 to a pot. Oppenheimer won when his entry, "It rolls off my back like a duck," appeared in the papers as a Goldwynism.

Goldwyn definitely did not say, "The next time I send a

fool for something, I go myself." That was Hungarian director Michael Curtiz shouting at a hapless messenger who had brought back the wrong article.

And Sid Grauman was responsible for the best reverse Gold-wynism: "I saw this empty taxicab drive up and out stepped Sam Goldwyn."

Anyone who visits Hollywood will find certain classic stories repeated over and over, attributed now to one mogul, now to another. "Never let that sonofabitch in this office again—unless we need him," is now most frequently credited to Louis B. Mayer and Columbia's Harry Cohn. In the era of Goldwyn's greatest activity, it readily attached itself to him.

Even a clever authentic phrase improves with time. Many in Hollywood considered Joe Schenck absolutely trustworthy. Goldwyn said of him: "His verbal contract is worth more than the paper it's written on," which transmuted to: "A verbal contract isn't worth the paper it's written on."

The producer was more pleased with a beefed-up version of his encounter with George Bernard Shaw. Goldwyn visited the great Irish playwright at his home and tried to sign him to a contract. Shaw, impressed by Goldwyn's appreciation of good things, jokingly questioned his commercial sense. Publicist Howard Dietz worked up a story that had Shaw saying, "The trouble, Mr. Goldwyn, is that you are only interested in art, and I am only interested in money." As such, it gained the widest circulation.

Many people close to Goldwyn were so acclimated to his speech patterns that they could not spot a Goldwynism at all. His son, Sam, Jr., swears he has never heard one. Irene Selznick, an intimate friend, similarly states she has been denied the privilege. Specialists of the genre, on the other hand, are quick to perceive the characteristic twist of phrase and to spot ersatz versions which lack the requisite rhythm.

In the growing stages of his career, Sam Goldwyn actively encouraged additions, manufactured or real, to the legend. Press agents Lynn Farnol, Jock Lawrence, and Harry Reichenbach responded perhaps too well. Goldwyn found that wherever he went, people expected him to sparkle with spontaneous wordplay. It was not easy to fulfill their desires. Too, a reputation for witty illiteracy might cause embarrassment to young Sammy, Jr., as he pursued his education. The device, in any event, had served its purpose, gaining attention for commercial ventures, and now it warred with Goldwyn's image as a film maker of quality. The order went out at the studio to cease and desist. Top publicist Ben Sonnenberg was hired to change the climate, to present Goldwyn to the public in the mantle of an industry statesman.

"None of them are true," the producer declared at one point of the much-quoted Goldwynisms. "They're all made up by a bunch of comedians and pinned on me." He went so far as to say that "Include me out" was spurious; what he had said to the producers was: "I'm withdrawing from the association."

Adela Rogers St. Johns recalls that at this period Goldwyn would sometimes be seated next to her at Hearst's San Simeon. She remembers how he would fix her with a piercing eye and talk determinedly about books, seeking no doubt to dispel the notion that he was uncultivated, that he had wanted to send for Shakespeare to rewrite *Othello*.

Samuel Goldwyn survived the laughter, and also the ridicule and abuse, of his early days and is today admired as one of the major film makers. His achievements are all the more remarkable in the light of his humble origins.

The melodious name Goldwyn came late in the day, but a strong personality characteristic developed earlier. Samuel was born in the Jewish ghetto in Warsaw in 1882. He was only eleven and working as an office boy when a fierce streak of independence came to the fore. He ran away from home, making his way to Germany and then on to England. In Manchester he became a blacksmith's helper and lived with relatives. As soon as he saw they were keeping a close eye on him, he again moved on. Traveling alone in steerage, the thirteen-year-old boy arrived in Castle Garden, the predecessor of Ellis Island. Busy officials listened to the rumbling Slavic syllables and wrote their closest approximation to the sounds, Samuel Goldfish.

Young Sam went to Gloversville, New York. He became a glove salesman at $3 a week, working the New England territory, transforming himself into a formidable Yiddish Yankee trader. Within five years his fantastic energy and persuasive harangues made him one of the masters of his métier, a picturesque supersalesman.

From the beginning, his commercial drive blended with a desire for the best. His lean, trim figure was clothed in a well-cut suit whose pockets were empty so as to keep the elegant line. His friends were from Gloversville's upper echelon, people like young Abe Lehr, whose father owned a glove factory, and beautiful doe-eyed Bessie Mona Ginzberg, also of a well-to-do family.

If Sam would have liked to cast a courting glance at Bessie, he was too late. On a trip to the Adirondacks, she had met debonair Jesse Lasky, a leading vaudeville producer; when he pursued her with theatrical flair and ardor, she married him. Bessie did the next best thing by Sam, however. She introduced him to Jesse's sister, Blanche. Blanche was very close to her brother, having been his partner in a vaudeville act. His marriage left her alone and lonely. When the impetuous Sam Goldfish proposed, she accepted. Sam and Blanche were both very strong-minded, as was her mother, who lived with them. The union, entered into in 1910, produced one child, a daughter, Ruth, and ended before many years in divorce.

Meanwhile, in 1912, a new Democratic Congress responded to President Wilson and began lowering the tariff on imported gloves. Wilson therefore deserves some credit for driving Samuel Goldfish into the movie business, or at least out of the glove business, whose bottom Sam could now see swiftly dropping out. He determined to move into a new field.

On the positive side, he was motivated by a visit to a theater on Herald Square in New York. The retiring glove salesman wandered into the noisy, acrid darkness only to be entranced by a Western film starring Broncho Billy. Broncho Billy used the name Gilbert M. Anderson during his immensely successful career as the first cowboy star of films. Actually he was a nice Jewish boy, Max Aronson, from Little Rock, Arkansas. Rather portly, he could not even ride and was thrown from his horse during the first day's shooting of *The Great Train Robbery*. Thereafter, he found his stride and made close to 400 one-reelers as Broncho Billy.

Sammy Goldfish sensed the magic fashioned by the flickering shadows on the silver screen. Even as a glove salesman he liked to surround himself with artistic people. To brother-in-law Jesse Lasky he suggested an entry into the new medium. When Sam suggested, he did so with vigor, with gestures, with a voice which resounded. Lasky said films were the last thing he intended to get into. Sam repeated his arguments six or seven times more, trying to wear his brother-in-law down by attrition, using the techniques that had sold many a glove. Lasky stood firm.

He was vulnerable, however; his closest friend and a partner in vaudeville ventures was Cecil B. DeMille, an actor-author with a zest for adventure. DeMille was tiring of vaudeville. To keep his interest, Lasky proposed a wild idea—to make movies. DeMille took the bait.

The Jesse H. Lasky Feature Picture Company was formed in 1913. Goldfish had been persuaded to try for the still unexplored market in long features by a lawyer friend. Lasky had come to the same turn after viewing an imported feature film starring Sarah Bernhardt. Lasky became president of the new company, Goldfish a general manager, and DeMille the director-general, each the owner of a quarter of the firm. The fourth share went to actor Dustin Farnum, who agreed to accept it in lieu of a salary for starring in a first production, *The Squaw Man*.

Former glove salesman Goldfish was the business genius who guided the film home. The story was an odd mixture of English drawing room comedy combined with Wild West scenes, and Goldfish approved of Lasky's decision to film at Flagstaff, Arizona, to be near Indian extras. He was dismayed when rain in Arizona prompted DeMille to telegraph: "Flagstaff no good for our purpose. Have proceeded to California. Want authority to rent barn in place called Hollywood for 75 dollars a month."

"Authorize you to rent barn on month-to-month basis," said the return wire. "Don't make any long commitment."

No one wanted to be stuck in California. On a month-to-month basis DeMille rented a barn in a clearing in the midst of an orange grove at Selma and Vine streets. The move frightened matinee idol Farnum, who now demanded $5,000 in cash rather than his quarter share. Goldfish raised it by selling exhibitors advance rights to *The Squaw Man*. The quarter share went to two of Bessie Lasky's relatives. *The Squaw Man*, the first feature film to be made in California, helped revolutionize the industry and grossed a fortune. A decade later the quarter share which Dustin Farnum relinquished was worth almost 2 million dollars.

The Lasky Feature Company followed up with a farce, *Brewster's Millions*, and made 21 films in its first year. Cyclonic Sam Goldfish handled all the selling, distribution, and exploitation. His greatest trauma came when DeMille began experimenting with the camera, devising a shadowy lighting effect to achieve a certain mood.

"I can't sell pictures that show only half the hero's face. I'll have to charge half price for them," stormed Sam in the office of Jesse Lasky.

"Tell him it's Rembrandt lighting," DeMille wired his worried president.

The phrase was just the right one to calm the aesthetically inclined business manager.

"I'll charge them double," said satisfied Sam.

The genial Lasky and the more fiery DeMille maintained an easy rapport. Restless Sam Goldfish, slamming doors, pounding down phones, shouting, was at times a source of friction. Once he was voted out of the firm, but within the day his passionate appeal to their sensibilities brought tears to his partners' eyes. They reinstated him, setting the stage for further bedlam.

The breaking point came not long after the company received and accepted a merger bid from Adolph Zukor, whose Famous Players in Famous Plays company was making a similar product. The soft-spoken Zukor, it was agreed, would be president in view of the top stars his company was bringing to the merger. As a result of DeMille's support, Lasky became first vice-president—to Goldfish's displeasure, for he wanted the post. DeMille was made director-general, and a compromise put Goldfish into the nebulous job of chairman of the board.

Here he exuded reckless energy. When Zukor ordered him to pay one of his players, Jack Pickford, $500 a week, he set up a fierce caterwauling. While Jesse Lasky was conferring with another Zukor star, Jack's immensely popular sister, Mary, Goldfish made the mistake of cautioning Lasky to keep production decisions out of the hands of Zukor. Mary Pickford, loyal to Zukor, told him of the incident. Zukor went into retreat for several days, then quietly informed Lasky he would have to choose between himself and the chairman of the board. After much agonizing, Lasky decided to back the thoughtfully coordinated Zukor over the dynamic but somewhat unpredictable Sam, a move which Sam did not forgive until many years later when both were elderly men. Zukor took his victory graciously, insisting that Sam be treated generously. The merged company bought him out for $900,000. It was 1916. Fewer than four years in the film business had made Sam Goldfish a near-millionaire.

The following year he formed a new company with Margaret Mayo, a popular playwright, and Edgar Selwyn, former actor and successful theatrical producer. All three were trying to decide on a name for their organization when director Allan Dwan somewhat facetiously suggested taking *Sel* from Selwyn and *fish* from Goldfish to form the Selfish Company. Goldfish did not take to the idea. Reversing the process worked much better, using *Gold* and *wyn* to form Goldwyn. After the company was launched, Sam grew to like the name so well he had his own legally changed to Goldwyn. It was certainly more appropriate for a presumed connoisseur of public taste. It was also one of the few cases in which a man was named after a company rather than the reverse.

The Goldwyn Company quickly signed up an impressive list of players, and for each Samuel Goldwyn chose an adjective which he used in his inaugural bath of ballyhoo. "Whimsical" Mae Marsh and "vivacious" Mabel Normand were his top film favorites. He courted "vivacious" Mabel but without success. From the stage came "dignified" Maxine Elliott, "soulful" Jane Cowl, and "winsome" Madge Kennedy. The opera contributed "elegant" Mary Garden and, later, "glamorous" Geraldine Farrar.

A series of "Eminent Authors" added their aura, important names such as Rupert Hughes, Rex Beach, Gertrude Atherton, Mary Roberts Rinehart, and Gouverneur Morris. They were Goldwyn's inspiration for competing with older companies whose star rosters were larger than his own. Throughout his career, he remained a champion of writers, even while occasionally driving individual ones almost berserk.

The tone of the new company was class, exemplified by a stunning series of full-page ads in the *Saturday Evening Post*. These spoke of pictures "built upon the strong foundation of intelligence and refinement." A recumbent lion graced the page, the invention of a bright young adman named Howard Dietz. Dietz was a Columbia University graduate and chose that school's mascot to compete with Bison's buffalo and Pathé's rooster.

The Goldwyn Company made hits, including Margaret Mayo's famous play *Polly of the Circus*, starring Mae Marsh; and some flops, such as *Fighting Odds*, with Maxine Elliott, and an expensive *Thaïs* with Mary Garden. Humorist Will Rogers joined the fold, starring in his first film, *Laughing Bill Hyde*. Tom Moore made a picture called *Thirty a Week*, in which a talented actress from the South named Tallulah Bankhead made her first professional appearance.

The expanding firm added new members. The Du Ponts put up additional financing. Theatrical producers Al Woods and the Shuberts joined up. They brought with them a quite extraordinary man named Frank Joseph Godsol, a relative by marriage of Woods. Godsol was one of those perplexing peripheral figures who shot into the film firmament like a comet and out again, leaving almost no trace.

Where Sam Goldwyn carried no bills in his pocket for fear of creating a bulge, Godsol liked to feel the pressure of a thick wad of greenbacks. A tall, handsome, athletic Don Juan, he drove a smart Hispano-Suiza or traveled by train with a retinue of valets and accommodating maids. Gambling dens and exotic night spots were his favorite haunts. He was a big spender, a heavy tipper. Wisely so, for few people other than servants had cause to like him, his career being that of a fast-talking swindler. During the First World War he sold mules to the French government, which later charged him with embezzlement. In another of his multifarious manipulations he imported pearls into the United States but neglected to tell his customers they were imitation.

Curiously, newcomer Godsol was able to convince people like the Du Ponts, the Shuberts, and the Woods that he knew more about film making than Sam Goldwyn. The two men loathed one another. In a company reorganization Goldwyn resigned, but he was persuaded to return two years later. In 1922 Godsol was elected president and Goldwyn left for good. Two years later, the failing Goldwyn Company merged with Metro, and Godsol was heard of no more.

"I was always an independent, even when I had partners," said Goldwyn near the end of his career, when his pictures had won more than a score of Academy Awards. After falling out with two sets of partners, he never took on any more. For the next three decades he made films, close to 80 of them, by himself, always putting up his own money. "It's not that I wanted all the profits," he explains, "but because I never wanted others to lose."

"I make my pictures to please myself," Goldwyn often said, and there is no question but that the vaunted "Goldwyn touch" was the reflection of one man. It meant taste, intelligence, consistency, and a fierce attention to detail. The topics had to be massive and appealing, the stars warm and winning. The story line had to be clear, the character development logical. In every realm it meant getting the best no matter what the cost. Goldwyn pictures had the glamour and glitter traditional to Hollywood. In midcareer, the remarkable onetime glove salesman, Samuel Goldwyn, moved from the business end of motion pictures into the creative end, producing pictures with a highly personal style, putting on a dazzling performance all the way.

Samuel Goldwyn, Inc., Ltd., was formed in 1924 with Samuel Goldwyn in complete charge, with no partners, no directors, no stock. As the years rolled on, "Samuel Goldwyn Presents" introduced a long line of quality features to a receptive public.

The Dark Angel (1925) was a tremendously successful vehicle for Goldwyn's European discovery, Vilma Banky. Stella Dallas (1925), adapted by Frances Marion from the novel by Olive Higgins Prouty and directed by Henry King, starred Ronald Colman, Belle Bennett, Lois Moran, and Douglas Fairbanks, Jr. Whoopee (1930), the first Goldwyn talkie, starring Eddie Cantor, was supervised by Flo Ziegfeld, who later hired many of the girls chosen by Sam, including Virginia Bruce and Paulette Goddard. Arrowsmith (1931), directed by John Ford, had a screenplay by Sidney Howard from Sinclair Lewis' novel, with Colman, Helen Hayes, Richard Bennett, and Myrna Loy. The Kid from Spain (1932), with Cantor and Robert Young, was choreographed by Busby Berkeley, whom Goldwyn imported from Broadway. Dodsworth (1936) was directed by William Wyler, with Walter Huston, Ruth Chatterton, Mary Astor, Paul Niven, Maria Ouspenskaya, John Payne, and Spring Byington. These Three (1936) was a version of Lillian Hellman's story of Lesbian love, The Children's Hour, which Goldwyn dared to slip by the Hays Office; it was directed by Wyler, with Miriam Hopkins, Merle Oberon, and Joel McCrea. Dead End (1937) was the Sidney Kingsley play for which Goldwyn paid the unprecedented sum of $165,000, with Wyler directing Joel McCrea, Sylvia Sidney, Humphrey Bogart, and the Dead End Kids in their first screen appearance. The Little Foxes (1941), the Lillian Hellman play directed by Wyler, starred Bette Davis, Herbert Marshall, and Teresa Wright. The Goldwyn

Follies (1938), directed by George Marshall, had music and lyrics by George and Ira Gershwin, with Adolphe Menjou, Zorina, Andrea Leeds, Kenny Baker, Edgar Bergen and Charley McCarthy, the Ritz Brothers, and the American Ballet of the Metropolitan Opera. *The Adventures of Marco Polo* (1938) starred Gary Cooper; *Wuthering Heights* (1939), Goldwyn's favorite, from the Emily Brontë novel, was directed by Wyler, with a screenplay by Ben Hecht and Charles MacArthur, with Laurence Olivier, Merle Oberon, David Niven, and May Robson. *The Westerner* (1940), directed by Sam Wood, starred Gary Cooper, Teresa Wright and Walter Brennan, who won an Oscar for his portrayal. Filming *The Bishop's Wife,* Goldwyn fired director William Seiter repeatedly, only to rehire him, as three successive scripts were junked at a staggering cost. *Pride of the Yankees* (1942) was the screen life of ballplayer Lou Gehrig, with Gary Cooper. *The Secret Life of Walter Mitty* (1947) was one of many Goldwyn films starring Danny Kaye. *The Best Years of Our Lives* (1946), directed by Wyler, with Myrna Loy, Fredric March, Dana Andrews, and Teresa Wright, won twelve Academy Awards. *Hans Christian Andersen* (1952) starred Danny Kaye. *Guys and Dolls* (1955), the Frank Loesser musical, starred Frank Sinatra, Marlon Brando, Jean Simmons, and Vivian Blaine. *Porgy and Bess* (1958), the great Gershwin folk opera, starred Sidney Poitier, Sammy Davis, Jr., Dorothy Dandridge, and Pearl Bailey.

Samuel Goldwyn discovered or greatly furthered the careers of a good many players. In the silent era, his most valuable find was a Rubenesque Hungarian beauty named Vilma Banky. Goldwyn saw her picture in a photo shop in Budapest. When the real article turned out to have curves that were overly substantial, he put her on a diet before starring her in a series of pictures, the most successful of which was *The Dark Angel.* Vilma's salary went from $250 to $5,000 a week in four years. Her marriage to male screen idol Rod La Rocque was one of the great Hollywood social events of the twenties. Banky's popularity faded with the advent of talkies, which exposed her broad Hungarian accent.

Goldwyn brought Will Rogers into motion pictures and gave him so substantial a salary that Rogers overpaid his income tax. When he had difficulty collecting, the humorist listed the overpaid amount the following year as: "Bad debt—government."

Lucille Ball, Susan Hayward, Merle Oberon, and David Niven all owe their careers to Sam. He ordered German comedian Danny Kaye to bleach his hair and made him a star.

Goldwyn made a number of blunders which he readily acknowledges. He saw Robert Montgomery in a Broadway play. Whereas everyone else said his neck was too long, Sam said his collar was too short. He signed him up, only to let him slip away after a time to MGM. He signed up a young cowboy named Gary Cooper at $50 a week in 1927 but released him to another studio because he thought he was limited to Westerns. Years later he rehired Cooper at 60 times his starting salary. Like almost everyone else, Goldwyn thought Clark Gable's ears were too big, and he also doubted Greta Garbo's star potential because whenever the actress came to visit the Goldwyn house she headed straight for the kitchen to talk to the Swedish cook. Goldwyn also made some story misjudgments, such as selling *The Wizard of Oz* to Mervyn Le Roy, who made a classic of it for MGM.

Far and away the biggest financial blooper on the Goldwyn record was Anna Sten. After seeing the Russian actress in a German version of *The Brothers Karamazov,* Goldwyn imported her from her native Poland, certain that he would repeat with her his previous success with Vilma Banky. He had forgotten that Sten's reputation was made in European silent pictures and that Banky had bowed out when talkies came in.

Anna arrived in America with an already flowing figure and a walloping appetite, with an almost impenetrable accent, and with a husband who tended toward the category of take-charge guy. Undaunted, Goldwyn saw what he felt was a beguiling if enigmatic smile and star quality. He hired an English coach. He hired a masseuse. He hired dancing and singing coaches and even demonstrated a few bunny hops himself. He ordered publicist Lynn Farnol to pull out all the stops. The entire country was deluged with seductive photos of Anna Sten, with reams of copy extolling her beauty, her glamour, her mystery.

Goldwyn chose *Nana,* the Émile Zola story of a courtesan, for his protégée's debut. Director George Fitzmaurice found her a good pantomimist but saw that she had difficulty with her lines, often gesturing first, then delivering the words afterward in a hurried, Slav-accented mumble. The cameras nonetheless rolled, with Richard Bennett and Phillips Holmes also in the cast. Goldwyn looked at the result, scrapped the entire version —at a cost of $411,000—and started over.

When the revised *Nana* opened at New York's Radio City Music Hall in 1934 it broke all records for first-day attendance, the result of Farnol's campaign. The next day the reviews appeared—most uncharitable. The crowds thereafter thinned out as if the plague had struck.

Steadfast Sam persevered by casting Anna and Fredric March in a screen version of Tolstoy's *Resurrection,* retitled *We Live Again.* When the film flopped, Goldwyn continued his march into the valley of disaster with *The Wedding Night,* an original story about tobacco farmers, headed in this case by Gary Cooper. Its dismal failure brought Goldwyn's patience to an end. He abandoned his *cause célèbre,* Anna Sten, who is today occasionally seen in a film role suited to her more limited talents. The case is a classic illustration of the fact that stars are born, not made.

Money was never an insurmountable object to Sam, nor was time, and in any event he continued throughout his career to place his main reliance on writers rather than stars. His early record with "Eminent Authors" such as Rupert Hughes, Mary Roberts Rinehart, and Rex Beach was not notably successful, their contributions usually falling short of the mark. In some cases, their efforts came to absolute zero. Belgian poet Maurice Maeterlinck, who wrote the popular fantasy *The Blue Bird,* at one point came under the Goldwyn wing after he was forced to cancel an American lecture tour due to his execrable English. Goldwyn pampered the poet, giving in to his many whims. Whether it was a mistake due to the confusion of accents or the

Belgian's lack of realism we will never know, but one day Goldwyn came from a meeting highly excited. "He wants to make a picture about a bee," he said incredulously. Reluctantly he let Maeterlinck return to his homeland.

"Everything—stars, directors, producers—depend on the story," Goldwyn continued to say with typical persistence. "I'd hire the devil himself as a writer if he gave me a good story."

The list of writers who worked for Goldwyn during his heyday is imposing: Robert Sherwood, Sinclair Lewis, MacKinlay Kantor, Sidney Howard, Frances Marion, Ben Hecht and Charles MacArthur, N. Richard Nash, Lillian Hellman, and Sidney Kingsley. Indeed, after the death of Irving Thalberg in 1937, Goldwyn was perhaps the producer most widely known as the writer's friend. His indefatigable, restless, impatient nature did not always make him an easy man to work with, however. Goldwyn squeezed minds like oranges. Ben Hecht compared his treatment of writers to an agitated man shaking a slot machine. His method seemed to be to make writers do a scene over and over until they threatened homicide. At that moment he took off the pressure and most of his victims were ready to admit he had forced them to surpass themselves. In later years Goldwyn joined the Shaw Society of America and continued to sponsor writers, establishing annual creative writing awards at UCLA; past winners of the $2,500 prizes have been Francis Ford Cappola, who wrote the screenplay for *Reflections in a Golden Eye* and *This Property Is Condemned,* as well as original scenarios, and Larry Johnson, coauthor of a recent film called *Lord Love a Duck.*

With writer and director alike, Goldwyn was often demanding and exasperating. "Boys," he liked to say, "I can't tell you what it should be, but I'll know it when you get it." Another of his favorite sayings, and certainly apt for his employees, was: "It's the survival of the fittest."

William Wyler was one of his all-time favorites, and their knock-down, drag-out arguments sent many an innocent bystander scurrying for cover. Those who stayed around, however, would be amazed at the end of one of these slugfests to hear Goldwyn shout after the departing Wyler, "By the way, Bill, are we eating at your house tonight or at mine?" To curb their tendency to shout, Wyler and Goldwyn one day made a wager. They would discuss their differences in quiet voices, with the first to raise his to a shout losing the bet. Associates were puzzled to see the two seated at a table, two $100 bills between them, launching vile epithets in the most civilized tones.

It was characteristic of Sam to fight and forget, the histrionics in between being part of the fun. During the filming of *The Bishop's Wife,* William Seaton was cashiered and brought back so often he must have felt like a yoyo. At times, however, the rupture was permanent. For *Porgy and Bess,* Goldwyn hired Rouben Mamoulian, who had directed the original nonmusical DuBose Heyward play on Broadway. There was difficulty from the start. Harry Belafonte turned down the role of Sportin' Life because he thought the all-Negro production might be viewed as an Uncle Tom show. Others felt similar apprehensions, and it was only Sam's persuasive powers which enabled him to finally sign up Sammy Davis, Jr., Sidney Poitier, Pearl Bailey, and Dorothy Dandridge. Mamoulian added to the controversy by giving interviews in which he outlined views to which Sam could not wholly subscribe. Sam did not like others to take the spotlight, especially to air opinions he did not share. Along with differences in interpretation of the screen treatment, it was sufficient reason for Goldwyn to give Mamoulian his walking papers. The director called the action "precipitate and irresponsible" and took his case to the Screen Directors Guild. While it debated the subject, Sam was cautioned to maintain silence. Eventually the Guild cleared him, and a New York *Times* reporter asked him how he felt. "I'm exhausted from not talking," said Sam. Otto Preminger replaced Mamoulian, and *Porgy and Bess,* somewhat static, opened to mixed reviews.

At one point in the thirties, Goldwyn hired writer Adela Rogers St. Johns, giving her an eight-week contract to work on a film. The contract was already in effect when the producer's favorite writer, Sidney Howard, became available. Goldwyn now wanted to get rid of Adela in the worst way. His first step was to tell her the work she had already done was far short of the mark. He suggested she relax, go home, have a nice ocean swim. She had barely arrived at her beach house when Sam appeared and told her he could not pay a writer who spent all her time swimming in the ocean; he would have to fire her. "You can't fire me. I have a contract," protested Adela. "That doesn't matter. You can't do anything if I fire you," said Sam. "Of course I can," Adela insisted. "No you can't," he countered. "You can't afford to let people say Sam Goldwyn fired you." Adela remembered all the prominent writers Goldwyn had fired in the past. "Oh, yes, I can," she said. "What I can't afford is for people to say I worked for Sam Goldwyn and he *didn't* fire me." The contract was honored.

In 1937 Goldwyn paid author Ben Hecht a total of $260,000, giving him an edge over Frances Marion, for years the best-paid screenwriter in Hollywood. At other times, he could be picayune. Also in the thirties, he asked author-magazine editor Allen Churchill to serve as his New York story editor without portfolio—and without pay. The Goldwyn name held considerable appeal for Churchill, and he undertook to ask various authors who had written for him on magazines to do brief screen treatments for a Goldwyn project—again on spec. When Sam came to New York, he invited Churchill to his Waldorf-Astoria suite, and they began discussing the project.

"Will you excuse me a moment?" Goldwyn interrupted. "I'm going to send down for a drink."

Churchill watched with astonishment as a single martini arrived, which Goldwyn sipped while his unpaid helper sat salivating. The two never got together again.

William Selwyn "found" some of the young players whom Goldwyn then "discovered." Joan Evans was one such star, and Goldwyn promised Selwyn rich rewards if he could bring him another such newcomer. Selwyn searched and found Phyllis Kirk, whom he brought to his boss in a New York hospital where Sam was recovering from a prostate operation.

"She's good," said Goldwyn. "I like her."

Selwyn was sure he would now get a bonus or some rich prize for succeeding. Goldwyn surprised him.

"Comes the time you need a prostate operation, it's on me," he told Selwyn, who was only forty and not in immediate need of surgery.

Goldwyn hirelings sometimes felt stifled by his methods. Lewis Milestone hesitated to work for him because he felt Goldwyn wanted writers to write, directors to direct, actors to act, with no interaction between them. He did, however, agree to direct *North Star* because Lillian Hellman, whom he admired, was doing the screenplay. He told her of his views, saying that the story was one to which he, a Russian, felt he could contribute, perhaps aiding her in technical points with which she might be unacquainted.

"The only way to work with Sam, and I know after these many times out, is to talk to me on the phone," she advised. "Sam doesn't have to know. I'll get the idea to Sam. If you do it, there'll be bedlam."

Milestone read the script, put his comments on it in red ink, then called Lillian up to draw her attention to these points. A few day's later, Goldwyn was on the phone from his office.

"Lillian has called up," he screamed. "She was in tears. You're monkeying with her script."

Milestone explained their arrangement.

"Why did you make an agreement like that?" Goldwyn demanded.

"To keep you the hell out of things," said Milestone.

Milestone felt double-crossed by Hellman, but he continued to work on the film. When Hellman came to town, however, and Goldwyn invited him to dinner with her, he refused.

"You have a contract," said Goldwyn ominously.

"There's nothing in it that says I have to have dinner with you and the writer."

"You're right," Goldwyn agreed. "Come after dinner for the discussion."

When Milestone arrived for coffee and talk, Lillian Hellman began complaining about the suggestions he had made on her script in red ink. To Milestone's surprise, Goldwyn started defending him, continuing at each point to support his side of the argument. Milestone, saying he was not needed, excused himself and went home. The next morning, Goldwyn called up. He had apparently had a vigorous argument with Hellman, one of his pet authors. It broke up an old friendship.

The lack of cooperation between the key production figures was reflected in the final product. *North Star* was one of the weakest of Goldwyn's efforts. When he himself did not believe in a product, Goldwyn made no effort to promote it, to send good money after bad. He let *North Star* die.

More often than not, however, Goldwyn made sound decisions. David Selznick, one of his greatest admirers, once reminisced and wondered how Sam so often saw the rightness of things, what it was that gave him his feeling for class. He finally decided it was what he called "a revolving stomach," Goldwyn's gut instinct. His stomach told him what was good and right.

Again and again, Goldwyn was ready to sacrifice everything to satisfy that instinct. During an early scene of *Wuthering Heights* he felt Laurence Olivier was not portraying Heathcliff correctly, that he was hamming it up. Olivier was in fact giving a flamboyant performance. Goldwyn asked him to do it over and was still dissatisfied. The scene was played a third time, and the producer remained unhappy. He called the company together.

"I'm calling the picture off," he said bluntly. "I don't like the results."

"Mr. Goldwyn," said Olivier, "I think you're referring to me. May I speak to you in private?"

"Certainly."

The two retired to Goldwyn's upstairs office. Goldwyn explained at length what he meant. He wanted total sincerity, complete credibility. Olivier began to see what was being asked of him and said he was ready to try again. The immensely gifted actor turned on a sterling performance which made *Wuthering Heights* one of the best pictures of the year.

The Goldwyn sense of fitness applied in many areas. At the

time his greatest silent star, Vilma Banky, married Rod La Rocque, he gave her a rousing send-off, one of many events in her honor. When she wanted to display her gifts in the heavily trafficked Robinson's department store, Sam said no. He was aware that the move might be considered exhibitionistic, in bad taste.

Publicist Pete Smith, later famous for the Pete and Jerry cartoon series, once came to him with an idea which sounded appealing. He wanted Goldwyn to say there were only 13 real actors in Hollywood and name them, a stunt bound to attract attention. Goldwyn liked the basic thought but feared that he would wind up with a limited circle of 13 friends among the actors, together with an angry regiment of enemies. Name 12, he suggested, but leave number 13 a secret. Everyone in Hollywood would put himself in the thirteenth position. The revised stunt became the talk of the town.

Goldwyn never lost his knack for getting attention. When he developed an aversion for bobbed hair, he did more than express it. He cabled the Pope at the Vatican and asked him to join him in his great crusade. The Pope wouldn't go along.

Sam could enjoy himself and use slang with the best of them, but he always kept his sense of measure. When he walked into a closed sound stage and found one of his authors atop a starlet, he thundered, "Not on my time!" before slamming the door. At fellow mogul Harry Cohn's house, he was outraged at Cohn's use of profanity, not objecting to it as such, but to the fact that Harry was foulmouthing in front of women and his young son.

Throughout his long career Goldwyn had a few close associates. His Gloversville friend, Abe Lehr, was his assistant for a time, and Arthur Hornblow, Jr., served as production head for a number of years but bowed out when Sam seemed unwilling to share the credits with him. Certain directors and writers and also actors were often found in the Goldwyn fold. But the greatest sense of continuity came from the producer's second wife, whom he married in 1925 and who has remained at his side ever since.

Frances Howard was playing a flapper on Broadway in the Gilbert Miller production *The Best People* when Sam met her. She came to a gala housewarming party for Condé Nast, the late publisher of *Vogue*. Among all the 300 guests, Sam spotted the slender, dark-haired ingenue with the enormous eyes set deep in a finely featured face. He cut in on a dance, proposed within days, and two weeks later the couple were married. It was an unexpected performance for a forty-three-year-old man who had been a carefree, fast-stepping bachelor for the past 15 years. Sam had never come close to a second marriage, certainly not the day a blind date turned out to be prankster Sid Grauman wearing a blond wig.

Goldwyn's new wife, only twenty-one, had made a number of films, but she gave up all career aspirations of her own after the marriage. Instead she became his inseparable right hand. "She's the only real close partner I've ever had," Goldwyn admits. After raising their only child, Sam, Jr., Frances took an office at the studio and helped actively with production—designing, counseling, guiding both business and creative matters, a virtual associate producer without portfolio. It was Frances who pointed out to Sam the magazine story that became *The Best Years of Our Lives.* When Sam had troubles with Rouben Mamoulian on *Porgy and Bess,* it was Frances who reminded him that Otto Preminger had directed an all-Negro cast in *Porgy and Bess.*

Her role had many facets, including that of mediator and protector. When Goldwyn collaborated with Alexander Korda on a film produced in England, costs ran over, and Sam refused to accept it for American distribution. Both sides sued. In the curious ways of show business, however, a personal friendship was not interrupted. The Goldwyns went on a trip to England, where they were entertained by the Kordas, each side reminding the other he was not calling off his suit despite the pleasures of breaking bread together. After dinner, they talked for long hours. Frances had been waiting for her opening. "Sam, Alex," she said at two in the morning, "don't you think it's time you started patching up that lawsuit?" They did.

Two days before filming was to begin on *Porgy and Bess,* a fire swept the entire set, destroying all costumes, props, and sketches, leaving a million-dollar heap of rubble. Frances took the call which conveyed the bad news at six in the morning. She made inquiries, found there was nothing that could be done to help, and let Sam sleep until his usual waking hour of seven. Over breakfast she told him of the fire. Very calmly he asked if anyone was hurt. Relieved that no one was, he shaved and showered and attired himself in his usual style before going to inspect the ruins. It was a typical reaction. When matters seem to be going well, Goldwyn has always been uneasy, ready to rampage, stirring up artificial storms. In a crisis, he has always been cool. "Usually when people are happy making a picture, it's a stinker," he explains these reactions.

Frances Goldwyn exercised great care and restraint in bringing up their only child, Sam, Jr. Just after the Lindbergh kidnapping, there were threats to various Hollywood families, including Goldwyn's. Many film families sent their children to the Black-Foxe Military Academy, founded by silent star Earl Foxe and a retired army major named Black, and until recently still operative at Melrose and Wilcox. Great limousines deposited progeny at the address, but after the kidnapping scare the showy automobiles gave way to discreet Fords, still chauffeur-driven, and watchmen were hired for day and night duty. Frances Goldwyn was as protective of her son as all the others were of theirs, but a curious circumstance might have been perceived in her management. After school, the chauffeur would drop Sammy, Jr., out of his car at Beverly Drive and Wilshire; there he would set up a stand and sell newspapers, with watchmen discreetly parked in a car across the way. Sammy, Jr., grew up learning the value of work and salesmanship.

In their early twenties, Sammy, Jr., and MGM producer Hunt Stromberg's son, Hunt, Jr., shared an apartment. As a housewarming gift, Goldwyn sent over a case of Scotch. It had hardly arrived when the chauffeur returned. Frances, hearing of the gift, sent him to retrieve all but one bottle of the premium bond.

For many years Frances Goldwyn has been the mistress of the couple's stately Georgian mansion high above Coldwater Canyon in Beverly Hills. Here she would supervise tasteful small dinners for four, her preference, or at times larger soirées for as many as 24 people. An invitation to the Goldwyns was long considered a signal honor, the film colony equivalent of a summons to Buckingham Palace.

Protocol at the palace could be amusing and confusing. After Joan Fontaine scored her great triumph in *Rebecca,* she married cultured actor Brian Aherne. To cap her ascent, an invitation arrived to dine at the Goldwyns. The couple, dressed in their appropriate best, got into their car and sped to the hilltop residence.

"We don't want to be the first," said Joan when she saw no cars in the driveway. "Let's take a little spin."

Twenty minutes later, they again approached the Goldwyn mansion. There were still no other cars. Once more they took to the road, returning to find the situation unchanged. It was now twenty to nine.

"Let's go back home and read the invitation," said Aherne. "Perhaps we made a mistake in the date."

At the house they saw that the day was correct, the hour eight o'clock. For the fourth time they approached the inviting gates, through which no motors had yet passed.

"We'll simply have to go in," said Joan.

The two put on a brave face as they parked the car and walked to the door. The butler met them with a gentle rebuke.

"Mr. and Mrs. Goldwyn have been expecting you since eight o'clock," he said.

Too late the Ahernes realized that in their eagerness to do the right thing, they had made a great gaff, appearing late for a signal honor, dinner alone with the Goldwyns.

The Goldwyns remain a dignified fixture of the Hollywood social scene, Sam, well into his eighties, still trim and erect, Frances aristocratically beautiful and entertaining. One of her favorite gambits is her party description of what she calls "the elegant rich." She has watched six or seven generations of the genre, and begins her story with a young actress who calls her up and speaks deferentially to her as "Mrs. Goldwyn." She gets a part or two, and when invited to dinner, is a bit late. Famous, she forgets invitations and has to be reminded through her secretary. Success makes her so elegant that she finally drops the Goldwyns entirely. Not very wisely, for her fame begins to wane. Her secretary is back on the phone to Frances Goldwyn. Soon she slides further down the scale. Now she herself is back on the line to Frances, her manner reverting to that of her beginnings.

"What's it like to be married to the same man for over thirty-five years?" Shirley MacLaine asked Frances at a recent gathering.

"It gets worse every day," she replied straight-faced. "Thirty-five years ago I told Sam to come home and I'd fix him lunch. He's been coming home for lunch every day for thirty-five years."

Her insight into Hollywood mores was further demonstrated at a party given by Charles Feldman for Charles Bluhdorn, who as head of Gulf and Western has become the top man at its subsidiary, Paramount. At first, Bluhdorn was standing by himself at the bar, an unknown figure. Gradually word got around who he was. Quietly, subtly, guests drifted his way until he was surrounded by a double ring of actors, writers, directors. Observing the scene, astute Frances Goldwyn turned to director Robert Parrish.

"New girl in town," she said.

Frances has been a serene influence on turbulent Sam, able to patch up many a situation, helping to thaw the frost which developed at one point between Goldwyn and his daughter, Ruth, who married designer Frank Capps. She had less success, however, with the most enduring feud of Sam's life, his running battle with Louis B. Mayer.

The animosity dated far back to the days when Goldwyn wanted to marry Jesse Lasky's sister, Blanche. Jesse had met Mayer, then a New England theater owner. He knew that Mayer had met Goldwyn, still Goldfish, when the latter trav-

eled north selling gloves. He asked Mayer what he thought of
the suitor. Mayer gave a most unfavorable verdict, counseling
Lasky to do everything possible to keep his sister from marrying
him.

A few years later, Sam sold Mayer certain rights to exhibit
The Squaw Man. Mayer reportedly agreed to pay $4,000 but
only remitted two thousand. Such defaulting on the part of
theater owners was common at the time; everyone found reasons. The bad feeling between the two men was not helped by
the incident.

When both arrived in Hollywood, the friction continued.
First came the merger of Goldwyn's old company into Metro-
Goldwyn-Mayer. Mayer at that time tried to restrict Goldwyn's
use of his own name in his film presentations, and lawsuits were
instituted to settle the point. From time to time, the two moguls entered into shouting duels, and on one occasion, in the
exclusive Hillcrest Country Club's locker room, pugnacious
Louis heard Goldwyn making remarks distinctly critical of him.
He dropped his towel and started punching.

Goldwyn was able to retaliate when, after divorcing his wife,
Mayer went off in ardent pursuit of beautiful, blond Jean Howard, a fledgling actress. Jean saw a good deal of Mayer but then
ran away to marry agent Charles Feldman. Mayer, his heart
and his ego equally assaulted, raged. He barred Feldman from
all MGM sets and influenced other studios to do the same. Feldman was effectively blackballed. Even his house was reportedly
under surveillance by Mayer henchmen, who reported to him
all who came to visit. Few came. When the couple were down to
their last dollars, Jean Howard, desperate, came up with an
idea. She called Frances Goldwyn.

"Frances," she asked, "if I gave a party for you, would you
come?"

Frances asked Sam, and Sam smilingly said yes, they would
come. Jean and Feldman then called 200 people by phone, the
top stars, directors, and producers, and asked them to come to a
party they were giving for Frances and Sam Goldwyn. The mag-

net drew a great gathering. The Mayer curse was broken, and Feldman went on to become one of the town's major figures.

Inevitably, affairs of the two moguls sometimes intertwined. On occasion, Sam called Mayer and began by inquiring about his health. Mayer, more than slightly hypochondriac, was disarmed and went into a lengthy discourse on the state of his nerves and glands. Goldwyn listened, then as an afterthought expressed an interest in borrowing two MGM players. Mayer saw the ruse and gave an exhibition of profanity which Sam quickly matched. No deal was made.

The two remained contentious until Mayer's death in 1957, but it is doubtful that Goldwyn made the remark attributed to him by several authors: "The reason so many people showed up at his funeral was because they wanted to make sure he was dead." In Hollywood one hears that sentiment attributed to other moguls at other funerals. It's a good story, and the temptation to use it is almost irresistible. Goldwyn, however, denies making the remark. He did not go to the funeral, was in fact not invited, but his son who was with him on that day says he was deeply moved despite the fact he never liked Mayer. Another reason for doubting the authenticity of the story is that Goldwyn was a close friend of David Selznick, Mayer's son-in-law, and remains even today a devoted friend of Irene Selznick, Mayer's daughter. Irene feels Goldwyn would have been incapable of making the remark.

He was often unpredictable, however. In politics, his leanings were heavily toward the right, although he voted for Franklin Roosevelt. He became a close friend of Dwight Eisenhower and once wanted to film his life. Above all, he loathes Russia and Communism. Nonetheless, when the case of "Hollywood Ten" came up, with writers accused of sneaking Communist propaganda into films, Goldwyn took a highly individual stance. He watched the hearings of J. Parnell Thomas' House Committee on Un-American Activities with increasing dismay because he felt this was not the American way of doing things; no congressional committee should be the arbiter of a man's right to work. He felt that producers like Mayer, who were loudest in their outcries, were themselves responsible if the charges were true. After all, they had made the pictures, approving each step of production. Goldwyn felt the entire industry was being hurt by the charges. When he heard that the committee was planning to call his close friend Robert Sherwood, in order to examine certain suspect scenes in *The Best Years of Our Lives,* Goldwyn spent long hours composing a telegram to Thomas. He explained his view and said he wished to appear before the committee to elaborate on it. He also said he would not speak publicly until he heard from Thomas, but that if he did not hear, he would make his telegram public. Goldwyn's stand is credited as a factor in Thomas' dropping his investigation.

At play, too, Sam's logic might take a surprising turn. In the grand old days, he was a poker player for high stakes, a willing gambler. Since the sums involved were great, outsiders sometimes financed a less rich but good player, or bought shares of the top money players. Thus, one might buy a quarter share in David Selznick's game. Not Goldwyn's; he wanted it all. And he hated to lose, a characteristic he carried over into his later years when he switched to croquet, a gentleman's sport.

A young studio executive recalls a recent afternoon when Goldwyn called to suggest a game. The man explained that he was tied up with production problems.

"You're absolutely right," said Goldwyn. "Your work, the picture, comes first."

A half hour later Goldwyn's secretary called, saying couldn't he play for half an hour; Goldwyn was edgy. The situation was again explained. A half hour later, an assistant called to repeat the request, saying it would be appreciated if he played just a little while, for Goldwyn was making everyone nervous. Still later, Frances Goldwyn called and the young executive rescheduled his conferences and headed for the hill to play croquet. The game began. Goldwyn started losing, becoming increasingly irritable. There were several arguments over interpretation. Goldwyn manipulated the ball a bit but continued losing. Finally, the game over and lost, he was in a vile mood.

"What are you doing here anyway?" he demanded of his employee. "A young man like you should be at the studio working."

The story illustrates the Goldwyn persistence which over the years won for him so many a day.

Another quality is demonstrated by a remark composer Richard Rodgers made one day to Goldwyn: "One of the most satisfying things about being successful is that it allows you to work with good people." His head bobbing approvingly, Goldwyn nudged his son and said, "Listen. He said it. Not just me."

Today Sam Goldwyn is a most generous contributor to various charities, one recent gift to the Motion Picture Relief Fund alone amounting to a quarter of a million dollars, and the recipient of a proliferating series of honors and awards such as the Screen Producers Guild's Milestone presentation for distinguished contribution to the industry. In the Goldwyn home sits an array of autographed photos from such friends, alive and dead, as Winston Churchill, Herbert Hoover, and Dwight Eisenhower.

It's all a far cry from those early days when two funmakers at a party played a practical joke on the young producer just emigrated from gloveland. Every time he passed by, they huddled secretively and snickered. Finally, Goldwyn accosted them, saying there was no reason to laugh that he could discover, since he was behaving himself and was as well dressed as anyone at the party. When he learned they were employees, he demanded a written apology, which arrived the next day at the office. He was indeed well dressed, said the note, and who should know better how to dress than a former clothing salesman?

The *New Yorker* magazine, darling of the smart literary circles, took a similar personal tack in an early issue, crediting Goldwyn with rising to a high perch in Hollywood as a result of one key factor—his ten-word vocabulary. A ten-word man can always triumph over minds befuddled by learning, said the

magazine, and Goldwyn had only one thing to worry about—
the man with a five-word vocabulary who could topple even
him.

As he was ridiculed personally, so Goldwyn was often criti-
cized professionally. As long ago as 1937, Edmund Wilson
wrote:

> I for one will be damned if I feel patriotic about Sam
> Goldwyn's silver jubilee. . . . It is plain that today's produc-
> ers, including the great Goldwyn and the late Irving Thal-
> berg, are the same megalomaniac cloak and suit dealers that
> their predecessors were. You have only to look at their products.
> . . . The myth is that he is a movie genius, as intuitive as he
> is uncultured, who has defied Hollywood conformists to make
> pictures that are different. The highest reach of his pioneering
> that my research has uncovered is importing into Hollywood
> Busby Berkeley to do the dance routines for "Whoopee". . . .

Critics dealt more kindly with Goldwyn as the years went
on. With his career in perspective in the sixties, Richard Griffith, curator of films for New York's Museum of Modern Art,
said:

> A movie connoisseur has not reached firm ground until he
> can enter an unknown picture in the middle and say to him-
> self with some confidence, Huston did this, or Ford. . . . By
> this test, the films produced by Sam Goldwyn are great films.
> King Vidor and William Wyler and Henry King and Robert
> Sherwood and Lillian Hellman have done some of their best
> screen writing for Sam Goldwyn, but it has been a specific
> kind of good work, possessing their own individual styles and
> values; they have when working for him worked in a style
> which perhaps they created for him but which is . . . his alone
> —the Goldwyn touch.

"The picture makers will inherit the earth," Goldwyn never
tires of repeating, insisting always that films are the one great
new art form of the century and that they must be considered as
art before they can succeed as business.

His policy over the decades never changed. "My idea of making motion pictures, the idea that fascinated me originally, was that films are family entertainment, a place where everyone can go and not blush over what they see on the screen," he has said. "I never made a movie that would embarrass a father who took his family to see it. People knew when they saw the Goldwyn name on a picture, it was a family picture. I've proved that fine things, clean things, can be done."

Goldwyn's view of his own work and of the Hollywood of which it was a part was characteristically expressed by him in the fifties:

> Hollywood has swaggered and boasted and roistered and shouted from the rooftops, to be sure, and admittedly been guilty of a variety of imperfections, exaggerations, and misrepresentations, but despite all the superficial faults which it has been intellectually fashionable to point to from time to time, Hollywood has nonetheless been the most influential and universal purveyor in this century of the potpourri, the hodgepodge of all the many influences and cross currents that go to make up that thing we call American democracy.
>
> The creators of motion pictures—the producers, writers, the directors, the actors, and all the other artists and technicians involved have always been interested in all the same things which interest most Americans—telling stories, making money, owning cars, having families, talking, singing, dancing, loving, history, sports, laughter—the entire catalogue of interests and emotion that is America. Overall, Hollywood has expressed America, and in so doing it has created an art form which is a real embodiment of the American democratic spirit . . . the mass expressions of the hopes, the aspirations, the dreams and the realities of the American people.

"Many years ago there lived in a crowded slum in a city under the leaden skies of Eastern Europe a poor little Jewish boy named Samuel," John Dos Passos has written of Goldwyn. "It was a city full of mud and misery. The police wore great heavy high leather boots just for the purpose of kicking poor little boys, and especially poor little Jewish boys, around. The little boy was very skinny and very weak, but there burned in his heart so great an ambition that he decided he'd run away far to the east beyond the Rhine and across the ocean. There was a country called America. 'What did I know about it?' he says to-day. 'It was a dream.' "

Samuel Goldwyn traveled from that grim ghetto in Warsaw to a masterly perch in another ghetto, this one going by the glamorous name of Beverly Hills. He moved with style. He made motion pictures in his style. "Hollywood owes me nothing. I owe Hollywood everything," he says. For what we owe him, we have to do what Edmund Wilson sarcastically suggested —look at the products. They're not hard to find. They're all over the Late Show and usually outrating everything in viewing range.

4

The Gentlemen from Paramount

LEGEND says that in the early days a homesick couple planted a slip of English holly in front of their adopted California home and tacked up a sign: HOLLYWOOD. The little bush withered and died, victim to a climate that was too warm. The name stuck, however.

The irony in the story is manifold. There is an air of unreality in Hollywood; nothing and no one remains the same in that strange, special, complex, compressed, self-fascinated, feverish, sensual, irresistible atmosphere. One has only to talk to a pair of cabdrivers to feel the mood. The first will say the haze in the air is a prelude to a rainy season that will probably last at least six unremitting weeks; the second will announce with absolute firmness that the rainy season is over and that you are in for six solid months of sunshine.

The climate is one factor that affects people. The peculiar quality of the film industry is surely another. There is something uniquely ephemeral about making motion pictures. Ideas and techniques are developed out of thin air and disappear again as readily as they were found. The studios have virtually no records, so that if a producer wants to know how the whale for an early version of *Moby Dick* was constructed, his only hope is to find still alive the man who did it. Metro's Louis B. Mayer used to boast that his was the only industry whose leading assets walked out the gates at night.

The transplanted, competitive, self-fascinated style of Hollywood naturally produced bizarre transmogrifications in the people who came to work there. Money was not the key to success; if it had been, Howard Hughes would have been the world's greatest producer of motion pictures. Adaptability was much more important, an ability to glide easily into the unpatterned avenues of thought and expression and action. For a man like William Faulkner, it was impossible. He insisted to Harry Cohn at Columbia that he would have to work at home. When he finally called in, it was from the family domain in Oxford, Mississippi. The writers who made it in Hollywood and who helped make Hollywood were not the Faulkners but the New York and London and Hungarian scribes who came dressed in business suits and driving conventional Fords which they swiftly exchanged for berets and turtlenecks and beads and low-slung convertibles with which to careen down Sunset Boulevard. As Ken Murray once put it: "Hollywood is a place where you spend more than you make, on things you don't need, to impress people you don't like." Or as Dudley Field Malone said: "Hollywood is the town where inferior people have a way of making superior people feel inferior." Not many who came succeeded, no matter what their specialty. And of those who did succeed for a time, a goodly proportion later lost their touch.

The men who founded and formed the companies which were eventually to turn into Paramount all spent their early years in the East—B. P. Schulberg, Jesse Lasky, Cecil B. DeMille, and Adolph Zukor.

From 1925 to 1932 Benjamin Percival Schulberg was Paramount's head of production, one of the dominant figures in Hollywood. In 1949, broke and unemployed, he begged for work in a paid advertisement in *Daily Variety*.

Known in his heyday simply as B.P., Schulberg was not the typical ill-educated Jewish immigrant from middle Europe. He was born in the less harsh environment of Bridgeport, Connecticut, in 1892, next to the last of fourteen children. The family moved to New York's lower East Side, where Ben attended public school and later City College.

Still in his teens, he gave up his studies to become copy boy for Franklin P. Adams on the *Evening Mail*. Graduating to reporter, he found that each year 80,000 New York children wrote letters to Santa Claus which were never answered. He induced the paper to respond, drawing on a sympathetic readership to raise $65,000. He himself spent long hours delivering Christmas gifts to neediest cases and years later remembered the experience as one of the most satisfying of his life.

At twenty Schulberg became an editor of *Film Reports*, a small trade paper. He met Edwin S. Porter, pioneer director, who asked him to become scenario editor of his film company, Rex. Both Porter and Schulberg were absorbed in 1912 by Adolph Zukor and his Famous Players company.

"That's when I turned out a scenario in one day," Schulberg later reminisced. "We'd be scheduled to start a picture on Monday morning. Along about Tuesday I'd think I ought to do something about it. Wednesday I'd remember it again. Thursday I'd finally sit down and write something. We'd talk about it Friday, maybe have some rehearsals on Saturday. Anyway we'd always start shooting Monday."

Adolph Zukor was certain that the future of films lay in features longer than the customary one- and two-reelers. Schulberg was the inspired publicist for his first venture. After purchasing the North American rights to Sarah Bernhardt's *Queen Elizabeth*, Zukor decided to offer it as his own production. Bernhardt had disdained the lowly film form, said the Schulberg press release, until Zukor persuaded her it was important to record her art for future generations. On seeing the finished product, her conversion was complete.

"Ah, Mr. Zukor," she reportedly exclaimed, throwing her arms around him. "You have put the best of me in pickle for all time."

The story was so widely circulated that Adolph Zukor gradually began to believe it genuine. At a dinner honoring his first five years as a company head, he was asked what had been his most thrilling moment in film making. He recited, word for word, the story of Sarah Bernhardt, his persuasive powers with her, and her embrace at seeing herself pickled for all time. Schulberg caught his eye near the end of the recital.

"You see, that's all your fault," Zukor said with a wry smile.

Schulberg was also responsible for dubbing Mary Pickford "America's Sweetheart" before leaving to go into independent production.

His greatest success on his own came with the signing of a pretty Brooklyn redhead named Clara Bow. Gum-chewing Clara came to films by submitting her likeness to a beauty contest in *Photoplay*. The magazine was her favorite reading. When Schulberg rejoined Paramount in the twenties, vivacious Clara went along, reaching the zenith of her fame as a twenties flapper after Elinor Glyn told the world she had IT.*

In addition to Bow, Schulberg was credited with discovering or developing Gary Cooper, Claudette Colbert, George Raft, and Fredric March, among others. He brought over Emil Jannings and Marlene Dietrich from Germany, working skillfully with both. He made widely acclaimed versions of *Dr. Jekyll and Mr. Hyde* and *The Way of All Flesh*. He helped touch off the gangster cycle with Ben Hecht's *Underworld*. His production of the aviation antiwar film *Wings* won the first Academy Award in 1928.

Working for him were young David O. Selznick and William Goetz. Schulberg's salary reached a splendid peak of nearly $10,000 a week. His wife, Adeline Jaffe Schulberg, was a vivid attractive woman who had given him three gifted children, Budd, Stuart, and Sonia. B. P. Schulberg seemed to have about everything that an ambitious man with talent could hope for.

Why did it all collapse? The advent of talkies did not help.

---

* In addition to crediting Clara Bow with the sex appeal symbolized by IT, she also bestowed the term on actor Antonio Moreno, a horse used in Westerns, and the doorman at the Ambassador Hotel. To Metro actor William Haines, on the other hand, she said he positively did not have IT.

"Madame," said Haines, "you left the *sh* off it."

Schulberg was schooled in silent films, and his protégée, Clara Bow, was terrified of the microphone and never adjusted to sound. Financial threats posed to the industry by the Depression raised special problems.

Then there was Sylvia Sidney. Oddly enough, it was Schulberg's wife, Ad, who first saw the actress perform in a Broadway play called *Bad Girl*. She urged him to sign the director and the star, only to find him unreceptive. She persisted, setting up a meeting with Sylvia which led to a Paramount contract. Even then Ad continued to help Sylvia's career, urging her husband to give her better roles. When Schulberg fell unreservedly in love with Sylvia Sidney, it broke up his marriage to Ad.

"Why did you insist I meet her?" B.P. later chided her.

It was more than a changing industry, the Depression, and a distracting love affair which toppled Ben Schulberg from power. It was getting to the top that destroyed him, in the view of his former wife, and the pressure of staying there. He had not drunk before, but now he began to tip the bottle. He became a compulsive gambler, dropping sums up to $25,000 in a night. Women went with the wine and the cards, all attempts to relieve tension. As anxieties and insecurities multiplied, so did the efforts to escape. Ben Schulberg became unstable.

It was easy now for him to fall into traps like the one set by that witty writer Wilson Mizener. Mizener tried to sell him a story, but Schulberg turned down successive versions. When he submitted a final outline, Schulberg tossed it away like the others, saying it was not good enough.

"I thought you'd say that," said Mizener. "It's a synopsis of *Deep Purple*, which ran for two years on Broadway."

"It's a dog eat dog business, and nobody's going to eat me," said Sam Goldwyn. To begin with, there were the built-in antagonisms between the money interests in the East and the production men on the Coast. There were the uncertainties of charting a course in a new field. It took a certain species of behemoth battler to endure the competitive squeeze in Hollywood. Those who survived—only a handful—played off pawns one against the other, seldom allowing a potential successor to develop in their midst. On all levels they sowed the seeds of insecurity. A familiar tactic, for example, was to put a fresh writer on a project without telling the original he had a collaborator. Terrified of scandal, of sound, of its own shadow, Hollywood has always been quick to panic.

A reorganization hit Paramount in the early thirties. When Schulberg's contract was not renewed, he went back to independent producing, drifting from studio to studio, the overall direction down. By 1949 the genial and generous and cultivated man who had once headed Paramount production was reduced to a last appeal, a full-page ad in *Daily Variety* begging for a job:

> As most of you know, I have devoted a third of a century to our industry. Yet at this time, when the industry demands and requires a fixed habit of production economy, I can't get a job. My friends tell me doors are closed because I have in my time talked back to some of the big boys. This is the only business I know. I am able to work as hard as anyone in it. . . . I believe the many creative artists I have discovered will agree with me that industry loyalty is a two-way street. Surely I have made some mistakes—as who hasn't. What is the juridical code of the industry? Life imprisonment for a misdemeanor and execution for violating a parking law? Must we always wait until a productive pioneer is found dead in some "obscure Hollywood hotel room" before reflecting upon an "indifferent and forgetful" industry?

One of the "big boys" that Schulberg had talked back to was Louis B. Mayer. They quarreled in early days when both briefly rented space at the Selig studio. Mayer was later incensed when Ben's son, Budd, wrote *What Makes Sammy Run?* a novel which took a hard look at Hollywood. He was also outraged at Budd's political liberalism, insisting that blackballing was too good for him and only deportation would be adequate punishment.

There was only one telephone call in answer to the *Variety* ad—and that led nowhere. B. P. Schulberg was bitter, but his spirit was not completely broken. Before he died of a stroke in 1950, he gave Budd instructions for a final gesture.

"Put my ashes in a box and tell the messenger to bring them to Louis B. Mayer's office with a farewell message from me," he said. "Then when the messenger gets to Louis' desk I want him to open the box and blow the ashes in the bastard's face."

"Happy families are all alike," Tolstoy wrote, and on a parallel plane, there is usually less to say about sweet and good people than about those who are contentious and irascible. When Ben Schulberg was in power at Paramount, his immediate superior was Jesse Lasky, a kind and debonair gentleman, a lamb who lay down with lions.

Lasky was an important vaudeville entrepreneur before he teamed with Sam Goldwyn and Cecil B. DeMille to make the first important feature film in America, *The Squaw Man,* in 1913. When the company merged with Adolph Zukor's Famous Players several years later, with Zukor becoming president and Lasky his first vice-president in charge of production, Lasky defined his duties as follows:

> In the producer's hands lies the supervision of every element that goes to make up the finished product. These elements are both tangible and intangible, the control of human beings and real properties as well as the control of the artistic temperament, the shaping of creative forces and the knowledge of the public needs for entertainment. . . . The producer must be a prophet and a general, a diplomat and a peacemaker, a miser and a spendthrift. He must have vision tempered by hindsight, daring governed by caution, the patience of a saint and the iron of a Cromwell.

Lasky had a sound business head and an uncanny gentle persistence. He was wise enough to lure opera diva Geraldine Farrar to Hollywood to make *Carmen, Temptation,* and *Joan the Woman.* He was able to rule over warring queens Gloria Swanson and Pola Negri, and to put up with the capers of Clara Bow. He was able to recruit such talented producers as Walter Wanger and Gilbert Miller to work for him. He inventively turned

Lucille Langehanke into Mary Astor, Jane Peters into Carole Lombard, Luis Alonso into Gilbert Roland, Augusta Appel into Lila Lee, and christened Ricardo Cortez, Gale Storm, and others with their screen names. Lasky signed Maurice Chevalier after Louis B. Mayer passed up the opportunity; he found Jeanette MacDonald in a Broadway show; and Bing Crosby singing on stage between films; and Charles Laughton; and on and on. He was able to ride out three studio scandals—the rape trials of roly-poly comedian "Fatty" Arbuckle, the mysterious murder of the company's most distinguished director, William Desmond Taylor, and the death through drug addiction of popular Wallace Reid.

With his natty pince-nez and his high, stiff collar, Lasky was an immensely likable figure around Hollywood, reigning over elite social gatherings at his town house and at his enormous 50-room beach mansion on the Santa Monica Riviera. His wife, Bessie, was a madonnalike Boston beauty who added to the charm of his entertaining.

One minor problem was that Jesse could not remember the names of the many people he asked to share his hospitality. When he announced one day that a famous English author was arriving, Bessie could not squeeze the man's name out of him, not even on the evening of the party she gave in his honor. The distinguished Englishman did not seem aware of her dilemma as she delicately introduced him to other guests, saying, "This is Norma Shearer. You know our guest of honor, don't you, Norma?" Everyone was wonderfully polite, pretending to know, and not once did the guest betray his name. The party ended, and he was still a mystery. Not until weeks later, when Lasky was at another gathering and heard the name by chance, did he recall that Guy Bolton had enjoyed his hospitality.

Lasky was always ready to make a speech, whether to declaim goals and ideals of the film industry or to present a new business associate or a fresh star. At one banquet he proudly presented a curvaceous Australian starlet whom he expected to do splendidly in Paramount films. His buildup was lengthy, and he was unaware that the girl was not fully aware of certain subtle language differences between her country and his—notably, that the English vernacular for salary is "screw." When he had finished he asked her to say a word.

"Thank you, Mr. Lasky," she said simply. "As long as I get a good weekly screw, you may be sure I'll do my job to the very best of my ability."

Because he was so affable and well liked, Lasky was an easy butt for practical jokes. Master prankster Sid Grauman knew of his readiness to burst into oratory and provided an occasion of his own devising. He faked a letter from the Pasadena Chamber of Commerce inviting Lasky to address its members on their forthcoming tour of the studio. Grauman and friends chose a Paramount projection room for the scheduled affair and proceeded to use trick lighting which kept the speaker from seeing that the seats were all filled with dummies from the prop department. As Lasky began, he was dismayed to find so little audience response. He told funnier jokes and grew increasingly puzzled by the silence. His voice rose but still no laughs. His agony was at its height when Grauman turned on the lights to reveal the hoax.

"What Jesse Lasky and I had was more than friendship," Cecil B. DeMille wrote of their relationship. "It was an affection warmer and closer than that of many brothers." Lasky and his president, Adolph Zukor, also had great respect for one another and in the manner of courteous courtiers addressed one another as Mr. Lasky and Mr. Zukor.

The Paramount business conferences were for many years open, friendly affairs where each executive aired his problems, candidly admitting mistakes if he had made them, and sought constructive advice and information. Harmony reigned most of the time until the early years of the Depression. At one meeting, in 1932, the group around the table was shocked by a man who had taken charge of one of the company's divisions.

"Lasky, you're finished here," he said to the gaping conference.

"But I'm a vice-president of this company," said the appalled Lasky.

The man went on to outline bad decisions he felt Lasky had made; his usefulness to the company was over, he said firmly. In the hysteria-ridden atmosphere of the early Depression he was able to make his dictum stick.

The astonishing thing was that Lasky was never able to express resentment, not toward this antagonist or toward any of those who failed to come to his aid, then or later. He went on to become an independent producer, his greatest success being *Sergeant York,* which won a 1941 Academy Award for Gary Cooper. Here, again, Lasky was overtaken unexpectedly by a cruel undeserved fate. He had taken a capital gains position of the film, using the profits to make excellent investments in stocks and real estate. More than a decade later, the federal government challenged his accounting and drew him into litigation which dominated the final years of his life. Because his assets were all in the open, with no such devices as deposits in Swiss banks, he was extremely vulnerable, ready to be stripped. Only by immersing himself in Christian Science and a religion called the Science of Mind was he able to keep his mental equilibrium. With all his tribulations, Lasky, in the memory of his widow, never spoke unkindly of another human being. The iron of a Cromwell he did not have, but the patience of a saint.

Ben Schulberg was unable to breath the heady air of Hollywood's stratosphere without feeling intoxication. Without too much help from others, he shook himself from the heights. Jesse Lasky's nature contained a spirituality which was out of focus on the competitive field of action but which yet enabled him to survive with an admirable personal grace. Both were Jewish movie moguls, but American-born, not of that resilient European stock shaped by early adversity.

Cecil B. DeMille was only one-quarter Jewish, on his mother's side, and he was not born in Europe, but he was nonetheless well equipped to do battle with giants. He revered his father, a Dutch Episcopalian of considerable sensitivity, and he was close to his mother, the former Gertrude Samuels, who later turned literary agent. The two directed his interest, and that of his older brother, William, toward the legitimate theater. William wrote *The Warrens of Virginia* and other Broadway plays before turning to films as a director-writer. Cecil was an actor and a play collaborator with William but found his true vocation as a film director.

In those early days, in the famous barn at Selma and Vine which served as the studio for DeMille, Jesse Lasky, and Sam Goldfish, the actors dressed in the horse stalls. While the horses and carriages were being washed down, the DeMille office would get a steady trickle of water. This led Cecil to buy a wastepaper basket into which he put his feet when the floods came.

The paraphernalia with which DeMille dressed himself, the leather leggings called puttees and the turned-around cap, became standard equipment and made him the prototype of his trade. In the primitive conditions of the time, the puttees were a protection against the wild undergrowth and reptiles, notably rattlesnakes. DeMille always carried a pistol to ward off such dangers.

When William went West with the company in 1914, he wrote:

> Hollywood itself is a suburban town, with lots of tropical vegetation, tremendous palms, etc., but it all has to be nurtured very carefully, the country being really desert and supplying best those things which grow in the desert. The general effect is rather tropical luxuriance with wild desert just outside and in plain view. . . .
>
> The usual thing seems to be to rent one of the very pretty furnished bungalows with which the place is filled and camp out, as it is always summer. Folks don't take housekeeping at all seriously and you can have your own house for $50 a month, furnished, or something like that. . . .
>
> I can't begin to tell you all the exciting things we have been doing. . . . You'll see when you see "The Rose of the Rancho" picture. I was one of the sharpshooters today, shooting with powerful rifles to break through doors, smashing the top of a stone wall, breaking water jugs, etc. It was very exciting Friday.

If I shot badly, I would be apt to kill someone but the effect will be fine in the picture. . . .

When the door was battered in, Johnson, the leading man, got hit in the head by a piece of flying board and knocked out, his head being rather badly cut. But we patched him up and made him play three more scenes afterward. . . .

Yesterday Cecil had an offer from a new combination of one hundred and twenty thousand a year to go with them. At the same time, companies are going to fail, but it is because companies like ours are putting them out of business. We'll have to wait a bit for the big money, but it is here, if we deserve it. . . .

Whatever else the life may be it is absolutely healthy . . . but the social atmosphere is that of an English regiment in India—dependent on its own members.

I don't think, however, you need fear our remaining here permanently. . . .*

As Hollywood came into its maturity in the silent era, Cecil B. DeMille sensed the public's interest in the mores of money and sex. His boudoir epics with Gloria Swanson, *Male and Female, The Affairs of Anatol, Her Gilded Cage,* showed the audience the objects of their dreams—beautiful clothes, rich jewels, champagne dinners—but within a context of high society that questioned whether they were sufficient to bring happiness. The DeMille insistence on authenticity was already much in evidence. The gowns and the champagne were real. The audience might not know that the Chanel dressing gown cost $7,000, but DeMille knew that the actress wearing it would know and that the expression on her face and her manner of walking would vindicate the expense.

DeMille's father wanted him to become a lay reader in his church until producer David Belasco persuaded him that he could preach to a much larger audience by writing for the stage. When Cecil B. DeMille came truly into his own as a director with his majestic Bible epics, the public itself showed him the way.

* These letters are now part of the Lincoln Center Library of the Performing Arts in New York.

"I make my pictures for people rather than for critics," De-Mille always maintained. As far back as the early 1920's, after making *Adam's Rib*, he decided to let the theater audience choose the subject of his next film. Publicity man Barrett Kiesling and press agent Al Wilkie organized a national contest with a first price of $1,000 for the best idea for a picture. The entries flowed in, ranging from themes sublime to themes ridiculous. Over and over again, to everyone's surprise, came the suggestion of biblical subject matter. Eight different letters referred to the Ten Commandments.

"Here was a theme that stirred and challenged in me the heritage of being Henry DeMille's son, a theme that brightened memories of his reading the Bible aloud to us and teaching his sons that the laws of God are not mere laws, but are *the* laws," DeMille later wrote.

Instead of dividing the first prize among the eight entries, he awarded each $1,000, and then took his idea to Adolph Zukor.

"Old men wearing tablecloths and beards?" demanded the incredulous company president. "What budget would you be thinking of?"

"One million dollars."

Since the figure rendered Zukor speechless, DeMille was able to overwhelm him with his enthusiasm for the project, outlining the great scenes showing the splendor of the Pharaohs, the Israelites toiling in the desert, Moses pleading for them, the flight from Egypt, chariots in wild pursuit, the miracle of the crossing of the Red Sea, to say nothing of the central scene, the orgy before the Golden Calf.

Zukor was won over and in turn won over the bankers he needed. DeMille flew into action, extravaganza and authenticity his uneasy co-bywords. Researchers ransacked libraries and museums for details of costumes and harnesses. Agents were sent to the Near East to purchase old goblets and knives and props of every order. Theodore Roberts was cast as Moses, Estelle Taylor as his sister, Miriam, Charles de Roche as the Pharaoh Rameses, Julia Faye as his wife, James O'Neill as Aaron. A hundred dancing girls began working on the colorful scene before the Calf of Gold. A group of 250 Orthodox Jews were engaged, people who spoke no English, to chant in ancient accents for one brief scene.

By the time filming began, the costs were beginning to alarm the home office in New York. More than 2,500 people and 3,000 animals were being fed each day at Guadalupe, near Santa Maria, California, where the crossing of the Red Sea was being relived. A bill for $5,000 came in for two perfectly matching coal-black horses purchased to draw the chariot of the Pharaoh.

Finally the pressure on Zukor became so great that he demanded a halt in expenditure. DeMille made a magnificently grand gesture—he offered to buy the film for one million dollars. To the astonishment of the home office, he was able to raise the money from banker A. P. Giannini, Joseph M. Schenck, and raw-film magnate Jules Brulatour. The home office refused his bid. DeMille finished the film.

The Ten Commandments wound up with a final cost of $1,-475,836. It opened at Grauman's Chinese Theatre in Hollywood on December 4, 1923, and on December 21 it opened at the George M. Cohan Theatre in New York, breaking all records by running for 62 consecutive weeks; *Birth of a Nation* had run for 44. By the end of the decade, gross receipts were a reassuring $4,168,798.

DeMille's extravagance was vindicated, but his relations with Paramount executives were severely strained. In a meeting which was distressing to all, one man—whom DeMille has never identified—told him: "Cecil, you have never been one of us."

The old ties with Paramount were severed, and in 1925 DeMille set up his own producing organization which did some releasing through MGM but eventually settled down into an adjunct, albeit completely independent, of Paramount. As his own master DeMille gathered about him the organization which made his name synonymous with biblical epics and historical spectacles, such well-known efforts as *King of Kings, The Sign of the Cross, Cleopatra, The Crusades, Reap the Wild Wind, Samson and Delilah, The Greatest Show on Earth* and a lavish Technicolor remake of *The Ten Commandments* in 1956.

The latter gave birth to the most famous of all DeMille stories. The second *Ten Commandments* was filmed on location in Egypt. For the great climactic scene which showed the Jews escaping from the Egyptian army and crossing the Red Sea, thousands of extras were hired, not on an individual basis but by village, so many hundred tribesmen under a chief, plus all the goats and sheep and geese and other animals. For the big scene, stars, stuntmen, horses, chariots, extras, all were in place. As the hallowed tale goes, the master camerman was seated on top of a hillock, commanding a battery of focused apparatus, when DeMille gave him the signal that set the massive crowd into action—Israelites running and shouting, Egyptians in shrill pursuit, horses and chariots and goats all blending in a magnificent panorama shrouded in a filmy cloud of dust.

"Well, how was it?" the satisfied DeMille shouted at the master cameraman when the tumult had died down.

"Ready when you are, C.B.," came the distant answer, accompanied by a snappy circling of thumb and finger from the cameraman, who had not heard the command to start shooting.

In fact, the circumstances were quite different. Henry Wilcoxon, the associate producer on the picture, remembers that he was on a camera down by one of the sphinxes; John Fulton was on top of the gates; DeMille himself was on the main camera. He did give the signal to begin the action, and once that immense conflux of people started to move it was impossible to stop them. Apparently, the boom lens was unsteady and got off its track.

"How are things going?" DeMille asked Wilcoxon.

"I think the film has buckled in the camera," the latter replied.

Actually, DeMille's footage was usable, as was Fulton's, and even some of Wilcoxon's.

"I'm a Welshman, and I say why let the truth spoil a good story," said Wilcoxon in urging that the classic tale be told as it has come down to us.

The DeMille technique of producing was organized down to the minutest details. He would begin with a 30-page treatment from the writer, working with him to expand this to perhaps 500 pages, then boiling it down again. In the process, DeMille himself did a good deal of writing. At times he liked to work with several men, each on a different segment. So extensive was the preparation that in the filming there would be few retakes, for each prop, each costume, was described and could be readied. Extremely visual, DeMille would have much of the film drawn for him. To get a point across, Henry Wilcoxon, his associate producer for the past fourteen years, would often make a sketch and slip it to him unobtrusively at conferences.

"Yes, here's what I mean," DeMille would say.

New writers were frequently mystified when he would ask them for a "Jody version." The old-timers would smile, knowing that Jody was DeMille's seven-year-old grandson. By a Jody version he meant he wanted a short treatment of five or six pages which he would take home and read to the boy. If Jody wriggled with delight, all was well; if not, the treatment would be scrapped.

"If I can't interest Jody, I won't make it," DeMille would say.

"All right, gentlemen," DeMille might tell his writers on another occasion. "Now I want you to prepare a short treatment for a circus story. No dialogue, just narrative style. And if anyone mentions the word circus, he's fired."

What DeMille wanted was a well-constructed tale which could stand on its own and then be transplanted to the circus. He frequently explained to writers that there was no point to building a house, putting in furniture and drapes and other comforts, when the essential base, the plumbing, was not yet in. The plumbing, the strong story line came first.

"Give me any couple of pages of the Bible and I'll give you a picture," he added, citing such examples as the story of Moses, whose identity problem he considered as modern as the current psychological thinking on the subject.

DeMille always went back to the Bible for subject matter. The fact that his scriptural epics were a remarkable blend of sensuality and morality should not blind one to the fact that he was a devout believer, that he saw great value in the lesson to be learned, that the films made him a sort of missionary of God to the modern world.

Science says the biblical line, "and the winds blew all the night," may give a logical clue to the parting of the Red Sea, for the winds in a certain area were of such intensity at the time that they might actually have blown a path which parted the waters, enabling the Red Sea to be crossed. DeMille knew of the theory but preferred to treat the episode as a miracle.

DeMille might give fleshy color to a skeletal situation, but he would not diverge from the moral and religious intent of the Bible as he saw it. He was too concerned with historical accuracy. For a giant set of the 1933 *Cleopatra*, a scene in Caesar's atrium with hundreds of extras crowded into an enormous hallway with great marble tables, goblets of gold, and a thousand other objects, the prop department was put to the test and passed it. DeMille noticed a small flagon so far removed from the camera that it was hardly visible. Inspecting it, however, he saw that it was encircled by an antique silver band engraved with the Latin *Vinum Purum*.

DeMille knew where each prop was from many years back. At times, he would demand a dagger that he had used in *Male and Female* or a scepter that had served in *The Crusades*. Preparing for his final version of *The Ten Commandments*, he held long conferences with the Oriental Institute of Art, in Chicago, with the curators of Egyptian museums, with the British Museum, and with the New York Metropolitan. His researcher, Henry Noerdlinger, spent a quarter of a million dollars on his investigations and wrote a definitive book on the period, *Moses and Egypt*, published by the University of Southern California Press.

DeMille was as demanding with actors as with his other departments when it came to assuring credibility. In his 1934 version of *Cleopatra*, starring Claudette Colbert in the title role, with Henry Wilcoxon as Marc Antony, there was one scene where the Romans and the Egyptian soldiers clash, an establishing shot for a later battle between Marc Antony and his own Romans.

"You want to rehearse it or shall we roll the cameras?" asked DeMille of the unit director, who had 150 extras set to do battle.

"Let's go," came the answer.

"All right, we'll rehearse with the cameras," said DeMille. "Cameras. Lights. Action."

After fewer than 20 seconds of the fight scene he yelled, "Cut," and began a patronizing explanation: "Gentlemen, because I said we'll rehearse on film, I didn't mean you should give each other little love pats. You are soldiers. You are enemies. You hate one another. You kill each other. Now, gentlemen, that is the general idea. Let's try it again."

Again the cameras started rolling but only for 20 seconds before the cry, "Cut!" rang out. This time DeMille framed his injunction to do battle in less polite terms. The cameras rolled for the third time, and once more the director stopped the action.

"All right, I can see that I made a mistake. One thing I want to know, gentlemen. Are you wearing lace on your panties?"

While this remark was sinking in, DeMille turned to Wilcoxon, carrying a Roman short sword and shield in preparation for his big scene.

"Henry, guard yourself," he shouted, grabbing a spear from an Egyptian extra and charging Wilcoxon like a madman.

For several frantic minutes he charged and the two hacked ferociously at one another, using, of course, real weapons of battle. Wilcoxon weighed close to 200 pounds and stood a towering six feet three against DeMille's 165 pounds and five feet ten, but so furious was the action that Wilcoxon feared he would be hurt or, more likely, hurt DeMille. This is crazy, he thought, and looked for an escape. He remembered a maneuver and used it now, a quick side step as he lunged, bringing down all his might on the shaft of DeMille's spear, cutting off the head. With DeMille weaponless, he could throw his sword with honor—and immense relief. The flushed DeMille thereupon resumed his directorial helm.

"Now anyone who doesn't want to fight like that can leave the set!" he roared.

Fully half the extras walked off.

DeMille employees of bygone days still enjoy telling an anecdote which occurred the following year on *The Crusades*, which starred Loretta Young and Wilcoxon. Although shot on the Paramount back lot, an epic scene pictured the gigantic crusaders' war machine rounding a corner in the French town of Marseilles. It had taken DeMille's many lieutenants long hours to set up the complicated set, but finally everything was ready.

DeMille put on a little show before signaling to the cameras: "All right, ladies and gentlemen, I want absolute quiet during this scene. I want you to know there are five hundred extras on set. The cost of this single scene is already over eighteen thousand dollars. So take off your dark glasses. Put your wrist watches into your pockets. Spit out your chewing gum. We can't afford to shoot this scene twice. Remember, absolute quiet from the time I say go: Lights, cameras, action!"

All three cameras were rolling when suddenly the cry, "Cut!" pierced the air. There was a fearful silence while DeMille glared at an extra perched high up on a Marseilles rooftop, a cute redhead as it happened.

"You," he shouted at her. "The woman on top of the building with red hair and the green dress. You were talking. Come down."

Bedlam ensued as ladders were wheeled up to the building in question and the shuddering extra made her way down.

"Bring her over here," DeMille commanded.

An assistant director led her to the platform, and DeMille escorted her to the spot where his chair was placed, overlooking the crowd.

"Now," he began, "since it was so important for you to say something even though I requested silence, since you felt it necessary to break into a carefully rehearsed crowd scene, I would like everyone here to know what was of such gravity that it could not wait. I would like for you to tell us all. All."

"I'd rather not, Mr. DeMille," said the redhead as he shoved the microphone in front of her face.

"Young lady, I've been directing for many years. I have asked you to do something and I don't expect to be refused. I can be quite tough, you know. Now what did you find so important?"

"I'd really rather not say, Mr. DeMille."

"I can see you're not grasping my point, young lady," said DeMille, his ire reaching a crescendo. "I want you to tell me what you said. And if you don't, I promise you'll never work in a picture of mine again. Now, out with it!"

"Well," stammered the redhead, "well . . . I was just turning to a friend of mine . . . out there on the roof . . . and I said, I wonder when the old bald-headed sonofabitch is going to call lunch."

DeMille stood transfixed—but only for a moment.

"All right," he said. "Lunch!"

The redhead played in many succeeding DeMille pictures. Another employee, starlet Ginger Hall, gave DeMille a similar ego jolt, which he also weathered. At the end of each picture an assistant would preside over a dubbing session. When it was over he would call DeMille. On this occasion DeMille entered while the session was in the midst of a short coffee break. Instead of coming in through the front door, he arrived from an upper story and stood in a little hallway landing overlooking the scene. Several people spotted him, but Ginger Hall was preoccupied by a book and went on reading. She was, moreover, sitting in the master's chair. Everyone was silent as DeMille stared at her.

"Mmmm . . . a sparrow in an eagle's nest," he remarked with a deliberately hammy intonation.

"Yeah," replied Ginger as swiftly as if she had rehearsed. "A *bald* eagle."

DeMille laughed with the rest of the group. He had no taste for lavatory humor but a great zest for ironies and oddities involved with film making. When a bit player, supposed to say "Cleopatra, daughter of Ptolemy," came forth with "Clara

Patrick, daughter of Talmadge," it touched his funny bone. Another time, an enormously handsome, muscular bit player began speaking in bizarre Bronx accent, "Caesar's been moidered," and references to the queen as "the quaine, the quaine," were puzzling indeed.

"Where did we get this?" asked DeMille, stopping the cameras long enough to learn someone had hired a good-looking cop in order to keep from getting a traffic ticket.

DeMille was wounded by the negative critical reaction to his work, occasioned, some astute observers feel, by the fact that his technique was so often pictorial, as in the silent days, whereas the reviewers tended to look for verbal content, for stimulating dialogue. Late in life, DeMille was gratified to win a special Academy Award for *The Greatest Show on Earth*.

"The trouble with Cecil is he always bites off more than he can chew—and then he chews it," said brother William De-Mille.

"Gentlemen," DeMille would often address his crew when tackling a difficult project. "I know you'll give me one thousand reasons why this can't be done. Now let's forget that and see how it can be done."

DeMille was self-centered in many ways, and he wanted complete loyalty and obedience from his studio family. He gained that to a remarkable degree, for while there was fire and frequent fury in his manner, there was also an underlying charm, an Old World courtliness evident in small matters and large.

At his home on DeMille Drive, named for him, he and his gracious wife entertained with quiet good taste. Lucky were those invited for a cruise on his yacht, the 109-foot *Seaward*, or for a weekend at the mountain ranch called Paradise. Here there was rustic peace, the chance for a dip in a pool filled by a fresh mountain stream, and excellent dinners presided over by a C.B. released from studio strain.

At Paradise the guest list was always small, for DeMille said he liked to enjoy his company. The custom was to dress for dinner. Ladies were asked to bring simple cotton dinner dresses,

men to bring dinner jackets and black trousers. DeMille himself
provided them with Russian shirts, deep wine red, high up on
the neck with a zipper, a modified turtleneck well ahead of
the vogue. He would furnish black cummerbunds and gold
chains, again a generation ahead of the fashion. Once in a while,
a good showman even at dinner, he would upstage the men by
wearing white. After the main courses, he loved to stand in
front of the fire and prepare a *café diablo,* making the flames
leap up, conjuring like a wizard, loving the drama of it.

Many of the DeMille studio family spent the better part of
their careers with him. He would torment them with his
exigent nature, but when it came time to make another De-
Mille picture he would call on them and they would be ready,
drawn by the expertise, by the skill, by the excitement, by the
tight-knit quality of the endeavor. Old favorites rejected by
other producers found a home with him, and all knew that if
they needed him, DeMille would protect them.

Stella was the oldest employee in the entire studio, harking
back to the days of the barn at Selma and Vine. Whenever he
saw her, DeMille would stop and say hello, often adding a
genial hug. One day as he arrived at the commissary he noticed
her turning away from him.

"Stella," he said, whirling to face her, "what's the matter?"

"Nothing, Mr. DeMille."

"Come now, Stella. You turned away. Something's troubling
you."

"It's nothing, Mr. DeMille. I don't want to bother you."

"Stella, I can see you've been crying. Now tell me. What can
I do?"

"You can't do anything, Mr. DeMille."

"Stella, please tell me."

"I've been fired, Mr. DeMille."

"Don't leave the lot, Stella. I'll see about this."

DeMille stormed straight to the office of company president
Y. Frank Freeman. Stella was instantly reinstated.

"You know," DeMille later confided to a close associate, "I

once fired Stella myself. She was the first employee we ever hired out in California. I needed a secretary when we were filming *The Squaw Man,* and it was Stella, in the old barn at Selma and Vine. The money didn't arrive from New York, and there was no choice but to let Stella go. She didn't say much. She simply picked up the typewriter and started out. 'Stella,' I said, 'where are you going with that typewriter?' 'It's my typewriter,' she said. 'I'm taking it with me.' 'Well,' I said, 'if it's your typewriter, we can't fire you.' Somehow we scraped up five dollars, or whatever it was, and we kept Stella."

Pauline Kessinger, the attractive lady who has presided over Paramount's commissary for many years, always prepared De-Mille's luncheon order. Every Monday the chef prepared pea soup, and for twenty years she never failed to begin DeMille's Monday lunch with pea soup. One day she apologized to him as he entered. There was a new chef, she said, and he did not know the custom. Should he ever omit Monday's pea soup again, he would be fired.

"You know, Pauline," said DeMille throwing his arms around her, "I don't like pea soap."

For twenty years he had eaten the dish because he did not wish to hurt her feelings.

As DeMille sheltered his people, so they protected him. For many, he could simply do no wrong. One day in the commissary, a familiar-looking actor walked by.

"Who is that?" DeMille asked Florence Cole, a trusted veteran in his service.

"Akeeem Tameeeroff," she replied.

"Is that how you pronounce it?" he asked.

"That's how *he* pronounces it," said Florence. "But of course, he may be wrong."

For the inner circle, DeMille was the patriarch, the power and the glory. Movements were measured by his anticipated reactions. "What will Mr. DeMille say?" was a frequent question, extending even to contemplated marital breakups. When DeMille died, there was a sudden falling apart at the seams.

Long-wed couples in his employ finally headed for the divorce courts at his death—but not until then.

Adolph Zukor, the president of Paramount, was receiving a female executive in his New York suite.

"Don't you get up when a woman enters the room?" she demanded.

"I am up," said the diminutive Zukor as he stood behind the desk.

He was one of the mighty midgets of motion pictures, along with little, round Carl Laemmle of Universal and short but dashing Darryl Zanuck of Twentieth Century-Fox.

In his seventies, Cecil B. DeMille vividly recalled his very first encounter with Zukor: "The steel and iron, the indomitable bravery and driving determination, in that little man. He is little in nothing but physical stature, and even that has still the tough stamina he gave it in his youth as an amateur boxer who could hold his own with professionals of the ring. In his ambitions and dreams, his shrewd judgment, his showmanship, his generalship, he has had no peer in the history of motion pictures. No one in the industry, including a septuagenarian like me, ever calls this man anything but Mr. Zukor."

Jesse Lasky was likewise impressed on first acquaintance by the vision, the astute theories, the quiet dignity and exceptional force which infused the mini-mogul. "That man is an inspirational force," he remarked to a friend. "I want to keep in close contact with him." Several years later they merged their two companies.

Nicholas Schenck of the giant Loew's theater chain called Zukor Creeping Jesus because in addition to his small stature he had a soft, almost sepulchral, speaking voice. But no one missed the strength behind the modest manner.

Adolph Zukor was born in the Hungarian country town of Ricse in 1873, arriving at Castle Garden in 1888 with $40 sewed into his vest. For the fifteen-year-old Jewish boy, America was at once the land of opportunity realized. Odd jobs gave him more than enough to pay the rent. Soon he enrolled in night school, learned the fur business, and set up his own firm in Chicago. He married a dark-eyed Hungarian girl named Lottie Kaufman, who bore him three sons.

Through a business partner he met another furrier, Marcus Loew, a man as tiny as himself but with ambitions easily as lofty. In 1903 both investigated the field of penny arcades. For a time they worked together, but soon each went his own way, Loew to become the head of a great theater chain, Zukor to go into motion picture distribution and production.

"I was struck by the moral potentialities of the screen," said the fledgling magnate after he successfully imported a three-reel passion play made in Europe. More importantly, he saw the potential in films of greater length than the customary one- and two-reelers. After importing the four-reel *Queen Elizabeth,* he decided to risk the savings of a young lifetime by producing his own features—against the advice of almost everyone, including pioneer Thomas Edison.

It was no easy matter to persuade the matinee idol James H. Hackett to star in Anthony Hope's *The Prisoner of Zenda,* for stage actors scorned the new film medium. Fortunately Hackett liked to tip the bottle, and Zukor offered him rich financial rewards to pioneer in motion pictures. Though the film was a great success, decades later the actor still refused to permit the credit to be added to his biography in *Who's Who.*

Zukor forged ahead by combining with Broadway producer Daniel Frohman, acquiring the rights to contemporary stage successes and cajoling recalcitrant players to re-create their roles for the screen. Under the Famous Players in Famous Plays slogan, the Famous Players company, the progenitor of Paramount, soon featured James O'Neill, father of playwright Eugene, Mrs. Minnie Maddern Fiske, and Lily Langtry, the celebrated "Jersey Lily," all legitimate stage stars who lent their dignified names to the screen.

The company's greatest asset, however, was Mary Pickford, who had performed for D. W. Griffith at Biograph and "Uncle Carl" Laemmle at Universal, but whose heart was with the stage. She was appearing in David Belasco's *A Good Little Devil* when Zukor met with her, hoping to persuade her to repeat the role for the screen. His offer of $500 a week was able to win over mother Charlotte and Mary.

The rise of Mary Pickford to unheard-of popularity as America's Sweetheart was swift, and the accompanying financial rewards staggering. In 1912 she received $40,000 for each picture; by 1914, $60,000; in 1917 Zukor paid her $2,000 a week plus a percentage of the profits. It was a race with the skyrocketing salary of Charles Chaplin at Mutual, and by 1918 Zukor felt he could no longer keep up the competitive spiral.

"Mary often called me Papa Zukor," he later wrote in his autobiography. "Mary and I went a long way together, and when we parted—a million-odd-dollar-a-year salary was all I felt I should pay—we were as good friends as ever."

Zukor decided to create a new Mary Pickford and chose young stage player Mary Miles Minter for the part. The public gave her a modestly favorable reception, but in 1919 her name was linked with that of director William Desmond Taylor, mysteriously murdered in his Los Angeles bachelor flat. The ensuing scandal wrecked her career.

There were many other stars in the studio's employ, however. From the stage came Marguerite Clark, Marie Doro, Pauline Frederick, Hazel Dawn, Elsie Janis, Florence Reed, Ina Claire, Laura Hope Crews, Lenore Ulric, the elder Tyrone Power, H. B. Warner, Victor Moore, William Farnum, and the fast-living John Barrymore. William S. Hart became the greatest Western star of his time. Douglas Fairbanks was the athletic, practical-joking Don Juan for an entire generation. Rudolph Valentino developed a more sultry, mysterious sex appeal that lasted until his wife, Natacha Rambova, exerted her influence on him. His ensuing Beau Brummel image was less successful, and Natacha's domineering stand led Zukor to release him from his contract. Mae Murray, Gloria Swanson, Pola Negri, Marlene Dietrich, and Clara Bow brought contrasting styles to the highly successful studio.

The Depression took its toll, but Mae West came in to help

save the day. And later Bing Crosby and Bob Hope, and a host of others.

"I was secretly envious of those who had an intimate hand in production, and making myself inconspicuous, often watched activities," Zukor has said.

His was largely the role of the entrepreneur, and as such he operated with dependable intelligence and a cool daring that impressed all around him. Dartmouth-educated Walter Wanger, one of his major producers, never ceased to admire his philosophical bent and the fact that he would always accept full responsibility when something went wrong, "Fish stinks from the head," being his rather unceremonious way of putting it.

In the early days especially, a go-ahead on the wrong project could easily wreck the company. "What is the story about?" Zukor would ask director Allan Dwan.

"I haven't the slightest idea," Dwan was forced to admit many times, for the shooting was done off the cuff. "I'll tell you when it's done."

With the company's future hanging by a thread, its hardworking president might at times find himself unable to focus too clearly. Author Rex Beach once went to Zukor to complain that one of his stories had been butchered by the director. Looking over a sheaf of papers, Zukor asked him to remind him which story he was talking about. Beach recounted. Zukor listened and suddenly interjected: "I'll give you ten thousand for it."

The grand gesture was characteristic of Zukor. At the time Paramount was gobbling up theater chains in competition with other major studios, a rich prize, the Comerford circuit in Pennsylvania, was about to fall into his hands. At the meeting to culminate the deal, Mike Comerford came up with a startling bit of news. He had agreed to sell to Paramount for $15 million but in the meantime Warners had offered $16 million. To Zukor he suggested that they call off their deal and split between them the added million which Warners was offering.

"I've known you for twenty years, Mike," said Zukor slowly.

"I have never known you to welch on a deal. When you sign this contract you will have enough money to enjoy every luxury that you, a simple man, could possibly desire. As for Paramount, I assure you that five hundred thousand means as little to us as the ashes on my cigar."

"If that's the way you feel, this is the way I act," said Comerford, and put his signature to a paper that signed away one million dollars.

The balance and proportion in Zukor's makeup was always one of his strongest points. In the early years, from 1904 to 1907, all went extremely well with his enterprises. The family moved to a fine new apartment dwelling at 114th Street near Riverside Drive in New York. In 1907, however, came a financial panic. People were unemployed, stocks lost value, and no one wanted to go to the movies. Zukor came home and spoke to his family in a quiet manner.

"I tried and it didn't work out as I expected," he began. "The conditions on which I based my plans have changed. There is unemployment, panic, and I think we must make a complete retrenchment. Let's not fight the storm by buying an umbrella. Let's get into a safe area."

"How far do you want to go?" asked his wife.

"Let's find a decent place to live, near a good school," said Zukor. "The neighborhood is very important. Let's find the cheapest apartment we can in the best neighborhood we can afford."

The Zukors took an apartment over a candy store at 149th Street and Broadway, making the transition without undue strain. Zukor went to his bankers and told them he could not meet payments on notes he owned, since his theater leases were worth nothing at the moment. He was aware of the dire situation, he explained, and was proposing to handle it by retrenching, by cutting expenses, by economizing in every area, knowing that an upswing would eventually be forthcoming. The bankers said that if he was meeting the crisis in his sound way, they would gamble on him and grant an extension of his loans.

When William Fox came to Zukor in 1929 and offered him a

startling sum of money to sell out to him, theaters and all, Zukor debated the matter at length. Since Fox had included in the deal a lifetime job guarantee for his son, Zukor asked Eugene to consider the offer, to weigh the pros and cons with him.

"We eat three meals a day," he said. "We have better than the normal comforts. I have no great desire for yachts, for getting into social areas where we don't particularly fit in. What will this add to our lives if we sell? Money. But what will we do with it? We already have enough. Now what will it subtract? The negatives are great. We have built up good will over many years. People have confidence in us, have invested in the business knowing that we were standing behind them. Now can I sell out and lose these friendships and this good will? How can I sell out and leave people in the hands of a man of an unpredictable destiny? We will have money but no place to go. We will be cut off from people, the most important thing in life."

Zukor went on to say that if they stayed with their business, refusing the Fox offer, they must expect that things would sometimes be very difficult. They must make up their minds now to have no regrets.

Zukor always met crises in the same thoughtful manner—and there were many. At Paramount he fought savage battles for control, and while he sometimes was forced to retreat, he had an uncanny ability to come back. One could attack him in the middle of the ring, but he was the sort of fighter who knew when to retreat to the corner, and there he was at his best. When all avenues of escape seemed to be cut off, he would throw his opponents off guard by behavior unorthodox and unpredictable. Miraculously, he would come out the winner.

His family was always amazed that after the worst day of battle he would come home and quietly ask what was on for dinner. He loved to listen to such comedians as Jack Benny, George Burns and Gracie Allen, and dialect comics Smith and Dale. Never outwardly disturbed, he would go to bed early and fall asleep immediately. Never in his life did he take a pill; seldom was there a doctor in the house, or medicines. It was his firm belief that the end of the day was the time to clear the mind, that in the morning there was a clean slate which could be wonderful and exciting and in need of his fresh strength.

The simplicity of Adolph Zukor is well illustrated by the story of the little Chinaman. As Zukor entered his office as president of Paramount, the policeman at the gate would always buzz him in, greeting him with a cheery, "Good morning, Mr. Zukor." One day in the entrance lobby, a distinctly Chinese voice added its greeting, "Good morning, Mistah Zookah." He acknowledged the salutation with a nod as he sailed into his office. The next morning the little Chinaman was there again, and the next. For the better part of a month the pattern continued until Zukor beckoned to the cop to come to his office.

"Who is that man sitting out there?" he asked.

"He's waiting to see you."

"Well, why haven't you sent him in?"

"I couldn't do that, Mr. Zukor."

"Why not?"

"There's something funny about him. He won't say what he wants to see you about. I can't send a man like that in to see you."

"Well, he's been out there for weeks. Send him in right now."

"If you say so, Mr. Zukor."

Reluctantly the cop ushered in the little Chinaman, who shall here be called Chang.

"Well, Mr. Chang," said Zukor. "What can I do for you?"

"Many years ago," began Chang, "perhaps you have forgotten, it is so long . . . many years ago . . . you were very young man . . . I employ you write mottoes in my fortune cookies. Perhaps thirty years ago. I use all mottoes you write and have been very successful and have been satisfied with mottoes, much satisfied. Only now has been thirty years and think would be good now have new mottoes in my fortune cookies. I have come ask you write new mottoes."

"How many do you think you will need?" Zukor asked, stifling a laugh at the recollection of the long-ago transaction between a Hungarian immigrant boy and a Chinese cookie manufacturer.

"Maybe fifty."

"All right."

"Must remunerate."

"Yes, the remuneration. Well, what did you pay me the last time?"

"Ten dollars."

"Ten dollars for the fifty?"

"That is correct."

"All right. We'll stay with that. Ten dollars."

Adolph Zukor, president of Paramount Pictures, shook the little Chinaman's hand and dutifully set about supplying mottoes for fortune cookies.

A recent book on the motion picture industry has a final paragraph which carries these words: "William Fox, Louis B. Mayer, Harry Warner, Adolph Zukor, Charles and George Skouras are dead." Actually, Fox, Mayer, Warner, and the two Skourases mentioned *are* dead. But Adolph Zukor at last report was alive and well. He is, moreover, still employed by Paramount Pictures, having survived the latest change in management, the company's acquisition by Gulf and Western.

He has not notably changed in recent decades. When, in the late fifties, Cecil B. DeMille announced at an executive meeting that he wanted to remake *The Ten Commandments* as a Technicolor talking picture, Paramount executives were astonished and almost unanimous in their opposition. Only one man in the assembly of 25 spoke out unequivocally. At eighty-two, Adolph Zukor was ready for another daring move—with no reservations.

On the day before his ninety-fifth birthday he went as usual to his office in New York's Paramount Building. In the lobby, he saw former employee Arthur Mayer, a man well into his eighties.

"Good God, Arthur, are you still around?" Zukor said and marched on by to his office, his New York office, for during his long career Adolph Zukor had never "gone Hollywood," a possible clue to his elephantine durability.

5

"White Fang"

"**W**HADDAYA been doing?" Harry Cohn, president of Columbia Pictures, asked a writer he hadn't seen for some time.

"I've been in retreat writing a book," said the writer.

"Is there a picture in it?"

"No, I don't think so."

"Too bad," said Cohn. "I'd like to have read it."

The encounter illustrates a trait that Cohn had in common with all the other moguls—an obsession with film making. "It's better than being a pimp," he told a reporter who asked him about his lifelong career, but actually there was nothing else Cohn really wanted to do. He was hooked. Like the other unlettered moguls of the movies, he never ceased to be amazed that motion pictures actually moved. And like them, to his obsessive preoccupation with the medium he added the instincts of the gambler and the showman.

The results were a four-decade regime from the early twenties to the late fifties which carried him from a small studio on Hollywood's Poverty Row to a halcyon period in which Columbia garnered Academy Awards at a rate rivaling the best of them. While the studio produced its share of bread and butter B's, items like the Blondie series, the Boston Blackie sagas, and program Westerns, the reputation came from one or two annual A's into which Cohn poured all his drive and daring, such as *It Happened One Night, Mr. Deeds Goes to Town, The Awful Truth, Cover Girl, All the King's Men, Born Yesterday, From Here to Eternity, Picnic,* and *The Bridge on the River Kwai.*

As the sponsor of these sophisticated comedies, tasteful musicals, and dramatic epics, Harry Cohn was about as improbable as hayseedish Harold Ross was at the *New Yorker.* Moguls like Mayer and Goldwyn and Zukor all came from humble backgrounds, but they acquired taste and civilized manners. Cohn, on the other hand, remained determinedly uncouth and vulgar. For those who could get past his shock barriers, there were rewards; for those who could not, humiliations and scornful dismissal.

The achievement and the apparently contradictory character are illuminated in two thoughts he frequently voiced. "I kiss the feet of talent," was a favorite Cohn saying, and the record confirms that he sought out highly gifted people and that many did some of their best work for him. In conjunction, one must refer to another Cohn maxim, not original with him but deeply felt: "He who eats my bread sings my song." The trick was evidently to reconcile the two. Cohn liked to kiss the feet of talent, lure it over to his banner, and then make it sing his song, a kind of Chinese torture updated with implements from the Inquisition.

The language he most frequently used was unpolished profane, the tone personal and accusatory and mercilessly abusive. Harry the Horror was his name until author Ben Hecht, a crusty type well able to defend himself, rechristened him White Fang. During one of their altercations over a script, the writer suggested the credits should read: "Written, directed and produced by Ben Hecht and ruined by Harry Cohn." Thus audaciously challenged, Cohn gave in.

He did occasionally bow to another, but more frequently he retorted savagely. A case in point involved a bright and sensitive young man whom Cohn long tried to bring to Columbia. When persuasion and charm—and Cohn could be immensely charming when he wanted to—failed, money and power were proffered. The man became Cohn's executive producer at a sweet salary. He was working on a script with a pair of writers when Cohn presented certain ideas of his own. These were discussed and found wanting. The young executive took the matter to Cohn and explained that the vote against him was three to one.

"You're wrong," said Cohn. "It's one to nothing."

He fired the writers immediately and proceeded to shower the producer with contempt and abuse. In the executive dining room he would turn to him and demand, "All right, Jew boy, what's your opinion?" On another occasion, as a group was piling into a studio car to go to a preview, Cohn turned to the man and said, "Who do you think your wife's fucking tonight?" It was understandable that the harassed employee eventually decamped.

Cohn admired two men intensely. He was largely apolitical, but after making a documentary on Benito Mussolini he went to visit the dictator and was tremendously impressed. He liked the pompous Benito's office, reached only after running a gauntlet of antechambers; the circular desk, at the far end of a spacious room, raised to give its owner added dignity. Cohn modeled his own office after it and kept *Il Duce's* photo on the wall until he became unpopular. Like *Il Duce,* Cohn refused to take novocaine for pain, following the dictator's stoic example.

The other man Cohn looked up to was Louis B. Mayer, the baronial head of Metro-Goldwyn-Mayer. Insofar as it was within his means, he tried to model his studio after MGM. He also liked the grand manner as practiced by Mayer with William Randolph Hearst, Herbert Hoover, Bernard Baruch, Cardinal Spellman, and other important figures.

With the other moguls, Cohn was often his insufferable worst. The Goldwyns were invited to dinner one evening when Cohn had a phone brought to the table and launched into some truly racy language. One of his young sons came down the stairs to say goodnight, but the swearing went on unabated.

"Harry," said Goldwyn, who could hold forth with the best of them in the proper situation, "you shouldn't talk like that in front of the boy. It's not right."

"It's time he learned," said Cohn, and finished his excoriation.

Even in the most casual conference, the language Cohn employed relied on profanity. He was hardly aware that reporters, especially female, were embarrassed when he confirmed recent castings. "So-and-so is playing the prick," he would say, referring to the male lead. "The cunt is. . . ."

At dinner with another mogul, Cohn drew crisp reference to the homosexuality of one of the guests.

"Harry, I'm going to have to ask you to leave the house," said the host. "There are certain things we just don't say."

Cohn hired Paramount production chief B. P. Schulberg after he was toppled from power, but often it seemed the motive was simply to have someone around to browbeat.

"You dumb sonofabitch, if you had any brains you'd still be running Paramount instead of working for me," Cohn sneered at a story conference; and when B.P.'s wife, agent Ad Schulberg, visited the studio, Cohn chirruped, "Hey, B.P., how does it feel to have a wife who knows more about pictures than you do?"

B.P.'s son, novelist Budd Schulberg, was asked by producer Jerry Wald to work at Columbia on the screenplay of one of his novels. Cohn clocked writers in at nine and out at five. Budd would take the assignment only if he could work at home. Cohn turned him down.

Budd further resented the fact that his wife, actress Geraldine Brooks, had had a bad experience with Cohn. When she was still an ingenue, he had offered her a role. According to her account, at an office interview he bounded around his enormous desk, ripped her blouse, and was ready to go further, when she fled.

Legends of Cohn's sexual escapades abound in Hollywood. Starlets newly signed to contracts supposedly had to go through an initiation week, a hell week of unspeakable indignities. At the same time, it is to be noted that many women found Harry Cohn extremely attractive. Well built, he was handsome of face, his intensely blue eyes his most striking feature. Cohn moved with an easy grace and exuded a strong masculinity.

He married twice. When his first wife, Rose, bore him no children, he offered a starlet on his contract list $125,000 if she would bear him a daughter and $175,000 if she bore him a son. The offer came with one other condition—that she never see him again after. The starlet refused and was fired. After divorcing his wife, Cohn married again in 1941. His second mate was a fashion model who changed her name to Joan Perry to enter films. She dropped her career on marrying Cohn, and bore him two sons, John and Harrison, who later asked permission to change his name to Harry, Jr. The couple also adopted a daughter, Catherine. From all accounts, Cohn was a dutiful father, the Goldwyn episode aside.

The family was very much with Harry Cohn, early and late, getting and coming, coming and getting. His relatives and those of his general manager, Sam Briskin, along with the relatives of Briskin's brother-in-law, Abe Schneider, roamed the lot. Employees often were forced to go to another studio for advancement because it was impossible to get past the Cohn-Briskin phalanxes. At one point, humorist Robert Benchley dubbed Columbia the Pine Tree Studio in tribute to its countless Cohns.

Like the Mayers and the Warners, the Cohns were a fighting Jewish family. The most intense battles took place between Harry in Hollywood and his brother Jack, the business head stationed in the East. At one time Jack mounted a cabal to unseat Harry. The plot failed. Thereafter, their quarrels were sometimes so virulent that they could only communicate through third parties. And yet, Jack's sons Robert and Ralph were given jobs at Columbia. Robert became a producer; while Ralph founded Screen Gems, a television subsidiary which enjoyed a startling growth before his untimely death. Jack's third son, Joseph, entered the advertising field in New York under the name of Curtis, which he thought would go better on that battleground. Joseph died at thirty-seven, but in turn left two sons. Tommy, the youngest, is today, at twenty-three, the operator of a discothèque in Washington named Wayne's Luv. The older, twenty-six-year-old Bruce Cohn Curtis, has produced his first film, *Otley,* with Tom Courtenay and Romy Schneider, for Columbia. Harry Cohn's two sons are about to begin careers, but it is too early to speculate on their progress.

Jack and Harry Cohn spent a lifetime having rows, but when Jack died, two years before Harry, in 1956, Harry called up associate Jonie Taps at four in the morning.

"Jack is dead," he said, crying bitterly. "He had many more friends than I had."

At the time of his firstborn's birth, Cohn had made a similar remark to a studio employee who offered a toast that the boy be like his father. No, said Cohn, angrily rejecting the toast, he wanted his son to have friends.

It was ironic that a man of Harry Cohn's temperament should want to be loved. "Harry Cohn was a man you had to stand in line to hate," wrote Hedda Hopper. Many people who had never met him refused to work for him, solely because of his unsavory reputation. To an emissary with a job offer, writer Nunnally Johnson explained, "He shouts. I could never work for a man that shouts." Writer Adela Rogers St. Johns did actually meet with Cohn after he bought one of her stories. In a brief 20-minute interview she, too, saw that she could not enter his employ. He shouted. Furthermore, he did not even know he was shouting.

The husband-wife writing team of Richard and Mary Sale had written a score of scripts for Twentieth Century-Fox before they were loaned to Columbia to do a picture. Because they had made their reputation, Cohn treated them well.

"Now you can hang your hat in this studio any time," he told them at the picture's preview.

"Don't listen to a word of the spellbinder," said their producer. "Once he's in charge of you, you'll get the same double whammy like everyone else."

"He would do anything to get a man he wanted," says former Cohn general manager Sam Briskin, now an elder statesman at the studio. "And he would do anything, go to the ends of the earth to get rid of one he did not like." He was a sadist with the weak or those he thought were weak, and an intriguing reprobate to those whose strength he could perceive.

After John Beck left Universal Pictures to set up his own producing unit, he contracted for one film at Columbia. *Kill the Umpire* was based on his original idea of a man who wanted to be loved but was hated. With Lloyd Bacon directing and William Bendix starring, Beck started the cameras rolling and immediately was called into the master's office.

"I looked at your first dailies," said Cohn brusquely. "They stink."

"Well, I'm doing a comedy, and I have a respect for the comedies you turn out here," said Beck, taken aback. "I've tried to please everyone I'm working with and I'll try to please you. But you'll have to be specific with me. Tell me what stinks so I can deal with it. I've been doing what I consider a good job."

"I told you. The dailies stink."

"I have only one answer. As Christ said, no man can serve two masters. You have to love the one and hate the other, or the other way around. Unless you can be specific I'll have to make this film the way I think it should be made. No man can serve two masters."

There was a long pause, while Cohn ruminated.

"I wish I'd said that," he finally declared. "Beck, you can do anything you want. I won't look at your dailies any more."

Beck went to the premiere of *Kill the Umpire* with several executives and Cohn. The audience at Pasadena's Crown The-

atre responded very enthusiastically. Afterward, Cohn gleefully went through the preview cards filled out by the audience, throwing out the few that were unfavorable.

"Well, Harry, I can't believe this reaction," said Beck. "It's
not that great a picture. I know the audience liked it, and
maybe we've got something that appeals to the general public,
but I'd sure hate to be sitting in a projection room with the
New York critics."

"Fuck the critics," replied Cohn. "They're like eunuchs.
They can tell you how to do it, but they can't do it themselves."

At a party at his home some months later, Cohn greeted Beck,
"Come on in and have a good time. Remember I'll never look
at your dailies." Despite the success of *Kill the Umpire*, Beck
did no further work at Columbia, refusing offers because he
was so appalled by Cohn's overall demeanor, his abuse of colleagues.

Cohn never forgot this. Years later, Beck was discussing with
director George Cukor the rights to a property by Dame Edith
Sitwell. Cuckor, then at Columbia, invited Beck to lunch at the
studio's private dining room. When he announced himself at
the desk, the guard made a call to confirm that he was expected. From on high came word that it was a private dining
room; Beck was not to have lunch there. Beck left and called
Cukor, who was immensely apologetic. He was also angry and
informed the studio he would not appear for work unless Cohn
apologized to his friend. Since Cohn needed Cukor, he agreed
to see Beck. When Beck entered the huge chamber, Cohn began mumbling something about the incident of the dining
room.

"I don't know why you did it," said Beck. "I'm no different
a person today than when I worked for you."

"You must be a Commie," said Cohn, somewhat puzzled by
this egalitarian statement.

"I could never be a Communist because they deny the Deity.
I'm a Catholic and believe in the Deity."

The strange colloquy ended with Cohn making some form of amends. Beck never worked for him again. It is worth mentioning that George Cukor has no recollection of the incident involving him.

Richard Quine began as an actor with Metro-Goldwyn-Mayer and arrived in Harry Cohn's office as the result of a screenplay he had written with William Asher.

"How much do you want for this script?" asked Cohn.

"It's not for sale," said the youthful Quine.

"Then what in the fuck is it doing on my desk?"

"Bill Asher and I don't want to sell it. We want to direct."

"You two punks who never directed anything before? You're crazy."

"I know what we want to do with it. We can turn it into a good picture."

"I want to buy the script. I don't want to hire a couple of amateur directors."

"Then no sale," said Quine and left.

Two hours later the phone rang at his home. It was the studio's general manager, Ben Kahane.

"I guess we've hired ourselves a director," he informed Quine.

In typical fashion Cohn was gambling but relying on the enthusiasm of others. If their voice and manner carried conviction, he gave them a go-ahead. Every Friday afternoon he would hold sessions at which his top-echelon employees would go over projects and problems. Once Quine was a regular, he attended these meetings. He found a property he wanted Cohn to buy, a New York play called *Operation Mad Ball*. Cohn didn't like it, but for 12 weeks in a row Quine brought it up. At the end of each meeting, Cohn would look defiantly at him and demand, "Anything from you, Mr. Quine?" When Quine again spoke of his pet project for the thirteenth time, Cohn bought it.

Operation Mad Ball was the story of a group of soldiers who encounter obstacles when they want to have a party with a group of nurses. It was produced on Broadway by Jed Harris, whom Cohn could not abide. Part of the deal was that Quine would see to it that the two never met. He gave Harris a small office without a window, relenting later and moving him to better quarters. In accordance with the plan, all story conferences were with Quine and Harris minus Cohn until the day before shooting was to begin. A Cohn secretary called to say he wanted a script conference with the two of them. Quine asked if he had heard right and was told he had.

"I know how to handle him," Quine counseled the apprehensive Harris. "I know his disposition. I'm skillful at working with him. Let me handle everything. This will go all right if you just don't louse things up. Don't say a word. Cohn won't speak to you, I'm sure."

Harris agreed, and together they went to the meeting. After a 20-minute wait, they were ushered in. Harris took a seat at a discreet distance and adopted an inoffensively neutral expression. Quine had calmed him but was now himself jittery. He sat facing Cohn.

"On page one, take out this speech," said Cohn, drawing a line through a piece of dialogue.

"Why?" demanded Quine.

"Because it's stupid."

"You can't take that speech out," said Quine. "It sets up a situation that develops later. It's a necessary speech."

"I don't give a damn. Take it out."

"You can't just take a speech out without giving a solid reason."

"The hell I can't. It's my studio."

"Then keep your fucking studio," said Quine, working himself up into a lather and storming out of the office, much to the amazement of Harris, who quietly followed.

"I thought you handled that very well," said Harris when the two had settled in Quine's office.

Minutes later the intercom erupted. It was Cohn.

"What the fuck's the matter with you?" he asked.

The argument began anew, and this time Cohn bowed to Quine's strong stand.

One of the key scenes in the film was the ball itself. Since it was hard to get the feeling of merriment at eight in the morning, Quine decided to shoot it at eight in the evening. He invited the cast, stars, and more than a hundred players to have real drinks at that hour. When shooting began at eleven, everyone was authentically gay. At midnight Harry Cohn, who was supposed to be in Las Vegas, came onto the set, glowering at Quine.

"How in the hell do you justify these extra costs?" he demanded.

Quine explained, only to arouse further ire. Since it was too late to draw back and dismiss everyone, he said, why didn't Cohn stay, have a drink, and watch the shooting? Cohn's expression changed. Sitting on the sidelines, he slowly sipped a drink, enjoying himself. He hated to be left out; now he was included. And he saw that things were going well.

The Cohn character was inordinately possessive. He was not averse to making trouble for a happily married couple that paid him little heed. Or to put the quietus on budding romances. One evening Quine went to Ciro's with Fred Karger, who was musical supervisor for the current film, *Pretty Girl*. Their dates were two of the starlets from the picture. Cohn seldom went out, but this evening he sat at a ringside table.

"I will not allow men who work for me dating girls from the studio," he told Quine on the phone the next morning.

"Then I won't work here," said Quine.

Several hours later, executive Max Arnow called to heal the breach. Three times Quine quit, and three times Cohn called him back.

Cohn was born in New York City of mixed German-Russian

parentage. In his early days, he was a pool hustler, a song plugger, and a trolley bus driver, so adept at slanting the finances of the latter operation that it was said company officials were always glad when he was kind enough to bring back the bus at night.

His education was negligible, and this was one of the bitter regrets of his life. His lack of learning showed itself in amusing ways. At a story conference for *The Solid Gold Cadillac*, Cohn, Quine, and author Abe Burrows were discussing whether or not to keep a scene from the play, the moment when the Senator, played by Paul Douglas, delivers "Spartacus to the Gladiators" with a high-schoolish declamation.

"It's got to go. It stinks," said Cohn after looking at the rushes.

The others tried to speak up for the passage, but Cohn insisted it should be cut. He did not understand it, and if he did not, neither would the public.

"What do you want in its place?" he was asked. "What do you think the public will understand? What sort of thing?"

"I don't know."

"Well, do you want something, for instance, like Hamlet's soliloquy?"

"Naw, I don't want Hamlet's soliloquy," said Cohn. "What it needs is something like 'To be or not to be, that is the question.' "

Cohn's second wife, Joan, became a convert to Catholicism. Cohn himself was not a religious man. Of Jewish birth, he was, some felt, on the verge of being quaintly anti-Semitic. Once at a large party he was giving for studio personnel, he looked at the crowd, which was storming the buffet table. "Look at those Jews eat," he remarked to an associate.

For a film he was directing, Richard Quine requested a certain actor.

"He looks too Jewish," said Cohn.

"But he's a good actor," Quine insisted.

"Around this studio, the only Jews we put into pictures play Indians," Cohn summed up.

It became a studio joke that the Indians in Columbia Westerns were really a band of Jews. Cohn's mentor, Louis B. Mayer, followed similar patterns. "I would put you under contract right now but you look too Jewish. I want you to have some surgery to straighten out your nose," he told comedian Danny Kaye. When Kaye voiced apprehension about the results of an operation, Mayer suggested he try it out first on his brother. Kaye demurred. In a like vein, Mayer cast elegant women in the role of the villainess, maintaining that it was bad enough to be a bitch without looking like one. Hollywood liked to improve upon reality. In the golden years, heroes and villains alike had a certain class and attractiveness.

As part of his possessiveness, Cohn liked to change the names of his players and even nonperforming employees. He wanted producer Leonard Goldstein to change his name to Leonard G. Leonard because that sounded better than the Jewish Goldstein. He got Sam Spiegel to become S. P. Eagle. When Eagle went to International Pictures, William Goetz said he'd have to change again, to E. A. Gull, for his new association. He produced his best pictures as plain Sam Spiegel.

The most important star Cohn developed at Columbia was a Spanish dancer, Margarita Cansino, who became Rita Hayworth. Even today Hayworth says, "Cohn was a monster. He thought he owned me." Rita managed some life of her own with Edward Judson, her first husband, with Orson Welles, her second, with Aly Khan, her third, and with Dick Haymes, husband number four. When Cohn's disputes with her, and with her succession of mates, rankled too severely, he sought a replacement. He found her in a Chicago salesgirl named Marilyn Novak. She would not sit still for a name change to Kit Marlowe, but accepted the compromise Kim Novak. Cohn soon found himself quarreling with her as violently as he had with Hayworth. He is credited with breaking up her romance with Sammy Davis, Jr. At the same time, a certain bond grew between them, and at Cohn's death Kim Novak was deeply upset. In tribute to him, she continued working on *Bell, Book and Candle* the very day he died.

Cohn turned Harriet Lake into Ann Sothern, and he tried to make George Murphy over into Gregory Marshall but Murphy balked. Jack Lemmon likewise refused to change a name that one might justifiably think needed alteration. Cohn seldom liked actors, reserving his minimal admiration for writers and, to a lesser degree, directors, but he did respect courteous, Harvard-educated Lemmon.

Director Lewis Milestone developed an easy rapport with Cohn when he made *The Captain Hates the Sea* for Columbia. During shooting at San Pedro, difficulties piled up—there was a waterfront strike and the cast was filled with performers whose alcoholic intake was truly impressive.

"Hurry up. The cost is staggering," wired Cohn from Hollywood.

"So is the cast," said Milestone's laconic reply.

"What made Cohn irresistible was that he had a star personality," says Milestone. "He could spot weakness, or sensitivity which he mistook for weakness. You might feel he was the meanest bastard on earth. But if he turned on his charm, you were completely disarmed. And of course he had that seventh sense of what made a successful picture."

Cohn himself described his unique ability in the following, more graphic terms: "I always know when there's something wrong with the story—my butt begins to itch."

One of the writers Cohn cultivated was Andrew ("Bundy") Solt, a young Hungarian émigré. At twenty-two, Solt sold a play to Columbia and was brought to the studio as a writer, receiving a standard minimum, $250 a week. He had been on the payroll for only a few months when a serious illness sent him to the Mayo Clinic. There he was surprised to receive a phone call from Harry Cohn, whom he had never met. He inquired as to his progress. There were regular messages until Solt returned to work.

A few weeks later, the writer found himself on the same plane with Cohn, both heading for a weekend in Las Vegas, a favorite Cohn diversion. Solt asked about a script he had prepared, wondering if Cohn had yet had a chance to inspect it. No, said Cohn. Solt explained that he had worked hard on it and developed ideas at length, submitting a 38-page draft. The two saw little of each other in Las Vegas but again took the same plane back to Los Angeles.

"How many pages did you say that treatment was?" asked Cohn.

"Thirty-eight."

"Thirty-eight pages is right," said Cohn, rifling through a document he pulled out of his coat. "I read it last night. Damn good."

"What do you know about Al Jolson?" Cohn asked Solt shortly after his arrival back at the studio.

"I remember going with my mother in Budapest to see *The Jazz Singer.*"

"What else?"

"I saw Jolson some years ago when I was living in New York. He was in a play, a musical, and the little I remember is that it wasn't very good."

"What else?"

"I hear he's washed up."

"Is there anything else you know about Al Jolson?"

"No."

"Good," said Cohn. "I want you to work on the script of *The Jolson Story.*"

Columnist Sidney Skolsky had come to Cohn with the idea of doing the life of Jolson. Cohn bought the idea, and Skolsky became the picture's producer. Cohn was aware, however, of the fanatic cult that had blurred the picture of the real Jolson. The Winter Garden, where the popular singer performed during his most successful years, was a constant sellout. Jolson, an intense egotist, would in fact not perform if he saw an empty seat in the house. On one occasion, a bitter cold night, he saw half a dozen empty places and swiftly entrained for his favorite hideout, Atlantic City. A hypochondriac, he was convinced he had tuberculosis, and at each cough, he headed for Atlantic City, where the winter breezes were somewhat milder than in New York. On the night in question, the management tried to convince Jolson that on a cold night people got colds and worse illnesses and were forced to skip the theater; the empty seats were no reflection on his drawing power. The explanation failed to satisfy. The singer left, and the management tried to placate the audience by offering to refund their money. The crowd refused. They had come to hear Jolson and they would stay until they heard Jolson. When a spokesman told them their idol had entrained for Atlantic City, they still refused to move. They would wait for him to return. In desperation the management called Jolson's hotel in Atlantic City. When he arrived there, he was informed that a clamorous crowd would not leave the theater until he returned to sing for them. The tribute moved Jolson. He took the next train back to New York at midnight; to thunderous applause, he began to wow them on the long runway of the Winter Garden.

It was because Cohn knew of the legendary character of Jolson, the sentiment which coated over the man and his real life, that he put Solt, a Hungarian, to work on the script. He was sure that an American would give him pap.

Solt went to see Jolson, trying to work out the main lines of the action. Much of the man's history had to be dropped because it was unfilmable; several wives before the then current Ruby Keeler also had to be relegated to the ashcan. The direct story line that developed had recourse again and again to Jolson's famous verbal gesture toward his audience: "Folks, you ain't heard nothin' yet." Larry Parks bore a remarkable resemblance to the young Jolson and was chosen to play the title role, lip-syncing words which on the actual sound track were recorded by Jolson himself.

The one big problem was the ending. Jolson's career had

gone downhill, and there was little punch in an ending which pictured him as a has-been. At the time, Jolson was touring American military bases in Europe. No one really wished the singer any harm, but repeatedly in studio conversations it was agreed that a splendid finale for the film would have his plane crash while he was entertaining the troops. The plane didn't crash. Parks gave a performance of refreshing insight. The film was a tremendous success, even without a smash close, and opened the door to a brilliant second career for Jolson. During the filming Cohn became a great friend of the singer, and when Jolson finally did die, he cried, a rare event indeed.

Solt liked Cohn because while he might be tough and behave like a monster, he would do it to your face so that you always knew where you stood, unlike several of the other moguls who would crack a dozen jokes, give an appearance of great joviality, and then do you in the moment your back was turned.

Solt was part of a Hungarian colony in Hollywood that included such figures as producer Joseph Pasternak, actor Tony Curtis—born Bernie Schwarz in Brooklyn—and the fabulous Gabor sisters. The Gabors had been close friends of Solt from childhood, and one incident involving them also involved Cohn. Solt had taken two of the three sisters, plus the mother, to a dinner party at Romanoff's. As they were leaving the large affair, two men also departed. The Solt car was brought forth first, and as the dazzlingly bedecked women were getting into the car, one of the men said in a loud voice, meant to be overheard, that he would not mind going to bed with any of them. The other said, in an equally loud voice, that he, in fact, *could* go to bed with any of the three if he wanted to. Solt thought the matter over for a second, debated launching some caustic remarks which would put the clowns in their place, then let instinct take over. He got out of the car, walked up to the first man, and hit him with a fast right. Back in the car, the Gabors were in a state of high excitement.

"It's not every day that you see someone belt the president of a bank," said Zsa Zsa admiringly.

"And one of the best friends of his boss," said the mother.

Solt found that he had hit Al Hart, a former liquor dealer, now the president of the Security First National Bank and an intimate of Harry Cohn. The ride home was a mixture of hilarious recollection and sober reflection.

The next day at the office, Solt received the expected call to Cohn's office. He entered the cavernous chamber with trepidation, only to find Cohn in a mellow mood. They talked about the script Solt was currently hatching. With each of his comments, Cohn would say, "Isn't that right, slugger? Do you agree with that, *slugger?*" Cohn had heard the story of the night before, and he said nothing of it. Ever after, however, it amused him to call Solt "slugger" and, on occasion, "killer."

As an admirer of the tight MGM organization ruled by his friend Louis B. Mayer, Cohn, at Columbia, adopted various Metro methods, adding a few touches of his own. His rule was despotic. Employees were clocked in and out. From his window he could see them arrive and depart and often called for an explanation when one left ahead of schedule. In addition to a network of spies and stooges who brought him news of every studio happening, he at one time had every sound stage wired so that he could overhear what was going on. It was an awesome moment when his voice suddenly boomed out of a loudspeaker with a harsh admonition for an unsuspecting director or star who had dared to criticize him. No one had to be told when Cohn was in the studio. One sensed it. When he was there, everyone was standing at attention, figuratively, all of the time.

A man of Cohn's nature had to have various whipping boys close at hand. He was drawn to easygoing Jonie Taps by the latter's background in music publishing, bringing him to the studio first in the music department, promoting him to producer, and making him his closest personal associate and friend of the later years. Whipping boy, says Taps, is a term which hardly applies. He loved Cohn and was happy to serve him 24 hours a day, as his contract specified. He is also sure Cohn loved him.

"Hey, knucklehead!" or, "Hey, stupid," Cohn would yell at Taps. Jonie knew that, coming from the unorthodox nature of his boss, these were compliments. If he didn't like you he called you "sir." Jonie was paid $75,000 a year for his services, for understanding things like that.

After divorcing his wife, Taps was for a time the only un-married executive at Columbia. There was a rule at the studio that the switchboard was to be in operation all night long and that Taps was at all times to keep the board informed of his whereabouts; Cohn might want to reach him at any hour. One day before leaving the office, he stopped to see Cohn. He wanted to let him know about progress on *The Eddy Duchin Story*, which he was producing.

"I've got some of the greatest recordings we've ever made," said Taps and went on enthusiastically.

"I'll listen to 'em before I go home," said Cohn. "By the way, where are you going tonight?"

"I've got a date."

"Who?"

Taps mentioned the name of a particularly stunning woman.

"You lucky sonofabitch," said Cohn and waved good-bye.

Taps went off to his date, spent the evening dining in town, then wound up at midnight in the woman's home in Benedict Canyon. They were inside only a moment, barely time to fix a highball, when the phone rang. Harry Cohn on the line.

"I thought you told me you made some wonderful record-ings," he began belligerently.

"I did."

"Did you listen to them? I did. They're out of tune. They're no good. They're rotten. They're junk."

"What are you talking about, Harry? Those recordings are great."

"They're junk. Where are you?"

"Up in Benedict Canyon with . . . uh. . . ."

"Come down here and I'll prove it to you."

Taps knew it was not a request but an order. He left his date and headed for Cohn's home at 1000 Crescent in Beverly Hills. His own house was nearby at 623 Canon—by Cohn's choice, to have him readily available. When the bewildered Taps walked in the door, Cohn gave him a defiant look and started playing the recordings. The sound was truly terrible. It took only a moment for Taps to realize that the strange garble he was hearing was the result of Cohn's playing a 33⅓ record at a 45 rpm speed.

"You're using the wrong speed," Taps shouted.

Cohn chortled. He had gone to the head of his sound department and asked how he could make the Duchin recordings sound awful. They had worked out the frameup which roused Taps from his pleasant midnight rest. It pained Cohn to see his buddy on the town when he himself was spending a quiet evening at home.

Through Taps, Cohn lived vicariously. First, he would call him from home at nine in the morning to see if he was at work. After berating him for one thing or another, he would go back to bed. Later, at the office, however, he would call half a dozen times until he had found out everything that was going on around town the night before.

Cohn used Taps as a heavy when it suited him. Once he called at 2 A.M. and asked him to hurry over. Taps arrived to find Cohn in his bathrobe, talking to a financier of great repute. The financier was accompanied by a pretty young girl under contract to Columbia. At the moment she had a small role in a film Taps was producing. The financier wanted to get her out of the picture and into his bed on a trip around the world.

"Jonie, can it be done?" Cohn asked after explaining the situation.

"We've already done some recordings with her," Jonie said.

"Her wardrobe was made up at considerable expense. We're ready to start shooting in two days, and we can't afford to delay the picture."

"Is that your final word, Jonie?"

"Yes."

"Is he running the studio or are you?" the financier asked in annoyance.

"He's working for me, and that's why he answered that way. He's not ready to do anyone a favor when the studio will suffer."

The girl stayed in the picture.

Difficult though he was, Cohn was at times thoughtful and benevolent. When the talkies came in, many players ran into difficulty with the new medium. Suddenly New York actors were hired en masse because they could presumably read lines. Silent screen actress Claire Dubrey found herself unemployed after having played leads. To gain a toehold in the talkies, she placed an ad in a casting directory of the time, stating her experience and offering to play bits, extras, and dead bodies off-stage. Years before, she had known Harry Cohn, but she had also worked for many of the other top producers. Only one man called in answer to her ad.

"What's this crap in the casting directory about you doing extra work?" Harry Cohn demanded on the phone.

"I want to get into the talkies. We West Coast defenders are not in the running. I want to at least have a chance."

"Well, you can work over here."

Cohn sent out word to his producers to use Claire Dubrey. They did, mostly bits, but enough to get her going again, and enough to help her get work as a character actress at other studios and later in television.

Cohn did not like Paramount mogul B. P. Schulberg, but this did not prejudice him against his wife, Ad. When the Schulberg family fell on bad times, Cohn asked Ad to become his New York story editor and talent scout. She used the position

as a stepping-stone and is today still a top New York literary
agent.

No less a figure than Louella Parsons was a staunch Cohn
supporter. Cohn liked Louella, favored her with scoops, and
inspired in her a considered affection. Another supporter was
doughty Ethel Barrymore, who said admiringly, "He knew the
score."

Jonie Taps probably knew Harry Cohn as well as anyone in
later years. He knew that he was stingy, watching every quarter. His tips were small, and he examined checks carefully. He
did not want to be cheated. He went around turning out lights
at the studio. Only anonymously would he express his kinder
side. When his chauffeur, Eddie Hahn, said he'd like to improve himself, Cohn got him a job in the sound department.
When one of his employees had gangrene in his leg, Cohn paid
all the hospital bills. When another worker was injured in an
accident and unable to perform his regular job, Cohn set him
up with a refreshment stand on the back lot. Cohn hated for
his kindnesses to be known. He was afraid others would demand more. And besides, he liked the image of himself as an
s.o.b. It amused him.

In the early days at Columbia, what amused Harry Cohn was
a rather childish device in the private dining room. He had a
chair wired so that when he pressed a button, the unwary guest
would get an electric shock, or if necessary, a progressive series
of shocks. Cohn was seated so that the occupant of the chair
was in full view. Usually the reaction was quite startling but
not in the case of Vicki Baum, author of *Grand Hotel*. On her
first day in the dining room, Cohn pressed the button. No reaction. He pressed a heavier charge. No reaction. The full treatment. Vicki went on gaily chatting and eating her lunch. Clever
sleuthing later revealed that the authoress wore an elaborate
girdle, so taut that it effectively insulated her from Cohn's device.

The Baum girdle had earlier gained notoriety. At the time
Grand Hotel was rehearsing in New York, Vicki was touring

Russia as a newspaper reporter, traveling in the bitterest winter along the Trans-Siberian railway. One night at a distant outpost, she got out to stretch her legs. To her amazement a porter approached with a telegram. *Grand Hotel* opened to magnificent reviews; she would be a rich woman. So chill was the atmosphere that the news literally left her cold, and she threw the telegram into the snow. As the days went by she recovered, and by the time she got to Japan, she saw it would be appropriate for a successful playwright to buy some flattering clothes—and help them along with a powerful girdle. Carried away, she decided also to lighten her hair a goodly number of shades.

In New York, Vicki was told reporters would be awaiting her, so stunning was the success of *Grand Hotel*. No one approached her, however. The other passengers debarked. All alone she waited. Finally a man walked shyly up to her.

"Are you by any chance Vicki Baum?" he asked.

"Yes."

"But we were told you were dark and fat," said the man, a reporter.

"I am," replied Baum and gaily marched down the gangplank.

Practical jokes were in the air at Columbia, a necessary relief to tension. Cohn was lacing into cameraman Rudy Mate when that hapless man, perspiring, reached into his pocket for a handkerchief. Mischievously, someone had devised a batch of double-headed prop nails and filled his pocket with them. As these started falling out, Cohn looked on with amazement.

"And not only that, you sonofabitch," he wound up, "you're also stealing my nails."

Studio manager Sam Briskin played a tough one on producer Sam Bischoff. Bischoff was forever talking of one of his inventions, a razor he had invented and wanted to sell. When the subject grew nauseous, Briskin sent a fake wire from an "American Razor Company" in New York, asking to buy rights to the razor. Bischoff went East; on his return he never again referred to the subject.

He did, however, swiftly retaliate. He told Briskin that a certain Senator and Congressman were coming to town, that both were great friends of the Jewish cause and deserved special treatment. Only he could properly arrange their welcome. Briskin went all out—banners of welcome, a special luncheon with dignitaries invited, speeches, a guided tour, calls to *Time* and *Life*. The hoax was assuming such proportions that a panicky employee tipped off the magazines involved. They printed a story, but not the one they had planned. Instead they told of two Central Casting dress extras who boarded the Chief at Pasadena, were met by Briskin and others, and were halfway through a splendid luncheon before their true identity was revealed.

In later years Cohn seldom laughed out loud, but he did manifest a quiet inner humor. His China-blue eyes would dance in merriment. When Jonie Taps wanted to get married again, Cohn found a dozen objections, so many in fact and so violent that Jonie sneaked off to Las Vegas without telling him. From there he sent a wire: "DEAR HARRY. JUST GOT MARRIED. JONIE."

The return telegram was quick in coming: "STAY THE WHOLE SIX WEEKS. HARRY."

Jonie was there when a call came from Joe Schenck of Twentieth Century-Fox. He had this girl named Marilyn Monroe, said Schenck, and he wanted her off the lot. If Cohn would only do him a favor and give her a 20-week contract.

"I don't want to tell the sonofabitch himself because he might turn me down," added Schenck. "Do you think you can arrange it?"

"I'll talk to him."

Cohn liked Schenck and approved the contract. Taps at the time was producing a film called *Ladies of the Chorus*. He gave Marilyn Monroe a small part in it. When he and Cohn looked at her first day's rushes, there was no enthusiasm from Cohn.

"Why'd you put that fat cow in the picture?" he asked. "You fucking her?"

"No, I think she's got something."

"I bet you a buck she never gets anywhere."

At the end of the 20-week contract, Columbia let Marilyn Monroe's options drop. John Huston later put her in *The Asphalt Jungle* for MGM and began her ascent toward stardom.

Jonie was also with Cohn at New York's Hampshire House when Frank Sinatra, far down on his luck, came into the room.

"If you give me the part of Maggio in *From Here to Eternity*, I'll do it for nothing," said Frankie.

Cohn said he'd think it over.

"They'll laugh at that skinny little runt," Cohn said after Sinatra left.

"What are you going to do—feel sorry for a fat man?" asked Taps.

Sinatra tested for the part, won it, and began his remarkable second career.

Cohn made errors aplenty, like the other moguls. He turned a deaf ear when Gloria Swanson brought him the script of *Dark Victory,* which later became a superb vehicle for Bette Davis. He let John Wayne drop off his contract list. *The Bridge on the River Kwai* had to be snowballed past Harry Cohn. He was insecure and indecisive at times, letting Elvis Presley out of a contract on the advice of aides and against his own better judgment. And, of course, he feuded self-destructively with major stars and close associates throughout his career, losing one great talent after another.

There is no patent on success in motion pictures, and for each bad gamble, Cohn made a remarkable number of good ones, as the record shows. Jonie Taps was with him when he saw Judy Holliday in *Born Yesterday* on the New York stage. They had dinner afterward with the show's author, Garson Kanin.

"I want to buy the play," said Cohn.

"It's not for sale at the moment," said Kanin.

"Everything is for sale. How much?"

"I told you it's not for sale."

"Everything has a price. How much, for Christ's sake?"

Cohn was so persistent, nagging and cajoling, that Kanin decided to shut him up by naming a figure completely out of line.

"How much?" demanded Cohn once more.

"One million."

"You just made a deal," said Cohn, shaking the startled Kanin's hand.

The price was an all-time record for a play, a great gamble which paid off.

Cohn was not in films with a mission, as was Louis B. Mayer. He was there to make money for himself and his studio. And he was ready to work until he dropped. Near the end, when he had a heart condition and was popping glycerine tablets into his mouth like popcorn, Taps told him one day to go home and take it easy.

"I can't go home," said Cohn. "I've got to save my studio."

On a plane trip from New York to California, returning from a board of directors meeting, Cohn had a heart attack. He refused to let the plane land until all arrangements had been made to take him to the hospital in secret. He was given oxygen on the plane, and an ambulance waited as they came in the runway. Cohn warded off publicity because he wanted to protect the price of Columbia stock.

"I would rather have had Harry Cohn's handshake than somebody else's signature," says Jonie Taps. "He never went back on his word."

Columbia floundered for some time after Cohn's death. White Fang was a tyrant, but he knew how to make pictures.

6

The Films' Forgotten Man: William Fox

IN HOLLYWOOD today one hears story after story about men long dead, people like Harry Cohn, or Louis B. Mayer, or Irving Thalberg. One almost never hears the name of William Fox, one of the founding fathers who gave his name to a great studio. Even the New York *Times*, which prides itself on careful research and historical thoroughness, seems to have contributed to his obscurity. "In a news story in the New York *Times* of yesterday," the paper acknowledged on February 8, 1949, "an erroneous reference was made to 'the late William Fox.' Mr. Fox, former theatrical man, is alive." When Fox actually died, in May, 1952, Hollywood's leading publication, *Variety*, printed a brief obituary which did not even begin on the front page. It was a strange neglect of a man who had played a key role in the industry for three decades and who had lived a life of high drama.

"No melodrama that I have been able to invent in my thirty years of inventing has been more packed with crimes and betrayals, perils and escapes, than the story of William Fox," wrote Upton Sinclair in his 1933 biography of Fox, *Upton Sin-*

clair Presents William Fox. Certainly the story was filled with unlikely events and none more so perhaps than socialist Sinclair writing a book in praise of the aggressive Fox, who tried to gain complete control of the film industry and make himself its sole producer and arbiter.

At the time of his greatest power, in the 1920's, Fox ran a motion picture empire with a value estimated at around $250 million. He was then a sallow-complexioned man, bald-headed, unsmiling. His prominent Jewish nose, dark, intense eyes, and black moustache relieved a face that was close to being round. Fox liked to wear white shirts and sweaters because they were to him a symbol of prosperity, and he could never forget his poverty-haunted childhood. His left arm was withered and hung limply at his side. As a child he had fallen off a delivery truck on which he was hitching a ride to save carfare. The family could not afford a good doctor, and so a makeshift operation removed the elbow joint and left the arm permanently useless. Despite the handicap, Fox became an excellent golfer, using only his right arm. Golf was a gentleman's game. Fox would never carry a watch because he didn't want to know what time it was. He worked until there was no more work to do, driving himself and those around him with a savage intensity. The blinds in his huge office were kept drawn, again to make time stand still, to allow all his energies to flow into the erasure of that poverty which he had once known.

The Fox family—the name was Americanized from Fried— came from Hungary, although both parents were of German-Jewish descent. William was less than a year old when the move to the United States was made in 1880, with the first residence a rear tenement on the teeming lower East Side of New York. Here twelve other children were born, six of whom died in childhood.

William worked as a boy to help support the family. He sold newspapers; he sold stove polish which his father made up in the house; he sold candy lozenges with riddles inside; he sold sandwiches and pretzels in Central Park and spent a night in jail because the wrappers made an illegal mess on the ground. More permanent employment came in the garment trade. Young William was eleven when a sweatshop operator gave him a job cutting linings for men's suits. The hours were from seven to seven, the wages $8 a week. From one firm to another he went, his salary going up to double his beginning scale. All the pennies and dollars were saved. With a partner named Sol Brill he opened his own business to examine and shrink cloth from mills. The cloth-sponging firm succeeded.

As the family prospered, Fox moved to a better neighborhood on Rivington Street. The day before his twenty-first birthday, William married Eve Lee, whom he had met six years before at a party. Soon she bore him two daughters. William was moving up in the world, but he would often betray his untutored background with a phrase such as, "He done it good," or, "I seen him there." His parents were Orthodox Jews who saw to it that he learned Hebrew; sparse hours of night school never perfected his English.

In his teens William had joined a boyhood friend, Cliff Gordon, to work up a vaudeville act to earn extra money. Gordon later went on to become a well-known comedian, but the young boys' act was poorly received and abandoned. Fox might well have continued to prosper in the garment industry if someone hadn't brought an interesting proposition to his attention.

Sol Brill told him of a penny arcade and picture show for sale at 700 Broadway in Brooklyn. Fox was intrigued by the peep boxes, weighing machines, punching bags, chewing gum machines, and phonographs which needed only a single attendant to collect the coins. Upstairs in a darkened room a recent invention called a "moving picture" was shown, people and objects actually moving on a screen, a man milking a cow, a tree bending in the wind. Some felt the new device to be the incarnation of evil, giving young men occasion to become pickpockets, young girls a temptation to go astray in the shadows. Feebleminded children would be the result of viewing, said one school. Certain medical authorities insisted the flickering pictures would cause a permanent squint, if not outright insanity.

Fox was troubled by no such misgivings. He saw lines of people filing into the establishment, leaving their money behind. His savings of $1,600 went into purchasing the place from J. Stuart Blackton, the clever, snappily dressed Englishman who was one of the founders of the Vitagraph film studio. His reason for selling, he told Fox, was the studio's increasing demands on his time. As it turned out, there were other factors. As soon as he began operating the house, Fox found the crowds of customers thinning to a trickle. Blackton had hired plants to people the premises on the day of Fox's visit.

Brill was so agitated that he moved out of the fledgling business. Fox determined to make it go. He refurbished the rooms, installed more comfortable chairs, and used vaudeville acts to lure people in off the street and then up to his moving picture show. In between the film showings he let a piano player sing illustrated songs, with the audience often joining in.

His first little theater, bought in 1904, became a success, and Fox bought another, checking the location more carefully this time. He soon owned 15 theaters in Brooklyn and New York, and money was flowing into his pockets at a spectacular rate. Even so, he saw that the people who leased him the films were making far greater sums. As a consequence he went into the distribution field, forming the Greater New York Rental Company.

To demonstrate how greatly the initial $1,600 had already grown in a few short years, it is only necessary to look at Fox's battle with the Trust. The "big ten" producers, Edison, Biograph, Vitagraph, Kleine, Selig, Essanay, Lubin, Kalem, Méliès, and Pathé controlled about 85 percent of all motion picture patents. As the industry expanded, they entered into the agreement whereby they forced manufacturers to buy licenses from them and film exchange owners to pay a $2-a-week fee for running their pictures. Their aim, as stated, was a complete monopoly of production and distribution, to achieve which they brought distributors out or forced them to abandon the industry.

The Trust set its own purchase price, usually far below actual value. They offered Fox $75,000 for his group of theaters. To their outraged astonishment, he asked for $750,000 and was adamant. The Trust thereupon canceled his license on the ground he had shown some of their films in a house of prostitution. Like the Blackton "customers" at the first theater, the situation was rigged. In retaliation Fox brought a lawsuit against the Trust for $6 million, saying the companies involved constituted a trust in restraint of trade, thereby violating the Sherman Anti-Trust Act.

The "big ten," headed by blunt, bellicose Jeremiah J. Kennedy of Biograph, were upset by the charge. They contacted Fox, who offered to settle out of court for one million dollars. This further infuriated Kennedy. Fox came down to $800,000. The Trust negotiator offered $200,000. It was Fox's turn to be enraged and walk out. The Trust came back with an offer of $300,000. Fox accepted.

A curious thing happened to the members composing the Trust. Many were businessmen with an actual scorn for the new medium of motion pictures. Although they settled with Fox, others later waged suits against them, and they were compelled to disband into individual units. Once forced to compete in the open market, they failed one by one, their products simply not good enough to win the public's favor.

William Fox's fight against this tough combine showed him to be fearless and capable of battling with giants on their own cutthroat terms. His theater chain grew, as did his leasing firm. In 1914 he also entered the field of production. He bought a story called "Life's Shop Window" for $100 and made it into a feature costing a total of $4,500. Filmed on Staten Island, it starred Claire Whitney and Stuart Holmes. Fox's sharp, metallic eyes narrowed as he watched the initial offering unreel in the projection room. At the end he was silent for several minutes. "Let's burn the damn thing," he finally said. Dissuaded from destroying the print, he released it for showing in his theaters, where audiences were delighted with it.

The Fox method of film making now quickly crystallized. Since he himself did not read, his wife, Eve, spent each day digesting a novel, current or classic. In the evening, she would recite the story to him, together with suggestions for the screen treatment. Fox would sit puffing away on a big, black cigar, asking questions, discussing. The next day he would narrate his interpretation to a director, who would prepare the continuity and drill the plot line into the actors. By evening, a good part of *Bertha the Sewing Machine Girl* or *No Mother to Guide Her* or Ouida's *Under Two Flags* or Dickens' *A Tale of Two Cities* would be in the can ready for the ceremony of the evening "rushes."

The most sensational success of the new company involved a wholly fabricated star personality, the first such case in the history of Hollywood. Fox bought a stage play called *A Fool There Was,* which derived from Kipling's poem "The Vampire," inspired in turn by a well-known painting by Burne-Jones. To play the lead, a wildly sensual *femme fatale* who uses men to satisfy her needs and then tosses them callously aside, director Frank Powell chose an unknown—not unknown for long, however.

Theodosia Goodman was a nice little Jewish girl from a middle-class family in Cincinnati. She had come to forge a legitimate stage career in New York, playing a few small roles before going to England to play Shakespearean roles with a touring company. On her return she met director Powell, who suggested she look into motion pictures, an idea which the young girl found repellent. The stage gave her little employment, however, and when a fire swept the apartment she shared with her mother, she was desperate. She went to Powell, lowering herself in her own mind by asking for a job on films.

Fox and his press agent, Johnny Goldfrap, realized that a

Jewish girl from Cincinnati did not create the proper aura for
the exotic heroine of *A Fool There Was*. A magical transforma-
tion began to take place. Theodosia was contracted to Theda;
Goodman became Bara, abbreviated from a Swiss grandparent
named Barranger. Even before the film was released, exhibitors' journals spoke of Miss Bara as a French actress who had
thrilled audiences at Paris' famous Théâtre Antoine. Her father, said the manufactured legend, was a French artist who had
gone to live in Egypt where he met Theda's mother. The
little girl was born in the shadow of the Sphinx and grew up
riding across the desert sands with Arab nomads.

The first showing of the film, in January, 1915, was preceded
by a dramatic reading of Kipling's poem. The audience was
therefore prepared for the havoc in the lives of men which
the heroine was going to wreak. A frenzy of applause greeted
the last image on the screen. Overnight, Theda Bara was a star.
Her line, "Kiss me, my fool," became a household favorite,
and the word "vampire" and its derivative, "vamp," entered
the common vocabulary.

For the next four years Theda Bara vamped at a rate that
makes the mind boggle. She made 40 pictures in which she se-
duced unwitting men, her ample bosom heaving, her curvaceous
figure draped with semitransparent silks, her undulating walk
an invitation to unbridled passion. Once the men were won
away from wives or lovers and completely under Theda's spell,
she began to reverse her course, scorning the advances of her
conquests, driving them mad with frustration. Daggers, poison,
fire and flame—by one desperate device or another their lives
came to an end. As one observer put it, an enterprising under-
taker could have made a fortune simply by camping on her
trail.

The American public reveled in the mayhem, which was
abetted and compounded by Fox, Goldfrap, and others. Bara,
they saw with delight, was "Arab" spelled backwards. Theda
was an anagram of "death." Theda Bara symbolized Arab death,
press releases said over and over. Her photograph began appearing in poses ever more alluring and at the same time menac-

ing, with skulls and snakes and glass balls and figures of Egyptian gods from which she was said to derive occult powers.

To a famous press conference in Chicago, Theda drove in a snow-white limousine attended by "Nubian" servants. She entered a hotel room which was dimly lit, draped in black velvet, and filled with the heavy fragrance of tuberoses and incense. Carefully rehearsed by Goldfrap, a languid Theda politely fielded reporters' questions, elaborating on her exotic childhood along the Nile, on the days of her stage successes in Paris, on the many men who in real life had gone mad with desire for her. When the last reporter had finally left, little Theda was almost suffocated by the incense. "Give me air!" she cried, raising a window.

Each new film brought forth astounding new revelations about the life of evil Theda. *The Clemenceau Case* was cited in court by a man who said it influenced him to try to do in his wife. *Carmen* was the occasion for Theda's statements intimating that she was the reincarnation of the actual seducer of bullfighter Don José. Even poor little Juliet turned into a vamp when Theda portrayed her on the screen.

Although Fox raised her salary from $150 a week up and up until she was getting $4,000, Theda Bara was unhappy. Children ran from her on the street, and women wrote her vile letters of abuse. Basically a simple woman with none of the characteristics ascribed to her by screenwriters, she wanted to play sympathetic roles. Several times William Fox indulged her wishes, but the public would have none of Theda Bara as a sweet girl, any more than it would accept sweet Mary Pickford in an unfavorable portrayal. Theda was convinced that Fox was deliberately ruining her career and demanded still higher wages to compensate for her suffering. Fox refused. The vogue for vamps was passing. After four halcyon years, Theda took to the New York stage in a supernatural drama called *The Blue Flame,* which received a merciless roasting from the critics. After a few comeback attempts she retired as the wife of director Charles Brabin and lived a long and quiet life as a Hollywood society matron. She died in 1955.

*   *   *

The Fox Film Corporation was far from dependent on a single star. Stage favorite William Farnum was becoming a popular screen idol for the studio. Also from the legitimate theater, Fox signed well-known players Nance O'Neil and Robert B. Mantell. Danish actress Betty Nansen was added to the fold. Before the vamp cycle thinned out, Virginia Pearson and Valeska Suratt joined the ranks of wicked women.

Thinly clad Betty Blythe gave a torrid performance in a superproduction called *The Queen of Sheba*. Annette Kellerman, reputed for her physical culture exercises, left Universal for Fox, where she made another early spectacle, *A Daughter of the Gods*, with leading man Stuart Holmes. The film was directed by imaginative, extravagant Herbert Brenon, who talked Fox into letting him shoot on location in Jamaica. Fox groaned as the bills came in—more than $100,000 for a complete Moorish city constructed near Kingston, $7,000 for a caravan of camels imported to appear in a fleeting sequence, additional thousands for a tower from which athletic Annette would dive into the sea. The final version ran so long that Fox hired an outside editor to trim it down and took Brenon's name off the credits. When Brenon insisted he wanted no credit for what he considered a butchered version, Fox put his name back on. Their arguments became virulent. Fox issued orders to bar Brenon from attending the premiere. To his annoyance he later learned that Brenon, wearing a disguise capped by false whiskers, saw the film from one of the best seats in the house —and furthermore seemed to enjoy it. The two men continued their spirited scuffling over the years.

The star who led the Fox ranks after the sinister seductions of Theda Bara and the cycle of lush spectacles was Western star Tom Mix. Born in Mix Run, Pennsylvania, he left for foreign adventures at an early age and then went to the American West, serving as a sheriff, a deputy U.S. marshal, and a Texas Ranger. In 1910 the Selig Company hired him as a technical consultant and began using him in films. He hit his real stride, however, after William Fox signed him to a contract which wound up ten years later paying him $17,000 a week.

Although Mix had actually started earlier, William S. Hart beat him to stardom. Fox decided that his new player should develop an original new personality of his own rather than imitate Hart. The Mix screen character was accordingly worked out with care. He never drank or smoked or used profanity. He would never kill his enemy but conquer him by clever horsemanship or lasso work. Breezy comedy entered into the characterization. The story line was direct and clear and the motivations realistic.

Tom Mix became a great favorite in such films as *Durand of the Badlands, Rough Riding Romance,* and *Tumbling River,* along with his horse of the moment, Tony, Old Blue, or Tony, Jr. More than 60 features rolled off the assembly line, filling the pockets of the star and his mentor.

The handsome cowboy used his money to establish a train of life befitting a screen hero. On a vast estate in Beverly Hills he built a mansion which rivaled the famous Pickfair. An English butler admitted guests to a living room which used saddles, rifles, and other Western gear for decorations. A huge sunken bathtub was another feature, and on the grounds a spacious swimming pool. A uniformed chauffeur drove the star's long limousine, which was custom built and lined with hand-tooled leather upholstery. Mix himself dressed in a white suit and white cowboy hat, attire which he made the symbol of the genre in the twenties. His large collection of fancy boots was unique. At formal dinners he sometimes liked to draw attention with purple dinner clothes, spotless white kid gloves, and a belt buckle with the letters T.M. spelled out in glittering diamonds. Talkies put a damper on Mix's career, but not on his personal style. With Tom Mix's Circus he made grand tours in the thirties, mixing with the noble and famous here and abroad until his death in 1940 in a car crash.

William Fox took some of the profits from the cowboy sagas and plowed them into artistic ventures, such as the 1927 production of *Sunrise*. This was directed by noted European film maker F. W. Murnau and starred Janet Gaynor and George O'Brien. There was assuredly plenty of financing around, for in addition to Mix's Westerns, many other films were reaching a large audience. One such effort, *Over the Hill*, dealt with children and their neglect of parents. It was based on an original idea by Fox, who spent $100,000 to make it and netted $3 million.

With the advent of sound, Fox Movietone News became extremely popular and Fox sound features followed the same pattern of success.

For some $50,000 Fox had also acquired all American rights to the German Tri-Ergon patents on sound devices, and he was waging a suit which if sustained by the courts would give him the right to collect damages against all theaters and every producer showing sound films.

In addition to his commercial films, Fox was a pioneer in other areas. His Movietone process was installed in a Chicago hospital to record the first surgical operation on film. Fox wanted to use talking films to aid medical studies. He also hoped to introduce audio-visual teaching in the areas of science and mathematics, and to make film libraries available for home use. Similar applications were under study for churches throughout the country. The overall plan was grandiose—to make film, under the direction of William Fox, a contributing, formative factor in the life of the nation.

In his majestic business manipulations Fox was a loner, but a key figure in the commercial film empire was Winfield Sheehan, a blond, blue-eyed Irishman who went from newspaper work to a job as secretary to New York's police commissioner. When bribery scandals rocked the department, Fox rescued Sheehan and made him his secretary at $100 a week, then his general manager. Eventually he rose to become chief of production for Fox films, earning $130,000 a year. Fox enjoyed his flamboyant protégé, and Sheehan was always ready with a show. He married opera diva Maria Jeritza and built her a splendid showplace in Beverly Hills, with lovely sunken gardens, frescoed ceilings imported from Europe, and landscaping that included trees from each state of the union. Sheehan acquired a stable of rare Lippizaner horses, which he liked to show off to guests. He and those he invited ate off solid gold plates and drank from solid gold goblets.

Fox himself lived well in apartments that were increasingly luxurious and at Foxhall, a well-kept estate in Woodmere, Long Island. Here he could well afford works of art by the great masters, but conspicuously on display was a reproduction of "Le Brun and Child" which had been acquired years ago by submitting Babbitt's soap coupons. It had graced the first modest Fox apartment and served as a reminder of those times of struggle. For the company Fox built a four-story structure on New York's West 56th Street. His own wood-paneled office was immense, with tall, colored-glass windows, thickly carpeted floors, and a desk behind which he sat in solitary grandeur, receiving visitors like the powerful potentate he was.

The drive for power overshadowed all else for Bill Fox. He could be patriotic, selling liberty bonds in each of his theaters for many wartime months. He could be generous, donating huge sums, time, and resources to such organizations as the Red Cross. He could on rare occasions laugh, as when he hired teetotaling Carrie Nation to occupy a vaudeville forum, only to find that she was also against smoking. During her run, he gave up his favorite cigars. He could also take pride in his friendship with Tammany Hall politicians Big Tim and Little Tim Sullivan, and in entertaining foreign dignitaries, including the young Prince of Wales, later King Edward of England.

Power, however, was what Bill Fox enjoyed most, and in its acquisition and exercise he could be fearless and fiery, inventive and indefatigable, cantankerous and cruel, single-minded.

Once, a new man he was sending West to run the studio asked how he could make the employees understand that he, unknown to them, was boss. "*Easy,*" said Fox. "The minute you get out there, fire everybody. Call them in one by one and fire every single one. After a day or two you hire them back, one by one. Then they'll know who's boss." The man followed the instructions, which worked out effectively. In addition to the people he hired back, he also employed 14 relatives from near and far.

By the late twenties William Fox had built up an empire whose proportions were truly staggering, so powerful in fact that he was ready to reach out audaciously for one more lever which, if acquired, would make him the single most important man in the industry.

The weighty business structure divided itself into two separate but related wings. The Fox Film Corporation expanded an initial output of four pictures a year to a film a week by the late twenties. Originally, Fox Film issued common stock as a bonus to those who had bought the preferred and made early moves of expansion possible. As such, it had no value at all. However, as the common began paying dividends of $4 a share annually, it acquired value. In 1925 the corporation was recapitalized and stock offered to the public, 900,000 of A nonvoting shares and 100,000 B voting shares. Old stockholders received the new A shares. Fox himself held on to a majority of the B voting shares and also bought 5 percent of the A. He continued to pay dividends of $4 a share on the A throughout his reign. Net earnings of the company in 1915 were $523,000; by 1920 they had risen to $1,413,542; and in 1929 they were a remarkable $9,469,051. During the course of this earnings rise, the shares of common stock shot up in value to $119 each, and the overall value of the company was estimated at $200 million by 1930.

In this period of expansion Fox watched his rivals building up theater empires which were naturally receptive to showing the parent firm's products. Adolph Zukor had his vast chain of Famous Players houses and was daily acquiring more. MGM was owned by the giant Loew's Incorporated. First National was served by a large list of franchise holders. Fox owned a few theaters but nothing to match these chains which ran into the hundreds.

With the money from his sale of stock to the public, Fox

determined to enter the race to acquire theaters. His first move was to spend $8 million for a third interest in Sol Lesser's West Coast Theatres. Next he made deals in St. Louis, Chicago, and Baltimore, and set up two corporations in New York to acquire theaters in the East. He made a further investment in the West Coast chain, gaining control and by astute aggressive management increasing its houses.

The competition was often intense in the swiftly expanding field. When the Balaban & Katz chain took over a small independent theater in midwestern North Platt, Fox built a bigger theater in the town. Not to be outdone, Adolph Zukor ordered his architects to draw up plans for a theater to outshine both his rivals'. As a result, the little prairie town of 12,000 inhabitants was blessed with three fine houses, all destined to lose money.

Within a year, Fox spiraled his small holdings into a formidable chain of 800 houses, with New York's 6,000-seat Roxy, the Cathedral of Motion Pictures, as his "flagship." He set up the Fox Theatres Corporation to run them and made the company public, with himself in control of voting power. Profits in the founding year of 1926 were $454,101, and streaked to almost $10 million within three years. The new corporation's market value in 1929 was estimated at $50 million.

At this stage, ambitious Bill Fox tried the audacious power play which briefly made him the kingpin of the industry. First he attempted to make a deal to burrow into the towering domain of Adolph Zukor, and was rebuffed. Next, he made an effort to splinter the franchise holders in First National, almost succeeding but encountering a last-minute resistance that killed his chances. Finally, he went after and gained control of Loew's Incorporated, the biggest prize of them all, owning as it did not only its well-run theaters but also the great Metro-Goldwyn-Mayer producing unit.

The circumstances of this singular coup were highly dramatic. The man Fox chose to deal with was powerful Nicholas Schenck, the perpetually smiling president of Loew's. The two men huddled in secret; then Schenck began to survey some of the leading Loew stockholders with a view to selling out to Fox and giving him, a rival, control of his corporation. If the plan seems preposterous, one must look at the financial blandishment which lay in store for Nick Schenck, who had come to this country as a penniless refugee.

The key to the scheme was the estate of Marcus Loew, founder of the mighty theater chain which bore his name. Loew died in 1924, leaving 400,000 shares of company stock to his widow and sons. The family now let Schenck know that they were willing to sell. The bloc constituted almost one-third of the outstanding total and so came close to carrying control. Loew's shares were selling on the exchange for $75 a share, but the asking figure for the sought-after prize was $50 million. Of this, $40 million was to go to the Loews. Nick Schenck was to receive the other $10 million!

Fox raised the money from various sources. The Fox Theatre Corporation floated $16 million of new shares through the banking firm of Halsey, Stuart & Company. The firm also advanced Fox $10 million. The American Telephone & Telegraph Company, involved in a sound patent dispute with Warner Brothers, was happy to see Warners out of the running for the Loew stock and loaned Fox $15 million. Several banks supplied the rest. It seemed a splendid deal for all concerned, the banks getting a heavy interest rate, Fox gaining power and almost a third of Loew's annual profit of $12 million, the phone company besting Warners, who had earlier tried to get the Loew stock, and Halsey, Stuart, picking up their regular commission plus another million from Fox as a "consultation fee."

To carry out the transactions, the Foxthal Company was formed by Fox and A. C. Blumenthal, a bizarre figure whom he had encountered during earlier real estate transactions. Blumenthal was a rather dainty and pale five-footer with a sharp eye for an easy dollar. A friend of New York's Mayor James Walker, he tried a delicate tightrope across legality and was eventually forced to flee to Mexico to escape one unsavory situation. He was also in the news for marrying showgirl Peggy

Fears, from whom he later separated after many a stormy scene.

While Nicholas Schenck was vigorously denying the fast-spreading rumors of his sellout, Fox went to Washington to try to protect himself against possible antitrust prosecution. He based his position on the necessity for American leadership in the world film market. The entire industry needed an expensive retooling, he told the Attorney General's office. His own plant and that of the Loew's Corporation duplicated facilities in almost every area, and only by merging the two could the necessary revitalization be accomplished. After his Washington conference, he was under the impression that he had a go-ahead from the government.

He was allowed to enjoy his sense of victory for only a short period. Halsey, Stuart came to him with a panicky thought. What if Mrs. Loew began buying Loew stock on the open market, thereby keeping effective control out of Fox's hands? The advice was for Fox to purchase additional shares immediately. He followed his bankers' directions, adding enough shares— a good portion on margin—to give him a majority control, increasing his indebtedness by $20 million in the process. As it turned out, Mrs. Loew stayed out of the market.

The country's mood of optimism seemed to justify the extraordinary expansion of Fox's reach. He was the president of two huge and highly profitable corporations. Everyone was buying on the market, which was rising dizzily. Moreover, he was acting on the advice of reputable bankers and industrialists. Under ordinary circumstances, he might have held on to his newly reached pinnacle.

On July 17, 1929, Fox climbed into his Rolls-Royce and headed for a golf date with Nicholas Schenck. They were to go over details of their complex adventure and seek means to calm the anxieties of rival magnate Adolph Zukor. Zukor was naturally unhappy over their agreement, perhaps doubly so because he felt his flank protected by a union of dynasties; his daughter Ruth had married Arthur Loew, son of founding father Marcus. On the winding Long Island road leading to Lakeview Country Club, the Fox chauffeur missed a turn. As they came to a crossing, a small Ford appeared suddenly from behind an incline. The two cars crashed, killing the chauffeur, injuring the woman driver in the Ford, and Fox in his Rolls. At the hospital Fox was found to be badly injured and to have lost nearly a third of his blood. For almost three crucial months he was immobilized.

On his first trip back to New York, on Thursday, October 24, 1929, he attended a banquet at which Secretary of Commerce Robert P. Lamont gave a speech. It warned that the nation's economy was grotesquely overextended and headed for an imminent explosion. The next morning, Fox instructed his brokers to sell every last share of his stock in corporations other than his own, a total of some $20 million. Three trading days later, after the disastrous Black Tuesday, the same stocks had dropped in value to $6 million and were still plummeting.

Almost miraculously, Fox had shored up assets against the coming storm. He was to be sorely in need of every aid. The market made periodic comebacks but continued its overall decline. Short-term debts came due, with their high interest rates. Margin calls on stocks further drained resources. The bankers who had advised Fox's expansion and promised to protect him withdrew their support.

To add to his dilemma, Fox found the government beginning to make antitrust noises. Since he had actively backed the new administration of Herbert Hoover, he used his influence to gain an audience with the President. Hoover reassured him, but the difficulties did not seem to subside. A government official hinted that MGM's head, Louis B. Mayer, was influential in the administration.

Fox had several meetings with Mayer, who was the treasurer of the Republican National Committee for California. Their encounters were frosty. Mayer held a number of things against Fox. Fox had negotiated his merger with Loew's without Mayer's knowledge, although one of his agents had offered to buy Mayer's stock. Mayer, as it turned out, owned none, and Fox chided him for having no confidence in his own company. Fox had furthermore neglected to renew the contract of William

Goetz, Mayer's son-in-law and an associate producer at Fox Film Corporation. Finally, shortly after Fox's deal with Nicholas Schenck, the sly A. C. Blumenthal had called up Mayer and boldly announced that his "new boss," Bill Fox, wanted to talk to him. Mayer, enraged, nonetheless met with Fox and immediately engaged in an argument over screen idol John Gilbert, an MGM contract player. Gilbert had once made disparaging remarks about his own mother, which caused Mayer to dislike him. Fox also disliked him and had once fired him from his studio. Fox now suggested to Mayer that he find a way to get rid of the high-salaried star, whose voice was proving a disaster in talkie experiments. Mayer came to Gilbert's defense and said he had a contract. When Fox suggested he could get rid of the actor by humiliating him with bad parts, Mayer had had enough. A contract was a contract, even when he disliked the man.

The collapse of Fox's position was gradual but steady. In two days alone, Monday, October 28, and Tuesday, October 29, his Loew shares tumbled in value from his purchasing price of $70 million to less than half that amount. As the market crash widened, Fox Film Corporation shares dropped from a high of $119 to $1, losing more than 99 percent of their value. At the same time, the government moved to dissolve the Fox ownership of Loew's Incorporated.

When various refinancing plans collapsed, creditors instituted receivership actions against both Fox companies. In March, 1930, Fox bowed to the mounting pressures and sold out his interests to a group of bankers. He came away with $18 million, which he swiftly pyramided by selling short in the still falling stock market.

The next years, however, were filled with legal wrestlings following the failure of his grandiose scheme for industry domination. In 1932 a Senate committee checked into his short selling and accused him of deliberately wrecking his own companies. The Fox Film Corporation instituted suit against its former head. Charges of income tax evasion complicated the already cloudy picture. Within a brief span, Fox paid one million dollars in lawyers' fees and another million in out-of-court settlements.

In October, 1936, William Fox declared bankruptcy. Before a federal referee in Atlantic City he estimated that whereas in 1930 he was worth "about one hundred million," he was now penniless save for "a few odds and ends."

The endless litigation continued. Under new management, the once prosperous Fox corporations floundered, to its former head's anguish. The previously dynamic Fox lost weight, grew lean and ill. In March, 1941, he was indicted on a charge of conspiracy to obstruct justice through bribing a judge at his bankruptcy hearing. In October, 1941, he was sentenced to a year in prison and fined $3,000 on his plea of guilty, one which he later tried to change but without success. He served almost six months in the Northeastern Penitentiary in Lewisburg, Pennsylvania, obtaining his release on parole in May, 1943.

Over the years he paid off the government's tax claims and eventually emerged from bankruptcy. From time to time, he spoke of a comeback in the film industry. None materialized. Various patents and projects launched long ago did, however, give him favorable returns as time went on. Fox was able to live comfortably and to provide sizable trusts for his wife and daughter.

He always maintained that his being cast out of the film industry was the result of a conspiracy of bankers, their object the rich 250 million dollars' worth of assets represented by the two companies he founded. He was particularly wounded when trusted associates like Winfield Sheehan, his "Crown Prince," threw in their hand with the men he considered his enemies. Evidently, too, he sometimes wondered, along with certain observers of the scene, if he would not have been wiser to work with financiers of his own race. Whereas Warners, Paramount, and Universal dealt with Jewish bankers, Fox, for reasons best known to himself, seemed to prefer dealing with conservative Christians like Harold Stuart of Halsey, Stuart, and John Otterson of A T & T, both strong Episcopalians. The man who bought his interests was Harley Clarke, utilities magnate and firm

Christian Scientist. All of these men disappointed him when he called on them for help. Another, whose refusal to aid was predictable, was Henry Ford, owner of the anti-Semitic Dearborn *Independent*. When that paper began preparing an unfriendly article about Fox, he informed Ford he would photograph accidents involving Ford cars, have experts analyze the cause, and discuss them on Fox newsreels. Ford stopped his article. He also later was swift in his refusal to help shore up the Fox interests.

William Fox was dour and pugnacious, and many think he was the most greedily ambitious of all the moguls. And yet Adolph Zukor, the Warners, Nicholas Schenck, and others all played the power game with equal savagery. Perhaps it was because Fox was a loner that he drew so little sympathy in his time of distress and was forgotten so soon after. He was poor at public relations, hating to be interviewed or have his picture printed. In his heyday he let his dark moustache grow thick, ordered himself photographed in a cold, forbidding pose which he decreed was official, and then shaved off the moustache. Few knew of his lavish bequests to artistic and charitable organizations, or of the fact that he dearly loved many of his employees and readily gave expensive watches as gifts. Forgotten were his pioneering contributions to the film industry. There were no sons, as in the case of Lewis Selznick, to carry on his name and fight to vindicate it.

Years after the loss of his empire, William Fox made a nostalgic return to Hollywood. At the airport, reporters and photographers were waiting for the plane because one of those aboard was actress Loretta Young. When a passenger, wishing to be helpful, told a reporter William Fox was also arriving, the newsman said, "William Fox? Who's he?"

"Our town worships success, the bitch goddess whose smile hides a taste for blood," wrote columnist Hedda Hopper.

Perhaps her words form the most appropriate epitaph for William Fox.

7

The Brothers Warner

IT was the San Francisco Film Festival, and Jack Warner was accepting an award. He had already accepted seven or eight Jack Daniels, so when he rose to speak he was in splendid form. His first move was to throw away a carefully prepared speech. His second was to launch into a ghastly, horrible, inappropriate tirade against Communism. The audience booed.

There were 800 people at New York's Waldorf-Astoria when Jack Warner arose to accept a citation at a March of Dimes dinner. He threw away his prepared speech. He clowned and wisecracked his way through an ad lib session, using such salty language that the New York *Times,* covering the event, found not one quotable line for the morning edition.

At a studio dinner party for *The Great Race,* a film with an international cast, Warner failed to respond to an introduction but finally appeared to explain his absence in a selection of four-letter words. To the large crowd which had assembled from several continents, he announced that the entire event reminded him of a bordello.

Following an old tradition, the film industry gives a dinner one year for the United States Navy, and the next year the Navy reciprocates. On one occasion the Navy hosted aboard a battleship at Greenwich, England, with Mountbatten, First Lord of the Admiralty, and other high dignitaries in attendance. Jack Warner, seated at the head of the table, looked at his prepared speech and rose to read the first sentence.

"Melords," he interrupted his reading, "this is a lot of ————— they've written for me," and proceeded to give one of his inimitable ad lib vaudeville acts.

At a studio dinner for Madame Chiang Kai-Shek, Warner cast a glance over the long row of inscrutable Oriental faces and was overcome by a fiendish impulse. "Holy cow," he remarked so all could hear, "I forgot to pick up my laundry."

Introducing the principals of *My Fair Lady* at a press conference, he began, "Does anyone mind if I say a few words? Who's going to fire me if I do?"

It was Samuel Goldwyn who was introducing Field Marshal Montgomery, the hero of El Alamein: "I should like you all to rise and join in a toast to our honored guest—Marshal Field Montgomery." Also on the dais, Jack Warner rose easily to the occasion: "Sam's got it wrong. What he meant to say was Lord Marshal Field Montgomery Ward."

To Albert Einstein, proponent of the scientific theory of relativity: "Well, professor, I have proved a theory of relatives, too—don't hire 'em."

To an interviewer: "It was nice meeting you, and when you come to Siberia I'll make my salt mine yours."

To an Italian who told him *"Arrivederci":* "A dirty river to you, too."

On meeting a director with a French-sounding name: "Chevrolet coupe."

*   *   *

"Jack Warner is a man who would rather tell a bad joke than make a good movie," Jack Benny has said, adding, "I know he must ad lib. No one would write that kind of stuff." Producer Robert Goldstein, who has worked for Warner, says, "If he had it all to do over, he probably would be a standup comic like Benny or Henny Youngman." "Hollywood's answer to Casey Stengel," says one columnist. "His very presence in front of a microphone can turn a hall into a disaster area," says another.

At a Friars black-tie dinner in 1965, Warner was "roasted" by a stellar gathering which used the occasion to raise $100,000 for the Motion Picture Relief Fund. "You're a very charitable man, and I think charity excuses a lotta lousy jokes," said Jack Benny. Dean Martin, parodying "Ol' Man River," sang "Jack L. Warner, that Jack L. Warner, he don't know nothin', but he must say somethin', he just keeps yakkin', he just keeps yakkin' along."

Jack Warner enjoyed the occasion. "Being roasted here tonight makes me feel alive and happy," he declared. "The day you don't enjoy being roasted—you're cooked."

He then went on in his usual mumbling, rambling, disjointed style, all ad lib and ad nauseam, controlling his tendency to use Marine expressions only because of the mixed audience.

"This is a lot better than some guy getting up with phony tears," said toastmaster George Jessel. "But what he said tonight, only God will know."

"How the hell did you become the head of a great studio?" Jessel shouted on another occasion when the Warner oratory got out of hand.

Hollywood has puzzled for years over the antics of Jack L. Warner. Why would he spend hours going over speeches, rewriting, changing words, commas, decimal points, having the major themes blocked out on cards in big print to obviate the need for glasses, and then toss the entire final draft away as he mounted the rostrum? The speeches, of course, were written for him, and even with his editing, he probably did not feel they were his own. Only his own inspired spontaneous words would do. He was so fond of his own witticisms that he wrote them

down the moment they occurred to him. Then, too, with a prepared speech, Warner could not indulge in one of his favorite
sports—picking at monuments. He himself wanted to be a
monument, but all the while he hated pretentiousness, hated
phoniness, wanted to strip off the veneer of affectation. Lastly,
the buffoonery of Jack Warner was a defense mechanism.

"As a little boy I started building up layers of insulation, and
now I have a skin like an elephant," he wrote in his autobiography, *My First Hundred Years in Hollywood.* "Without this
armorplate I would have been carried out long ago with ulcers,
brain clots, fallen arches, and a lot of other executive ailments
I don't have now."

Whatever the reasoning, the incongruities remain. It is puzzling to hear the head of a magnificently successful film studio
talking like a third-rate comic. One adds to this the plethora of
stories which testify to artistic insensitivity, and the wonder
grows.

Warner was watching the screen test of a new actor with his
then son-in-law, Mervyn Le Roy. The short scene infuriated him.

"Why do you throw away five hundred dollars of our money
on a test of that big ape?" he demanded. "Didn't you see those
ears when you talked to him, and those big feet and hands, not
to mention that ugly face?" The player's name was Clark Gable.

In 1936 Le Roy made *They Won't Forget,* casting young Lana
Turner in a brief role that had her wearing a tight sweater.
When Le Roy moved over to Metro-Goldwyn-Mayer, he asked
Warner if he could take Lana along. "She hasn't got it," Jack an-
swered, letting her go. "She's just a kid."

Talent scout Solly Baiano brought a high-school girl named
Debbie Reynolds to Warner but couldn't sell her. Similarly,
Warner refused to sign up a statuesque blonde who was modeling
for his own newsreel division, one Grace Kelly of Philadelphia.
Alfredo Cocozza, rechristened Mario Lanza, had a good loud
voice, but Warner thought he was too fat to have romantic appeal and let him go to MGM.

Over the years, Warner turned thumbs down not only on players but on plays. On seeing a rough cut of *Johnny Belinda,* he

fired everyone involved except producer Jerry Wald. The same year, he watched with dismay as the rushes came in of *The Treasure of the Sierra Madre,* with Humphrey Bogart lurching through the desert looking for water.

"If that sonofabitch doesn't find water soon, I'll go broke," said Warner.

He fought hard to make director John Huston change the ending. He didn't want Bogey to die at the picture's end. Huston won out, following the B. Traven novel in which the Bogart character is murdered on the banks of a water hole by Gold Hat and his bandits. Again, Warner fired right and left when shown the finished film. Between them *Johnny Belinda* and *Sierra Madre* won half of the year's Academy Awards. Even today, Warner persists in not liking some of his top pictures, the most recent example being *Bonnie and Clyde.*

How is one to account for a man who could call so many wild shots, who could quarrel so violently over the years with his major players, and yet produce *Little Caesar, The Jazz Singer, Public Enemy, I Am a Fugitive from a Chain Gang, The Petrified Forest, The Life of Emile Zola, Disraeli, Casablanca, Sergeant York, Yankee Doodle Dandy, Four Daughters, Captain Blood, The Private Lives of Elizabeth and Essex, The Green Pastures, Dark Victory, Jezebel, Dr. Ehrlich's Magic Bullet, The Adventures of Robin Hood, The Nun's Story, My Fair Lady, Who's Afraid of Virginia Woolf?* and countless others?

One follows the classic pattern. First, one is born to poor Jewish parents who emigrate to the United States. Benjamin and Pearl Warner came from Krasmashhilz, near Warsaw, in 1882, settling briefly in Baltimore before moving on to Youngstown, Ohio. Over the years, 12 children, a number of whom died before reaching maturity, were born to the couple. The father became a cobbler, then opened a bicycle shop, responding to a national fad for that two-wheeled vehicle.

It was 1903 when the family gathered together its resources and made a daring gamble, entering the chancy new field of motion pictures. The father pawned his prize possession, a watch brought from Poland. Despite initial failures in various nickel-

odeon ventures, the Warners refused to abandon the infant industry. They became film distributors, failed again, and turned
to production.

Years later the Warners were to become one of the great feuding families of Hollywood, but of this early period the New
York *Times* could accurately write: "Pooling their talents as
they had pooled their assets, the family worked together in perfect harmony and survived numerous setbacks and disappointments. Their loyalty to one another and their remarkable coordination became almost legendary as the Warners, coming
late in motion picture history, finally forged to the forefront of
the industry with their first talking picture."

The first notable film made by the Warners was a feature
called *My Four Years in Germany*. Appearing in 1917, it was
American Ambassador James Gerard's account of his dealings
with Kaiser Wilhelm.

In the twenties the Warners survived on a remarkable combination of talents, on the one hand matinee idol John Barrymore, on the other the most famous of all dog stars, Rin Tin
Tin.

Rinty, as the handsome German shepherd was called, was
found in a French trench during the First World War by Lee
Duncan, who brought him to California. Duncan trained the
police dog so that he responded superbly to his least command.
On the Warner lot in Burbank, where an earlier dog star,
Strongheart, roamed long before the land was taken over for
motion pictures, Rin Tin Tin made a score of films, many
scripted by young Darryl Zanuck. He was known as "the
mortgage lifter" because of his extraordinary box office appeal.
These were the days when the Warner financial status was so
precarious that producer Henry Blanke would take the company's Mitchell cameras home with him at night so that the
sheriff wouldn't get them.

"He was the only leading man—or her, if you prefer—who
never gave a bad performance," a nostalgic Jack Warner has written of Rin Tin Tin. "He faced one hazard after another and was
grateful to get an extra hamburger for a reward. He didn't ask

for a raise, or a new press agent, or an air-conditioned dressing-room, or more close-ups."

With money from the dog dramas, the Warners were able to finance such Ernst Lubitsch efforts as *The Marriage Circle* and *Lady Windermere's Fan* and to garner further prestige with John Barrymore. The Great Profile must have made them long for docile Rin Tin Tin. An extravagant character at best, Barrymore came to the studio fresh from his great London stage triumph in *Hamlet*. He arrived in Hollywood with Blaney, an English valet, and Clementine, a pet rhesus monkey, plus a remarkable capacity for alcoholic intake. The valet was grand, and the monkey tended to relieve himself on the nearest shoulder, often that of Jack Warner. To make sure that party-loving Barrymore appeared sober for early morning calls, Warner induced him to sleep in an empty office on the lot, guarded by a beat-up former prizefighter.

The Warners coddled Barrymore. They paid him a high fee of $75,000 a picture and gave him script and costar approval. Barrymore profited fully by the arrangement. When asked to make *Don Juan,* he agreed on the condition that he follow up with a version of *Moby Dick*. The Warners were not too keen on the commercial potential of the Melville story, fearing that the lack of love interest might hamper the box office. Barrymore insisted. If necessary, he said, he would fall in love with the whale. That great beast, constructed at a monstrous cost, sank into the sea during the first day's shooting and had to be recast. Dolores Costello was eventually recruited to provide a romantic interest, and *The Sea Beast,* as the film was titled, was one of the year's prestige successes.

It was the Warners' pioneering in sound, sponsored by brother Sam, which vaulted the struggling studio into the first ranks. Working with Western Electric, Sam put together an organization called Vitaphone to capitalize on the results of sound research. The original intention was only to provide musical backgrounds for film. The actual breakthrough to dialogue came as an accident during the filming of *The Jazz Singer.* Al

Jolson, taking the role of the cantor's son which George Jessel had created on Broadway, was recording a song for the film version when he was carried away by excitement.

"You ain't heard nothin' yet, folks. Listen to this," he exclaimed, using the trademark phrase with which he had regularly captivated audiences at New York's Winter Garden.

Sam listened to the words on the soundtrack and saw the immense potential of using dialogue. Contrary to general opinion, the original nine words were not in the final edited version, but a soliloquy in which Jolson spoke emotionally to his screen mother was inserted. "Did you like that, Mama? I'm glad. I'd rather please you than anybody I know of. . . ."

The effect on the audience was climactic. *The Jazz Singer* brought the film industry out of a serious economic decline and inaugurated a new era of extraordinary expansion. Sadly, Sam Warner died of a cerebral hemorrhage the day after it opened on October 6, 1927.

While other members of the family participated at various periods, the Warner brothers of the company title numbered a basic four. Good-natured Sam was the most likable and was deeply mourned by those who remained. Albert was called the Major because he retained his commission as a reserve officer in the Army Signal Corps. In his role as treasurer, he was the great economizer, cautioning against great star salaries and harking back fondly to the days of reasonable Rin Tin Tin. Harry was the business brains of the tribe, credited by Jack with having "the toughness of a brothel madam and the buzzing persistence of a mosquito on a hot night." Like other industry figures, Harry at first believed sound to be a passing fad, changing his mind swiftly, however, on seeing the indisputable rise in profits. Jack was the frustrated vaudevillian who sang illustrated songs in the very first Warner theater. As the man in charge of all production for the studio, he became the best known of the brothers.

The three remaining brothers took advantage of their lead in sound, spiraling the company to spectacular heights. On June

25, 1930, *Variety* devoted a special section to Warner Brothers. The facts and figures presented were as awesome as the policy statements were fascinating.

The Warner empire as of this date had grown into a giant complex, headed by the parent company and the recently acquired First National studio, itself a complete producing unit with top talent. Fifty affiliated companies and subsidiaries had been acquired, so that Warners could now handle every phase of their business without calling on outside sources. At home, the firm had bought theaters at an average of 1.3 a day since the first of the year, the total having mounted to more than 800 theaters seating close to one million patrons. Distribution was worldwide in scope, with foreign branches in 43 countries.

Warner Brothers went public in 1925. As of early 1930, there were 16,250 stockholders in a company employing 18,500 people. The market value of the securities was staggering: stocks worth $204,497,287 and bonds valued at $75,000,000. The last year's dividends alone amounted to $11,600,000.

Warner Brothers-First National Pictures and Vitaphone Varieties were advertised every day in the year 1930 in 92 percent of all newspapers in the United States. Every community in the United States large enough to boast a theater was visited at least once every two weeks by a company salesman. At the Warner theaters, 296,360,605 admissions were taken in during the past year. The public saw the best of some 7,000 miles of film, over half a billion frames.

"Motion pictures have become the world's greatest matrimonial agency," said sales manager Gradwell Sears. "They keep the world in love with love, even during periods of financial depression, when the stress and strain of life operates to deter men from marrying. It is a fact that civilized man cannot live without motion pictures."

Another set of brothers, the incredible Skourases, Charley, George, and Spyros, were in charge of the theater division. Impoverished immigrants from Greece, they had risen from menial occupations to ownership of their own theater chain before being absorbed by the Warners.

"Since the inception of Vitaphone, it has been the policy of Warner Brothers to present to its vast picture audience all over the world only entertainment which conforms to the highest moral standards," spokesman George announced. "The motion picture wields a far greater influence than any other form of entertainment. We should recognize the necessity for wholesomeness. Yet our motives are not only altruistic. We have discovered that clean pictures earn greater profits because they attract wider audiences. When you produce a story that may be enjoyed by every member of the family, you are automatically eliminating the risk of failure."

"Each of our managers is awake to his personal responsibility —alive to the moral obligations a theater manager assumes in soliciting public patronage," echoed Spyros, managing director of the 812 Warner houses. "To bring recreation and happiness to millions; to invite the public to share the comfort of beautiful, clean, and wholesome theaters; to make those theaters a place where citizens can congregate in perfect safety—these are commitments that demand and shall have the best of thought and studied action experience can provide. And to what more useful and purposeful work can a man devote himself?"

The list of Warner contract players included George Arliss, John Barrymore, Joe E. Brown, Noah Beery, Charles Butterworth, Betty Compson, Lila Lee, Winnie Lightner, Conrad Nagel, Ole Olsen and Chic Johnson, Walter Pidgeon, Vivienne Segal, Grant Withers, and Jack Whiting. The First National list boasted Richard Barthelmess, Douglas Fairbanks, Jr., Marilyn Miller, Frank McHugh, James Sidney Blackmer, Otis Skinner, and Loretta Young.

Warner Brothers-First National directors were a formidable group: William Seiter, Howard Hawks, Clarence Badger, Frank Lloyd, Edward Cline, Roy Del Ruth, Lloyd Bacon, John Adolfi, Michael Curtiz, William Wellman, Archie Mayo, and young Mervyn Le Roy, who married Harry Warner's daughter, Doris.

Under Jack Warner's overall supervision, Harry Rapf was at first the company's major producer. When he went to MGM, dynamic Darryl Zanuck left some of his writing and publicity chores to head production.

"Many great products are ruined by overfootage; many fair pictures are improved one hundred percent by clever and intelligent cutting," he announced. "Now Warner Brothers pictures are recognized for their tempo, speed, and direct continuity of thought and action."

Advertising and publicity chief A. P. Waxman handled the immense promotional operation, feeding material to the more than 400 newspaper and magazine reporters who were permanently stationed in Hollywood. No Warner picture ever opened "cold," he boasted proudly. In addition to on-scene coverage, concise studio news was sent weekly in mimeo form to the country's 2,000 principal newspapers, syndicates, and press associations. *Studio Highlight Starlights,* an illustrated clipsheet, was mailed every two weeks to 5,000 papers. On alternate weeks, the Vitaphone clipsheet, *Varieties,* went to 7,000 editors. *The Woman's Page,* with articles and illustrations of stars designed to capture female interest, was mailed fortnightly to a list of 4,000. Some 400 selected editors received exclusive stories each week. In addition, timely production stills and art portraits were mailed out by the thousands.

The hoopla surrounding Warner Brothers premieres came under the jurisdiction of publicity chief Charles Einfeld. When *Gold Diggers of 1933* opened in New York, the *Sun* reported in advance that a ribbon-cutting ceremony would release 5,000 gold balloons. "Chorus girls will sweep up and down Broadway on roller skates for an hour before," said the story. "An automatic girl, whatever that may be, will play a phosphorescent neon-light violin, whatever that may be, in front of the theater. It promises to be another of those dignified Warner openings."

Although Jack Warner was a staunch Republican, he supported Franklin Roosevelt. As a result, he was among the Hollywood figures invited to the inauguration in 1933. Taking full advantage of the situation, he ran a special train to Washington, in attendance such stars as Bebe Daniels, Ruby Keeler, Joe E. Brown, James Cagney, William Powell, George Bent, Warner Baxter, Bette Davis, Joan Blondell, Warren William, Guy Kibbee, Douglas Fairbanks, Jr., Loretta Young, Una Merkel, and Ginger Rogers. A good many of these were in a forthcoming Warners picture, *42nd Street,* and at stop after stop along the route, platform appearances plugged the film. In 32 cities in 32 days the glamorous stars also descended and marched to the local department stores. There they demonstrated General Electric kitchens, Einfeld having arranged a tie-in with that company. When the special gold-leafed Pullman reached New York, they entered a parade which skirted the width of Manhattan from river to river. It was an exhausted troupe that finally arrived in Washington to see F.D.R. sworn in as President.

Each year the Warner openings grew splashier. By 1940 the premiere of *Dodge City* saw a special train of 150 Warner stars and executives head from Hollywood for a two-day celebration in the onetime Kansas frontier town. A fleet of 50 privately owned planes formed an aerial convoy into town for principals Errol Flynn, Olivia de Havilland, Ann Sheridan, and others on the "beauty salon on wheels." Perc Westmore, head of makeup, was on hand to demonstrate his wizardry to the town's residents. Governor Payne Ratner provided companies of the state National Guard to oversee enactment of early days of the "bibulous Babylon of the Western plains." The promise of the film, the glamorous stars, rodeos, and Wild West shows bulged the city from 10,000 inhabitants to a festive 150,000. Even Franklin Roosevelt, Jr., was corralled into attending the ceremonies.

During the early Depression years, the Warner company experienced financial difficulties from which it eventually extricated itself. The brothers Warner as individuals fared quite well throughout. In 1932 Harry was called before a Senate investigating committee looking into stock manipulations. It was revealed that he had been trading in his own company stock, selling at an average of $54 a share and buying back at an average price of $23 a share. Under various names, his total transactions had netted him a profit of more than $9 million. At the time such trading was not illegal, but committee members made it clear they did not consider it nice, especially when Warner could guide himself by advance knowledge of such matters as passed dividends.

The company righted itself, and by 1934 dividends were once again being paid. Warner pictures kept their swift tempo, realistic big-city dramas, fast action melodramas, biographical histories. Darryl Zanuck was a key figure in the organization. In 1933 he quarreled with Harry Warner. Employees had taken a voluntary salary reduction, which was to be reinstated when business reached a certain level. At the appropriate moment, Harry wanted to wait a little longer before bringing pay back up to scale. When Zanuck insisted on immediate action, a rupture ensued.

"Due to a disagreement of policy in company management, Darryl Zanuck tended his resignation to Warner Brothers Picture Corporation, which the company accepted. The resignation is effective April 15. The future business policy of the company will be handled by Jack L. Warner," read the terse statement issued at the time.

As Louis B. Mayer survived the loss of Irving Thalberg, so Jack Warner surmounted the defection of Zanuck. In his place he appointed Hal B. Wallis, who had long been production chief at First National. Wallis was a modest, thoughtful, painstaking executive, the very opposite of the more flashy, swaggering Zanuck. "I wonder if this business will ever turn honest," was his favorite expression then, and today, after a long record of immensely lucrative producing, it so remains.

"We'll make the pictures; let Western Union deliver the messages," was the oft-repeated thought of Harry Warner, but it was belied by the daring gambles and innovations made by the brothers.

Harry himself was a strong advocate of topical themes, such as the first big company success, *My Four Years in Germany*, back in 1917. *I Am a Fugitive from a Chain Gang*, in 1932, made a powerful social comment on prison conditions of the time, leading in fact to substantial reforms. Directed by Mervyn Le Roy, it also portrayed a Negro prisoner in a remarkably intelligent, nonstereotyped fashion. *Dr. Ehrlich's Magic Bullet* treated the taboo theme of venereal disease, with Edward G. Robinson playing the German biologist whose research led to the first proven cure for syphilis. At the outset of World War II, Warners produced *The Confessions of a Nazi Spy,* an early attempt to alert the country to the menace of Fascism.

Sam, of course, was the driving force behind sound innovations, but the brothers stood behind him for *Don Juan* in early 1926, the first film to have a synchronized musical accompaniment. The following year came *The Jazz Singer,* and in 1928 Warners released *Lights of New York,* the first all-talking feature film ever made.

Overall, it was Jack Warner whose influence on policy matters was predominant, first through the agency of Zanuck and then through Hal Wallis. Warners made the first all-color feature as early as 1929, and the first all-star picture came in the same year. Rex Ingram starred as De Lawd in Marc Connelly's Pulitzer Prize play *The Green Pastures* in 1936, one of the first films with an all-black cast.

With *Little Caesar* in 1930, Warners launched a fantastically successful cycle of gangster films. The film made Edward G. Robinson a great star. *Public Enemy,* in 1931, did the same for James Cagney. Although Jean Harlow and Joan Blondell were in the film, attention focused on Mae Clarke when Cagney shoved half a grapefruit in her face. Apparently the nation's women longed for lovers who would treat them rough. Poor Mae Clarke went into film after film in which she was pushed, shoved, dragged, and knocked down by brutal men. Humphrey Bogart, Pat O'Brien, George Raft, and John Garfield joined the casts of the studio's "gat and gag" epics.

The genre developed so extensively that Warners employed its own gun and explosive experts. On one occasion, a group of visiting United States Army officers, watching the shooting of a gangster film, expressed amazement that certain machine guns were used without jamming. They themselves had had trouble with the same guns. Jack Warner explained that the cost of filming was so great that they could not afford delays. His experts demonstrated their work on the guns, and the Army adopted the devices.

Warners made *42nd Street* in 1933 when everyone said musicals had had their day, launching a new trend in mammoth musical extravaganzas. Two years later the studio imported Max Reinhardt, famed European stage director, to guide home an expensive imaginative production of *A Midsummer Night's Dream*. Again there were warnings that the public would not buy Shakespeare. The film turned out to be a box office favorite.

The brothers were aware that they might lose money on *Disraeli,* with George Arliss, but they went ahead because they were conscientiously trying to bring a new audience, the reluctant theatergoer, into movie houses. They succeeded. Because Paul Muni was not the kind of actor one could put into ordinary parts, they cast him in a series of screen biographies—*The Life of Emile Zola, The Life of Louis Pasteur,* and *Dr. Ehrlich's Magic Bullet.* The films again expanded the audience by luring a new type of customer into movie houses.

"Every worthwhile contribution to the advancement of motion pictures has been made over a howl of protest from standpatters, whose favorite expression has been, 'You can't do that,' " Jack Warner told a reporter. "I do not mean we should strive for so-called intellectual films, but we should strive for pictures that provide something more than an idle hour or two of entertainment."

Through the years, Jack Warner managed to wage more battles with his contract players than any other mogul. Bette Davis, Jimmy Cagney, Pat O'Brien, Olivia de Havilland, Humphrey Bogart, and other stars were so often on suspension that one wonders how all the studio's films ever got made. More money and better roles were their rallying cry.

Bette Davis survived her Slim Summerville characterization at Universal and also that studio's attempt to change her name to Bettina Dawes. She would not, she said, go through life known as "between the drawers." At Warners she gained stardom but suffered from the studio policy of giving her one good role and then putting her in a potboiler to capitalize on her popularity. The temperamental Bette must have been a formidable opponent for Jack Warner. When upset, she would make a noisy progression from outer office to outer office, giving secretaries sample indications of her state of mind. By the time she reached the office of Jack Warner she was in high dudgeon indeed, peering at her boss through dark, horn-rimmed glasses. "Mr. Warner," she always called him as she launched into her complaints. Jack would pacify her with difficulty—until the next time. On one occasion, her fury was such that she tried to break her contract. Warner followed her to England, where she had agreed to make pictures for a European producer. In a celebrated court case she was told she must honor her Warners contract. Jack welcomed her back to Burbank and paid a good portion of her court costs.

"In all fairness to Jack Warner, I will add he was singular as a movie mogul," Bette wrote in her autobiography, years after ending her brilliant career at Warners. "No lecherous boss was he! His sins lay elsewhere. He was the father. The power. The glory. And he was in the business to make money. . . ."

Humphrey Bogart battled with Jack Warner throughout his career, calling him a "creep," among other epithets. After a quarrel over a newly assigned role, Bogey often found solace in the bottle. Sometimes he surprised Jack and other executives by riding around the lot on a bicycle, his dress a pair of crumpled pajamas. The celebrated tough guy was obviously ambivalent toward his antagonist; the morning after, he frequently apologized.

"I kind of miss the arguments I had with Warner," said Bogart after leaving the studio for good. "I used to love those feuds. It's like when you've fought with your wife and gotten a divorce. You kind of miss the fighting."

Swashbuckling Errol Flynn made his debut with Warners

playing a corpse on a slab in *The Case of the Curious Bride,* a role which Jack called typecasting since he was later so often under the sheets. Brash, handsome, charming, Flynn would arrive on the lot escorted by a phalanx of blond beauties and hangers-on. The seats in his sports car reclined into a convenient bed, and the Flynn sexual prowess gave rise to the expression "in like Flynn." When Flynn got into trouble with a teen-age girl, the studio stood behind him, despite recurrent arguments over contracts.

"Only Jack Warner's faith in me set off my career—for whatever it has meant to me and to the world, for good or ill—and started me on that road which has so often made the public acquainted with my wicked ways," Flynn wrote in his autobiography, *My Wicked, Wicked Ways.*

James Cagney battled with Jack Warner but came back again and again to star in gangster pictures and later in screen biographies like *Yankee Doodle Dandy.* Kay Francis fought for good roles and more money and got plenty of both. George Raft fought with Jack Warner and has no kind words to say.

The star-producer relationship at Warners is typified by the case of Ann Sheridan. Jack Warner saw potential in the Texas-born redhead. In March, 1940, the studio publicity department boldly announced that 25 men of the world, such connoisseurs of female beauty as Lucius Beebe, the Earl of Warwick, Robert L. Ripley, Bob Hope, Busby Berkeley, and Earl Carroll, had chosen Ann Sheridan "America's Oomph Girl." At a dinner celebration, to which she wore costume designer Orry Kelly's "Oomph gown," she was presented with a two-inch solid gold wrist band attesting to her new title and a five-year contract with Warner Brothers Pictures.

One year later, after a nationwide promotion campaign and several launching-pad films had made her an almost instant celebrity, Ann Sheridan decided that her $600-a-week salary was too low, that the Warners were trying to "starve" her. It would take at least $2,000 a week to get her to oomph any more, said her agent, for she needed oomph clothes, in which she could give oomph parties, to say nothing of oomph funds for the charities to which she was expected to contribute. Jack Warner refused the increased salary demand, and Ann Sheridan left the lot to go for a cruise with George Brent. Her strike lasted for six months. At the end of that time, she oomphed back on the lot to resume her career in *Navy Blue*. Eventually her salary was given a substantial boost, but not before Jack Warner was ready to grant it. Underneath the practical joker lurked the hard-headed realist, the businessman who had made an investment which he wanted to pay off.

During this heyday of Hollywood there were so many sexy starlets sitting on the bony knees of producers that one old actress dubbed the town Lapland. Jack Warner was not numbered among those who used and abused their position of power in this fashion, but one tale clings to an executive producer on his lot. A young starlet found herself alone with this man on a closed set. As the story goes, he snapped the latch, and the accommodating girl dropped to her knees and began performing fellatio on him. It was a closed set, but what the producer had forgotten was that it was open at the top. Suddenly he looked up and saw that cameramen and grips were watching the scene with intense if silent interest. With a burst of energy he shoved the girl away from him, quick-wittedly shouting, "Get away from me, you crazy girl! What in the devil are you trying to do to me?"

Warner was at his irritating worst with writers, clocking them in at nine and out at five. There was a couch in each office, however, and the scribes could frequently be found stretched out, sleeping off hangovers. At other times, they would check in and then head across the street, where a drugstore had its convenient location. One day Warner called for one of his writers and found that he had gone to the drugstore. He called a second, who was also across the street having coffee. Furious, Warner sent a lackey across the street.

"Get the name of every writer in the place," he ordered.

The man went on his mission but found the writers monumentally uncooperative. He told Warner his problem. Warner himself called the drugstore manager and asked him to get the names of all Warner employees on his premises.

"Who's over there?" he asked an hour later.

"They all say their name is William Orr," the manager sheepishly replied, Orr being Warner's not-so-popular son-in-law.

Writer-director John Huston managed on one occasion to vent his dissatisfaction with the Warners by rather diabolical means. Working on *Across the Pacific,* a war film with Humphrey Bogart, Mary Astor, and Sydney Greenstreet, Huston was called into the Army as he was completing the script. In his final hours at the studio, he produced a scene which had Bogart in Panama, the prisoner of Japanese who were about to bomb the Panama Canal. Gleefully, he wrote a sequence of events which saw Bogart trapped in a room full of Japanese soldiers, his hands tied behind his back, more Japanese outside armed with machine guns. He filmed right up to this point, then departed for the Army, leaving the studio with the problem of extricating Bogart. The Warners fumed. They called in director Vincent Sherman. After mulling things over, Sherman had one of the Japanese soldiers go berserk and start shooting at random. In the ensuing confusion, he had Bogart grab a gun and manage his escape. The improbable but not impossible ending saved the day.

Warner Brothers was often referred to by writers as the Buchenwald of Burbank. Jack Warner made little secret of his low regard for word craftsmen and seemed almost to pride himself on being relatively illiterate. As in the case with his running rows with star players, one could never be sure just how much of his attitude was sincere and how much was a put-on. Now, long after the fact, it is easy to see that the constant contract disputes served at least one positive purpose—they gained an enormous press coverage for Warner players and forthcoming Warner films. Often, too, Jack Warner was right and his players were wrong. George Raft, for example, refused good roles which subsequently went to Humphrey Bogart and hastened his stardom. On a parallel note, Warner was right and MGM was wrong in the case of Joan Crawford. Released by Metro, Warner gave her career a remarkably fresh impetus.

Overall, the Warner artistic instinct produced a notable track record. Before selling out his studio in 1967, the last films produced under his regime were *Up the Down Staircase, Camelot, Wait Until Dark, Cool Hand Luke, Bonnie and Clyde,* and *Petulia,* not a bad skein on which to exit.

Those who saw only corny humor and insisted Warner had no taste are contradicted by William Haines, former silent star and interior designer. Haines recalls how Warner would walk into his place of business, glance about, and say, "That's beautiful." Invariably he would be pointing at the best piece in the house.

Certainly Jack Warner was demanding and despotic, surrounded by yes-men, quarreling not only with writers and stars but with producers, and finally his own family. Costume designer Orry Kelly had daily disputes with Warner which were, however, patched up over dinner at the Warner house, where Kelly, a close friend of Jack's wife, was a frequent guest. For years the studio's key producer was Henry Blanke, who had come over in the twenties as Ernst Lubitsch's script boy. So successful were his films that the studio signed him to a 25-year contract at $5,000 a week. When the industry suffered setbacks and Warners wanted out of the long-term deal, they submitted Blanke to every legal indignity within their power, hoping he would break his contract. Blanke surrounded himself with lawyers. When the gatekeeper said, "How are you?" as he entered the studio gates, Blanke turned to one legal minion and asked, "What do I answer?" Finally he refused to eat in the studio commissary, and when Jack Warner asked why, he declared flatly he was afraid of being poisoned. Blanke was paid in full, but the experience was shattering.

Whereas the family had stuck together during early days of trial, success split it at the seams. In the fifties Harry and Jack started to sell the studio to a group of bankers but changed their minds. Some years later they made an agreement to sell.

Harry dumped his stock, but then Jack pulled back, unable to release the reins. Where Harry sold out at $25 a share, Jack later got $80. The two stopped speaking and were on bad terms when Harry died in 1958. Jack also quarreled with his son, Jack M. Warner, and locked him out of his office. Harry's daughter, Doris, participated in family disputes in between marriages to Mervyn Le Roy, Charles Vidor, and Billy Rose. And finally, Jack divorced his first wife, Lorna, whom he called Ben Turpin because like that comic she could make her eyes play cross-eyed tricks. He was separated from a second wife, Ann, later reconciling, however.

There was always a job for relatives, of course. In addition to Jack's son, son-in-law Mervyn Le Roy was long on the payroll. Harry's second daughter, Betty, married Milton Sperling, who became a Warner producer. Harry's only son, Lewis, worked on the lot during summer vacations. At twenty-two an ulcerous tooth brought on an infection, and he died. Harry Warner never fully recovered from the tragic death of this son and heir apparent.

Always a headache but never a bore is the way one associate characterizes Jack L. Warner, known for years simply as J.L. The sobriquet gave way during World War II to Colonel. Jack took that rank in the Army, upstaging his brother Albert, who was after all only a reserve major. Albert died in 1967, leaving Jack the only surviving member of the illustrious brothers Warner.

"Make it," Jack said bluntly when Hal Wallis outlined the Emile Zola story during a long-ago car ride to the studio. By nature a gambler and a showman, Jack, in recent decades, has alternated between his villa on the French Riviera and the French provincial chateau which Bill Haines decorated for him far back in the Depression thirties. At Cap d'Antibes he rubbed shoulders at the roulette tables with King Farouk, Elsa Maxwell, and others of international café society. Bronzed, jaunty, with a villain's moustache acquired in middle age, he returned from European hegiras to rule over his studio, making news by such moves as spending a record $5.5 million for film rights to *My Fair Lady*. Honors came to him from many governments and charitable organizations. Yet, to close observers, Warner seemed a lonely man with no close friends, hiding his sensitivity behind the clown's mask.

His obsession with films never abated. He looked at every daily. He cut with skill. If pictures flopped, he was nice to everyone; when business was good, he was distant and irascible. An aide figured out this was because he knew no one would ask him for a raise when things were bad; he could afford to be nice then. It was when all went swimmingly that he became defensively ferocious. Always, he remained the captain of the ship, the man almost everyone loved to hate.

After he sold his interest in the company in 1967 to Seven Arts Productions, his old private dining room, where he had lorded it over so many stormy luncheon sessions, was converted to other uses. Jack Warner was to produce independently for the new Warner Brothers-Seven Arts, but it was clear that things would never again be quite the same. People began referring to the abdicating king in the past tense.

At a final meeting, Warner called in his employees and told them not to worry, that he would watch over the transition, that everything would be all right. Producer Bill Conrad listened and thought of the $32 million Warner had pocketed for his stock.

"Colonel," he said to the departing boss, "why don't you shift that money over to the other side? You're leaning too far over to the left."

Smiling, Jack Warner waved farewell.

8

The "Goy" Studio: Twentieth Century-Fox

"SAMUEL GOLDWYN, Louis B. Mayer, the Warner Brothers, the Schenck brothers, Adolph Zukor, Harry Cohn, Irving Thalberg, Carl Laemmle, Jesse Lasky, B. P. Schulberg, and their *mispochas* were conducting a Semitic renaissance, sans rabbis and Talmud," wrote Ben Hecht of the Hollywood he knew as a screenwriter and maverick critic. "The fact that they were flinging at the world the ancient Greek credo that deluding the mind of the public with tommyrot was better medicine than torturing it with truth (Plato) cut no ice about who was running the renaissance—Greeks or Hebrews."

"Sans rabbis and Talmud" is perhaps the operative phrase in the statement. Louis B. Mayer, Jack Warner, and Harry Cohn all shed Jewish wives in later years, replacing them with younger women of Christian backgrounds. Symbolically, they were asserting their independence of race.

Virtually every studio head numbered Gentiles in his immediate entourage; most of whom, incidentally, were often mistakenly thought to be Jewish. Among Louis B. Mayer's closest studio aides was Irishman Eddie Mannix. Another Irishman,

Winfield Sheehan, was head of production for William Fox. A Georgia Methodist, Y. Frank Freeman, long served Adolph Zukor and Paramount. The Greek Orthodox Skouras brothers were associated with several studios.

Key decision makers, however, were predominantly Jewish, a unique breed drawn from marginal enterprises, from nickel-odeons and vaudeville, from sales and petty trade, from the fringes of the garment industry. If they had all been thrown out of Hollywood by decree, it seems likely that the industry would have been forced to invite them back to survive, for they were men of gargantuan energy who combined a striking variety of talents—gall, persistence, artistic impulse, imagina-tion, showmanship, the gambling instinct.

One mogul who carried all these traits and headed policy at a major studio and was non-Jewish was Darryl Zanuck. To a sa-tirical *New Yorker* profiler, Zanuck was an anomaly indeed, for he had come not from the ghettos of middle Europe but from Wahoo, Nebraska. Nor was he altogether illiterate, having managed to reach the eighth grade before abandoning his ed-ucation.

"Generally speaking, the university alumni are working for the high school alumni and the high school alumni are working for the grammar school alumni," said the *New Yorker* writer. "College men have not covered themselves with glory in Holly-wood. Some have been billed successfully as directors and writ-ers but few are in places of power. Generally, you can roughly measure the importance of a man in the movie industry by the number of stories told about his ignorance. University train-ing appears to be a handicap in a new changing experimental calling in which imagination and judgment are more impor-tant than specialized knowledge. The semi-literates seem to have a vehemence, decisiveness, and singularity of mind which are commonly educated out of college men."

How Darryl Zanuck overcame the handicap of eight years of grade school and acquired screen power makes a beguiling tale. It does have its unlikely beginnings in 1902 in Wahoo, the authentic Indian name of a town in the Nebraska sandhills.

Father Frank Zanuck, of Swiss extraction, operated Le Grand Hotel in Wahoo. The mother's maiden name, Torpin, was English and presumably changed from Turpin in order not to be confused with Dick Turpin, the famous highwayman who was hanged in the eighteenth century. Louise Torpin was reading *Darrel of the Blessed Isles,* a turn-of-the-century best seller, when her son was born. She liked the book so well that she named him after the heroine, changing the spelling to accommodate his male gender.

Blue-eyed, sandy-haired Darryl was only eight when he visited California with his mother, sent there for her health. At the old Essanay studio in Glendale he earned a dollar a day playing an Indian papoose. The following year, back in Nebraska, he joined the ranks of the literati, publishing the story of his return train trip in the Norfolk, Nebraska, *Sentinel.* The account relied heavily on his imagination, interspersing descriptive passages with presumed encounters with Indians and cowboys.

Nothing ever happened in Wahoo, the young boy felt. The day before his fifteenth birthday, he quit Page Military Academy, took the braces off his teeth so he could lie about his age, and joined the Nebraska National Guard. His unit was sent to Mexico to chase Pancho Villa and later saw service in France. Darryl worked for the American Expeditionary Forces newspaper, *Stars and Stripes,* along with such men as Harold Ross and Alexander Woollcott. He also sent letters home which were published in local papers as "A Doughboy's Letters to His Family."

He was only seventeen when he returned from France and settled in California with his mother, who had divorced and remarried. In short order, he tried a dozen occupations, including prizefighting, laborer on the San Pedro waterfront, riveter in a shipyard, arranging window displays, press agent, and working in a drugstore. He was fired from them all.

His writing eventually lifted him out of the morass. His favorite authors were Mark Twain and O. Henry. In the short stories he submitted to magazines he tried to model himself after them, with scant success. His stories were rejected. At last, however, came a small check for an acceptance from *Argosy.*

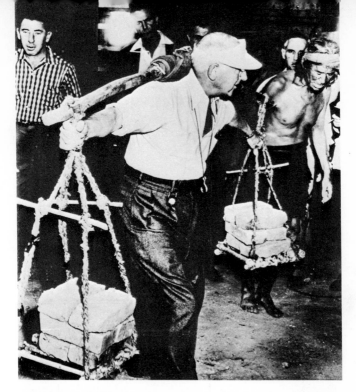

Cecil B. DeMille showing an extra how to carry bricks in
The Ten Commandments

Harry Cohn and director Frank Capra at 1939 Academy Awards ceremony

Harry Cohn, producer Walter Wanger, and Charles Boyer at a preview of *Mr. Deeds Goes to Town*

William Fox at his Hollywood studio in 1920

Mervyn Le Roy's fiftieth birthday party: Le Roy, Gower and Marge Champion, Jack Benny, Louella Parsons, Jack Warner

Harry Rapf and Sam, Harry, Jack, and Albert Warner

Jack Warner, Lloyd Bacon, and Darryl Zanuck

Left to right, first row: James Stewart, Margaret Sullavan, Lucille Ball, Hedy Lamarr, Katharine Hepburn, Louis B. Mayer, Greer Garson, Irene Dunne, Susan Peters, Ginny Simms, Lionel Barrymore. *Second row:* Harry James, Brian Donlevy, Red Skelton, Mickey Rooney, William Powell, Wallace Beery, Spencer Tracy, Walter Pidgeon, Robert Taylor, Jean-Pierre Aumont, Lewis Stone, Gene Kelly, Jackie Jenkins. *Third row:* Tommy Dorsey, George Murphy, Jean Rogers, James Craig, Donna Reed, Van Johnson, Fay Bainter, Marsha Hunt, Ruth Hussey, Marjorie Main, Robert

Benchley. *Fourth row:* Dame May Whitty, Reginald Owen, Keenan Wynn, Diana Lewis, Marilyn Maxwell, Esther Williams, Ann Richards, Martha Linden, Lee Bowman, Richard Carlson, Mary Astor. *Fifth row:* Blanche Ring, Sara Haden, Fay Holden, Bert Lahr, Frances Gifford, June Allyson, Richard Whorf, Frances Rafferty, Spring Byington, Connie Gilchrist, Gladys Cooper. *Sixth row:* Ben Blue, Chill Wills, Keye Luke, Barry Nelson, Desi Arnez, Henry O'Neill, Bob Crosby, Rags Ragland

Darryl Zanuck and Hedda Hopper

Darryl and Virginia Zanuck

Darryl Zanuck and Tyrone Power

Academy Awards 1947: Darryl Zanuck, Loretta Young, Ronald Colman, and Celeste Holm

Louis B. Mayer with Judy
Garland and her mother at
Judy's eighteenth birthday
party

Louis B. Mayer and Lorena
Danker at a party given by
Bundy Solt

Irene Mayer, Mrs. Louis B. (Margaret) Mayer, director Fred Niblo, Louis B. Mayer, Edith Mayer, and scenario writer Bess Meredith in the 1920's

Irving Thalberg and Norma Shearer

Shortly after, *Physical Culture,* a Macfadden publication, accepted his serial "Mad Desire." Here is a choice passage:

> A hateful sneer parted Loma's lips as her breasts arose and fell. She stepped back, acidly eyeing me.
>
> "As if I'd give him up," she snarled, a row of ratlike teeth catching a reflection of candlelight. "After we've gone this far together, after he talked me into the looney idea in the first place. What do you take me for, boy? I know I'm about as rank as women get—maybe a notch or so worse than his wife—but I'm no recruit. I've sinned and I'm paying for it. And if my daddy is gonna profit, I want my share, too. Understand, if he goes back, I go with him—arm in arm—or else we both stay. Get me, we both stay. Don't we, daddy?"
>
> "We do," he calmly replied.

The story subtitle read: "Determined to die in a futile effort to make amends, love points him a better way and rekindles his desire to live."

Success rekindled Zanuck's ambition. He sold other stories, including one to the Fox Film Company. When he learned that the adapter earned more for his work than he had for the original, he entered that field. Several lucrative years were followed by a dry period. Studios were suddenly buying only stories by authors who had published books.

Habit and Other Short Stories, by Darryl Zanuck, was published in 1923 by the Times Mirror Press of Los Angeles. The extraordinary work was sent to every production office in Hollywood. It consisted of one short story, two rejected scenarios, and a 100-page testimonial he had written earlier for Yuccatone Hair Restorer. As a published author, Zanuck regained entrée to the studios. Incredibly, the short story, both scenarios, *and* the hair restorer testimonial were sold to the movies and found their way to the silent screen.

The following year, Zanuck joined the staff of Warner Brothers and became one of the most prolific writers in Hollywood, turning out material at such a rate that he was forced to use a variety of names to market his product. His most notable con-

tributions were the dog dramas of Rin Tin Tin. In many ways
his scripts were dreadful, ungrammatical and inconsistent. A
character killed off in one scene would make a startling reap-
pearance with no explanation whatever. On the positive side,
however, there was always fast dramatic action, scenes alive
with plot ingenuity and invention. The lack of logic could always be fixed later.

The brothers Warner responded to the dynamism of Zanuck.
In short order he moved up in responsibility, becoming studio
manager in 1928, helping to guide the transition from silent to
talking pictures. In the late twenties and early thirties he served
as Jack Warner's right hand in production; here he was influential in establishing the gangster cycle and other efforts which
formed the studio's style of fast-paced realism. Many felt that
he butchered pictures with his cutting shears. But while motivations did sometimes disappear and while character development was sometimes sacrificed, Zanuck films always showed a
great story sense, a swift continuity. The audience was seldom
bored.

In early 1933 Zanuck quarreled with his chiefs over policy
matters and resigned. Already known as the bantam Teddy
Roosevelt and the boy Napoleon, his move caused wide specu-
lation. Job offers came from many sources but were turned
down. In late April the industry learned that he was founding a
new company, Twentieth Century Pictures, and that his associate would be Joseph Schenck.

Genial Joseph was perhaps the most widely liked of all the
moguls, his warm outgoing nature a contrast to his more taciturn brother, Nicholas. Both were Jewish immigrants from
Russia, and both entered the motion picture field after building up successful careers as owners of Eastern amusement parks.
Befriended by theater owner Marcus Loew, they joined his organization, Nick eventually becoming president of the amalgamated Loew's-Metro-Goldwyn-Mayer.

Joseph set up producing companies for early players like
Buster Keaton, Constance Talmadge, and Norma Talmadge,

whom he married in 1917. George Jessel was named as the third party in their divorce in 1934, but so easygoing were all the participants in the suit that they were called "the world's friendliest triangle." Schenck settled a good deal of money on Norma, but when she hired a new country lawyer a year after their separation, he told her that Schenck still owed her close to a million dollars as a result of various agreements. On being told, Schenck checked the books, found his casual bookkeeping was at fault, and without further ado paid the amount owed. He also hired the country lawyer.

"Well, that's the limit," said Brooklyn-born Norma to a friend. "From now on I'm not even going to trust the ass I sit on."

In 1918 director D. W. Griffith and actors Charles Chaplin, Mary Pickford, and Douglas Fairbanks, Sr., set up their own studio, United Artists, incurring the scorn of Metro's Richard Rowland, who declared, "The lunatics have taken over the asylum."

Schenck became president of United Artists several years later and functioned with great success. He maintained his reputation for geniality through various stratagems. He seldom fired anyone, but that did not mean employees did not get cashiered. On one occasion, producer-theater owner Sol Lesser was hired at $1,000 a week. Schenck welcomed him, assigned quarters, and then left on a trip. Lesser was puzzled because he had been given no duties whatsoever. As he sat in his empty office, a telegram arrived from his traveling boss.

"This will give you full authority to fire Johnny Considine," it read.

Considine was the studio's general manager. The startled Lesser carried the message in to him.

"I've been expecting it," said Considine, and evacuated his office.

After his divorce from Norma Talmadge, Schenck never remarried, preferring to enjoy more casual liaisons with pretty women—whose number included Marilyn Monroe. He enjoyed the good life, especially travel in Europe. His guttural accent remained with him all his life, and he never made any attempt to hide his humble background.

Taking the baths at Carlsbad, he enjoyed reminiscing about his sea voyage to America and his first days in his adopted country. He would never forget one incident, he told Ad Schulberg, wife of Paramount mogul B. P. Schulberg. Arriving in New York, he went to the Bowery and took a room for 10 cents a night. Lonely, frightened, speaking no English, he lay in the dismal quarters and stared up at the ceiling, where a naked bulb blazed away. He was wondering how to turn it off when he saw a cane reach through a hole in the ceiling. Dropping down, it hooked his trousers, whose pockets contained every cent he had in the world. Only a frantic lunge saved him from complete penury.

Schenck was already a rich man when he and Zanuck formed Twentieth Century in 1933. His brother, Nicholas, was a heavy investor in the new company, as was Louis B. Mayer, production chief of MGM. Mayer made his investment on the condition that his son-in-law, William Goetz, be taken on as Zanuck's assistant. In addition to financing, Mayer and Shenck loaned some of their top players to Twentieth in the early years.

The new company quickly signed up its own contract players, with George Arliss, Constance Bennett, and Loretta Young in the vanguard. Arliss made the tremendously successful *The House of Rothschild,* and Fredric March starred in *The Affairs of Cellini* in the first year. *The Gallant Lady, The Firebrand,* and *Bulldog Drummond Strikes Back* all made money and the company was on its way.

Visiting New York, Zanuck was interviewed by a youthful reporter, Joseph Alsop, Jr. In his suite at the Sherry Netherland, "Hollywood's newest Napoleon" greeted Alsop dressed in a vermilion and yellow silk dressing gown bedecked with painted polo ponies. Zanuck had taken up the noble and rugged sport and laid claim to being a two-goal player, although he was a short five feet five, a light 140 pounds, and slim. A large cigar jutted from his mouth, partially hiding two protruding buck teeth. A blond moustache compensated to some degree for a very high receding hairline.

"Movies have the greatest potential of any industry in the country," he told Alsop, marching back and forth in his natty bathrobe. "You see the public taste is an ascending spiral."

Like all the moguls, Zanuck liked to pontificate, but the new studio was certainly on the ascendant. The following year it merged with the old Fox company, which had been rescued from financial straits by a group which included Spyros Skouras, the onetime shepherd boy from the village of Skourihourian in Greece. Skouras eventually joined the company as president, with Schenck taking the post of chairman. Both functioned mainly as businessmen, however. The man who guided Twentieth Century-Fox's destinies was its chief of production, Darryl Francis Zanuck.

At Warners, Zanuck had helped guide the careers of male stars James Cagney, Edward G. Robinson, Paul Muni, and Humphrey Bogart. On his own he had developed the so-called period pictures with George Arliss, starting with the exposé of both anti-Semitism and international banking in *The House of Rothschild* and quickly going on to film *Cardinal Richelieu,* one of the best pictures of 1935. The same year Charles Laughton and Fredric March appeared in *Les Miserables,* which Zanuck called "an *I'm a Fugitive from a Chain Gang* in costume," and Loretta Young joined Clark Gable, on loan from MGM, in *The Call of the Wild.*

Female stars played an increasingly prominent role as Twentieth Century-Fox veered away from early topicality and realism toward a style that was warm, folksy, and sentimental. Far and away the biggest moneymaker on the lot was inherited from the old Fox studio—Shirley Temple.

"She's the world's eighth wonder. . . . Nobody has ever written the true story of that remarkable child," exuded Zanuck. "I'm uncomfortable every time I confront her because I feel that her intelligence is superior to mine.

"Why—why, Shirley Temple is endless," he gave the ultimate compliment on another occasion. "There is no one in the world to compare her with—why, she's a wonder. Beyond the case of her being—she isn't a freak or anything like that. Why, this child has rhythm. I always thought when we dropped the curls—this is the end. This mint, this gold mine, has gone dry. But now she's good for years."

Several suspicious minds indeed suggested that Shirley Temple was a midget who was being exploited as a child by Zanuck. The gifted Shirley survived such scabrous innuendo. *Captain January, Dimples, Heidi, Rebecca of Sunnybrook Farm,* and others reached an eager public; none of them was a big-budget picture, but all were healthy moneymakers. Even Franklin Delano Roosevelt succumbed to Shirley's charm.

"When the spirit of the people is lower than at any other time, during this Depression," said the President, "it is a splendid thing that for just fifteen cents an American can go to a movie and look at the smiling face of a baby and forget its troubles."

Shirley's popularity did not far survive the Depression thirties, as the mounting years forced her into a different type of role. The studio backstopped her, however, with Sonja Henie in an ice-skating extravaganza and with Alice Faye in a series of warmhearted musicals, supported by male stars like Don Ameche and Tyrone Power. On hand were the Dione quintuplets, Annabella, Simone Simon, and Gypsy Rose Lee. There was also Jane Withers, whose tough-girl appeal counter-pointed the saccharine Shirley Temple sagas.

"God, man, the movies are the greatest political factor in the world today. For propaganda, I mean," said Zanuck in his slapdash style. "If I use in a picture a bed that will put on your shoes when you get up, there will be a million orders for that kind of a bed pouring into Sears and Roebuck in a month. You remember how the head of the Soviet Russian movie industry said, 'Give me control of the movie industry in all nations for one year and I'll rule the world'?"

As the decade ended, Zanuck made such meaningful films as *The Grapes of Wrath,* for which he paid a record $100,000 in 1938, and Erskine Caldwell's *Tobacco Road.*

By the time Zanuck himself went to war in 1940, he had made Twentieth Century-Fox into a major studio and himself into one of the most discussed moguls, pro and con, in the industry.

Volatile, competitive, disputatious, immensely creative, his energies flowed into every area of production. Original ideas for films often came to him from reading the newspapers. His staff also prepared digests—one paragraph, a page, and a complete outline—of virtually every novel and play on the market. Once a property was chosen, Zanuck put his imprint on it at hectic story conferences, pacing back and forth swinging a polo mallet, his Rocky Mountain twang spilling words at such a rate that stenographers could not keep up. Each role he would play, moustache twitching, eyes dilating in sign of terror, the voice shrill for feminine characters and dropping in pitch for male roles. At other times he would sit back and seem to be almost asleep. His quiet pose was deceptive, for Zanuck had a unique ability to listen. Suddenly he would burst forth volubly with an elaborate solution to a plot problem.

"The reason that I got on so well with Zanuck was because he had faith in his own judgment and in mine," wrote actor George Arliss. "He talks a blue streak with the full intention of exposing his own weakness. He will pour out his ideas one after another, tumbling them on each other's heels, lashing himself into such a state of excitement that the words can't come out fast enough. When he is holding forth in this manner he is really having what to an actor would be a dress rehearsal. He is not only watching others but he is listening to himself and registering his own weaknesses as he goes along. He is trying to stimulate the others into going one better, but most of all he is trying to expose to himself the vulnerable points in his own arguments. It is an ingenious method, but in using it you must be careful not to be surrounded by too many yes-men."

After World War II, writer Nunnally Johnson came to Zanuck with the idea of doing a film on Nazi general Erwin Rommel, who led the German forces in Africa. Johnson warned that a picture about a German general might not be well received, but Zanuck said if the story was good, go ahead. He ordered a script, and after the first draft was prepared, he began conferences with Johnson, working with him on a line-by-line basis. His concentration was unbelievable.

"Here." He would stop abruptly. "Something's wrong here. I'm not interested."

He would leaf back in the script and find the exact spot where he had lost the thread. There would be specific suggestions, never dictatorial, at three- and four-hour sessions. There might also be rather silly ideas put forth, but Johnson saw that these were simply a device to get him thinking in a new pattern. To him, Zanuck was a genuine collaborator.

"I consider myself fortunate to have served an apprenticeship as a writer," Zanuck once said. "Writers deal, or try to, with the universality of human experience with which motion pictures must deal. And universality surely is the basis of every art."

The Zanuck schedule was demanding and compulsive. He did much of his best work at night, not leaving the studio until the early morning hours. He slept only six or seven hours at best. At the studio and at home, dictaphones were in every corner so that the endless flow of ideas could be recorded on the spot.

"Take a chance and spend one million dollars and hope you're right," he explained as his philosophy of film making.

To help him keep a grip on reality, he maintained several surprising characters in his entourage. Mike Romanoff, the self-styled but fake prince, was put on salary as a technical consultant because he amused Zanuck. Gregory Ratoff was given a giant salary so that he could afford to play poker with his boss—and hopefully lose it back to him. Rather shadowy studio scripts sometimes bore the credit line: "Based on a remark by Gregory Ratoff." A man named ———— was always around, and no one could understand why until someone asked.

"He's really the dumbest s.o.b. in town," Zanuck answered. "What I do is when there's a question of the public understanding some element of a film, I ask ————. If he understands it, everyone in the United States will understand it."

Relaxation for Zanuck came from poker, from polo, and from hunting. Studio personnel were unmercifully recruited for polo and duck and other game shoots, risking life and limb for one or the other.

"I had no idea about duck hunting, and neither did anybody else in the studio," confesed director Michael Curtiz. "The casting director almost shot my head off. They put us in those damned trenches in the rain early in the morning, three or four or five o'clock, I forget, but that was the order from Zanuck."

"You had to shake the porcupines out of the trees at night," said director William Wellman of a forced hunting trip to British Columbia. "It snowed. We had to break trail for the horses. We were snowbound for three days. We made twenty special fordings. We lost the horse carrying our medicine. I got blood poisoning. It was the ruggedest damn trip you ever saw. But do you know what? Zanuck loved it."

The big black cigar was another Zanuck symbol of virility, and he smoked 20 a day while strutting about his lavish office on the lot, dictating to three secretaries at once. Green and gold, the high-domed sanctuary boasted stuffed heads of water hogs and antelopes, skins of lions and jaguars, even the severed feet of elephants and rhinos, all mementos of African safaris.

The practical joke was a favored Zanuck defense against ulcers. One of his weak-stomached friends had an allergy to cheese. Zanuck delighted in slipping a sliver of odorous Limburger into his ice cream and watching him rush away to retch. He kept a small manufacturer busy making rubber chocolates, which he passed around with secret glee. On occasion he put a trained ape in his own chair, dimmed the lights, and had his secretary summon aides for a conference. More elaborate was a gambit which saw him pass off a bit player as the British ambassador to Mexico, with himself, in disguise, as the ambassador's secretary. An entire vacation trip south of the border was built around this charade.

Occasionally the joke was turned on Darryl. A favorite device of the time was to send gifts, the more unwieldy and outlandish the better. Crates of live chickens were popular, later outdone by baskets of slithering snakes. One of Zanuck's directors bribed his household staff during a period when he was out of town. He dismantled a huge field plow, brought the pieces into the Zanuck living room, and there had them all welded irrevocably together. It was almost as amusing as Ida Lupino's party, where she enticed her formally clad guests to look at the new swimming pool and blithely pushed them in.

Zanuck, like many of the high-powered Jewish moguls, smelled out weakness in others and pounced when he found it or thought he found it. He sensed a flaw in none other than Otto Preminger and baited that director in both subtle and simple fashion, something he would have never done with Lewis Milestone or Henry King.

When tough, crusty John Ford was making *Prisoner of Shark Island* with Warner Baxter, writer Nunnally Johnson observed that the actor was using what he knew to be a very phony Southern accent.

"There is no need for an accent in the characterization at all," Johnson, a North Carolinian, told Zanuck.

Zanuck told him to talk to Ford, which he did. Ford talked to Baxter, who liked what he was doing. The accent remained. Johnson told Zanuck again, and together the two went to talk to Ford.

"I agree with Nunnally," said Zanuck, looking up at Ford, towering above him on a sound stage. "The part doesn't need an accent. You've got to get Baxter to stop using it."

"Look, if you don't like the way I direct, I'll leave," said Ford, employing his familiar tactic with producers.

"Are you threatening me?" shouted the peppery Zanuck even before the sentence was out. "Don't you threaten to walk off this picture. I *throw* people off pictures. Don't ever threaten me!"

So vehement was the response that Ford mumbled a few pacifying words and went on with his work.

Once a decision was made, Zanuck wanted absolute acceptance. Until then, however, he liked argument, and there is his classic remark to an aide who was too eager to agree with him: "For God's sake, don't say yes until I'm finished talking."

A group of cronies sitting around were talking one day about Zanuck's needs, real or imagined, and how to meet them. Each invented ways of pleasing him. "When I die," said the winning entry, "I want to be cremated and have my ashes sprinkled on Mr. Zanuck's driveway so his car won't skid."

Zanuck liked to test people, to see if he could intimidate them into yessing him. Sports editor Mark Kelly of the Los Angeles *Examiner* came to work for him after leaving his paper. At his first story conference, Zanuck was in full regalia, black cigar, polo mallet, rattling off dialogue which everyone seemed to think was extremely good—except for Kelly, who sat stone-faced.

"Don't you like it, Mr. Kelly?" Zanuck asked defiantly. "Don't you think it's funny?"

"I thought it was funny when Weber and Fields first did it," said Kelly dryly.

Zanuck was amused. Later, however, when he found that Kelly hated child actors, he made a point of putting him on the script of *The Boy with the Green Hair*.

There was also a distinct madcap element in Zanuck. Director Richard Fleischer was suggested for *Compulsion,* Meyer Levin's novelistic account of the Leopold and Loeb murder case. "Fleischer?" said Zanuck. "He's good for your big imaginative extravaganzas. We're doing a psychological drama here. He'd be no good for that." Eventually he decided to go with Fleischer. *Compulsion,* under his direction, was a success. Next came the moment to choose a director for *Dr. Dolittle.* Fleischer was proposed. "Fleischer?" said Zanuck. "He'd be no good for this. He's your man for the intimate psychological drama. We need someone who can handle the extravaganza type thing." Zanuck eventually decided to put Fleischer on *Dr. Dolittle,* which garnered healthy grosses. Now came the time to put a director on *The Boston Strangler,* and again the name of Richard Fleischer was proposed. "Fleischer?" said Zanuck. "He's your man for the

big splashy musical like *Dolittle*. We need someone who understands psychology."

Giddy and grotesque, too, was Zanuck's comment to friends
in Paris who visited the Louvre with him.
"All right, we've got twenty minutes to do this joint," he said
with the taxi outside waiting.

It would be a mistake to take the jokes of this highly talented
man too seriously—for Zanuck as a film maker was certainly
gifted. While he was serving in the Army, producing training
documentaries, William Goetz tried to supplant him as head of
production. Joe Schenck appeared to back Goetz but at the last
minute swung his support back to Zanuck, who resumed his
role. Goetz left. Schenck, who had served a year in prison for
income tax evasion, retreated ever further into the background.
Back at the helm, Zanuck made *Woodrow Wilson,* an expensive object lesson against isolationism. He made *The Snake Pit,*
a searching study of insanity. *Pinky* and *No Way Out* dealt
with the racial problem, and *Gentlemen's Agreement* won
an Oscar for its trenchant depiction of anti-Semitism. The
studio made any number of brash parlor comedies, merry musicals, and bedroom farces, but along with them came *Young Mr.
Lincoln, Laura, The Razor's Edge, Twelve O'Clock High, Song
of Bernadette, How Green Was My Valley, The Ox-Bow Incident,* and *All About Eve,* among many others. In the postwar
years, Fox films led the field in quality, in serious commentary.
"We are in this business primarily to provide entertainment,
but in doing so we don't dodge the issue if we can also provide
enlightenment," commented Zanuck.
In the middle fifties, he resigned from the board of directors
and went into independent production. He was still married to
his first and only wife, Virginia, who had given him two
daughters and a son, Richard. Their living arrangements were
extremely casual, however. Zanuck headed for France, where

he became adept at the language and a connoisseur of good food, fine wine, and attractive women like Juliette Greco and Bella Darvi, with whom he conducted widely publicized romances.

In his absence, Spyros Skouras moved into the spotlight. He was one of the three brothers who were all supersalesmen, operators of theater chains throughout the country. Their accomplishment was remarkable when one considered their limited understanding of English. Told that Indianapolis was calling, one of the brothers said irritably that he had no time to talk to any damn Greek. Few knew what the Skourases were saying in their unique guttural delivery, but their persuasiveness transcended language.

After Zanuck convinced Spyros to take over the business end of his studio operation, he developed misgivings. Would Spyros, with his mangled English, make the right impression on distinguished bankers like Winthrop Aldrich, former ambassador to Great Britain? Fortunately, at this time Zanuck started playing golf with Skouras and his brother Charley. He watched with awe as they made fantastic bets after each hole.

"What reassured me was that they made each other settle after every hole," Zanuck told a friend. "If they're as careful as that, I guess we'll pull through."

Zanuck lived the high life on the Riviera but came back when the trouble-ridden production of *Cleopatra* made it seem as though Twentieth would never survive to become Twenty-First Century-Fox. With his customary daring, he looked at the 35 million dollars' worth of film and gave the order for $2 million of additional shooting. Because he wanted more action and less talk, he released writer-producer Joseph Mankiewicz. He cut the film himself.

His own effort, *The Longest Day,* gave the studio a financial shot in the arm, and eventually *Cleo* started paying off. Zanuck placed his well-trained son, Richard, at the production helm and himself assumed the complex business direction of the firm, an astonishing feat. Today, Twentieth Century-Fox, under father and son, is one of the most active and successful studios during a period of uncertainty.

From old-time employees and bright new faces alike one hears praise for thirty-four-year-old Richard Zanuck. His accomplishment is a tribute to the father, a rare case of one of the "sons of the pioneers" fulfilling promise and providing new-generation leadership.

9

Mayer's-*Ganz-Mispochen*

MORE THAN a decade after his death in 1957, the prevailing mood toward Louis B. Mayer seems to be changing, mellowing, turning nostalgic. Fresh source material is sometimes actually flattering.

It used to be far different. In 1960 Mayer's major biographer, Bosley Crowther, referred to his subject as violent, stubborn, arrogant, unmercifully rude, ruthless, tyrannical, sentimental but hardheaded, sexually a satyr. Film educator Robert Gessner spoke of Mayer's rages and thespian poses, of his jealousy, chicanery, spite, avarice, pretensions, and unbridled lusts, of his drive for power and his awesome egomania, calling him an emotional crook and a Satanic demigod. A *Variety* article referred to his character of unspeakable arrogance mixed with unspeakable naïveté, said he was intolerant of all who disputed his cornball taste, and summed up: "One does not remember his achievements so much as his monumental pettiness, his savage retaliation, the humiliations he heaped upon old associates. . . ."

There are still many in Hollywood who detest the memory of Louis B. Mayer. But there are also many once vicious critics of L.B. who are beginning to moderate or mute their dislike, to speak of regret at the passing of a great era, to realize that in some strange way they miss the stern patriarch who ruled the lives of his film family with a regal hand. For it was a family. In that heyday of the thirties and forties, it was laughingly said that MGM stood for Mayer's-*Ganz-Mispochen,* the Yiddish equivalent of "Mayer's whole family." The reference was to nepotism, the presence of relatives all over the lot, but in retrospect it is clear that everyone who worked at MGM was a member of the family. There was a great pride in working at this Tiffany of studios. Those who didn't make waves, who kept their noses clean, were guaranteed well-paying positions for as long as they cared to stay. For those in the top echelon, there was comfort in knowing that if they got into trouble, they would be bailed out of their difficulty by the head of the family, sexual transgressions would be covered up, alcoholic binges kept from the newspapers by crossing official palms with silver. On the other hand those who were disputatious, too independent, could have a very rough time. They might even be driven out of Paradise. The family, after all, was run by a Jewish elder who liked order and obedience. His was the largest and most fascinating family in Hollywood. Difficult it might be to remain part of it. Dull, never.

The feeling of a family and the excitement—these were perhaps the two most important things that Louis B. Mayer brought to his people at MGM, the two things those who are left today miss most. Through the great studio gates in Culver City walked "more stars than there are in the heavens," a publicity boast that few cared to question. King Clark Gable led the list, but no one overshadowed such players as Norma Shearer, Spencer Tracy, Greta Garbo, Jean Harlow, Joan Crawford, Robert Montgomery, James Stewart, Mickey Rooney, Jeanette MacDonald, Nelson Eddy, Walter Pidgeon, Freddie Bartholomew, Red Skelton, Greer Garson, William Powell, Robert Taylor, Myrna Loy, Elizabeth Taylor, and Eleanor Powell. High-powered directors W. S. Van Dyke, Mervyn Le Roy, Norman Taurog, King Vidor, Victor Fleming, and Clarence Brown were there. Gifted Irving Thalberg ruled his topnotch staff of producers. Every department head was chosen because he was the best in his field or at the least one of the best. The air bristled with competitive and creative drives.

This was the studio family of Louis B. Mayer, the single most powerful figure in the history of motion pictures. His blood genealogy could be traced back to Russia, to a ghetto in Minsk where his father, a laborer, married a peasant woman and began raising a family. Louis, the Anglicization of Lazar, was born in 1885. Along with an older sister, Yetta, and the younger Ida Mae, he migrated with the parents to the New World in the late 1880's. After a sojourn in New York, where two other sons were born, the Mayers settled in a small town called St. John in the Canadian province of New Brunswick. The father was a junk collector, and Louis, a chunky, dark-haired boy, first faced the world in this capacity. In later years, at elaborate studio banquets he would recall for visiting celebrities and statesmen those ragpicking days and the taunts of "Kike! Kike!" that would often echo in his ears as he gathered up forgotten bolts, pieces of piping, and rejected cans.

Junk collecting paid off. Jacob Mayer set up a ship salvage operation, aided by his fourteen-year-old son. Young Louis disliked his authoritarian father, a conscientiously Orthodox Jew, at the same time giving him the respect he considered his due. Although in his declining years Jacob became a sickly, difficult man, Louis continued to quarter him in his elegant Santa Monica home. From that base the father occasionally made unannounced and embarrassing sorties to the studio, still under the illusion that he was the reigning head of the family.

The mother was a remarkable woman who won the complete devotion of Louis, far beyond the ordinary Jewish reverence for the matriarch. As a boy his tendency to swear at the cruelties of life led her to teach him an enduring lesson. She led him by the hand to the top of a hill in St. John. "Say, 'Damn, damn, damn,' " she ordered. The boy said the words and listened to the harsh echo. "Say, 'God bless you,' " she then commanded. The moving reply came back. As the greatest mogul of them all, Louis B. Mayer's violent temper could elicit startling bursts of profanity, but never casually—only when provoked. And never in the presence of women.

The sale of scrap metal led young Louis to various cities, including Boston, where he lived briefly and found love. In June, 1904, he married gentle-natured Margaret Shenberg. The daughter of a kosher butcher, she was his age and a darkly beautiful girl. Their first daughter, Edith, was born in August, 1905, and during a short residence in Brooklyn, a second, Irene, was born in April, 1907. As is often the case when the father originally wanted sons, Mayer became exceedingly fond of daughters.

At the time of his marriage, he added the middle initial *B* to his name, later saying it stood for Burt or Burton, at the same time patriotically choosing the Fourth of July to stand as his day of birth. It was as Louis B. Mayer that he entered the amusement field. To a friend in Boston, Joe Mack, he talked of the difficulties of the scrap metal business. Mack told of a small theater for rent in Haverhill, Massachusetts, some 30 miles away. With a 600-dollar down payment, Mayer took possession of the 600-seat Gem, a former burlesque house which the townspeople called the Germ. He renamed the theater the Orpheum, refurbished its interior, and opened in November, 1907, with an announced policy of high-class films. One of the first attractions was a passion play filmed in Germany. It attracted a large audience. The next high-class film was *Bluebeard, the Man with Many Wives*.

Four years later, in 1911, the prospering Mayer built and opened a second theater, the 1,600-seat Colonial, following the pattern pioneered by Marcus Loew and others of alternating films with vaudeville acts. In 1913 Mayer and an associate leased the venerable Walnut Theatre in Philadelphia for a season of touring legitimate attractions. In the same year, he turned the Orpheum into a legitimate theater with a resident stock company.

Only a word is necessary to describe Mayer's next stops. From theater ownership, he followed a characteristic route into distribution, making a quarter-million-dollar killing in 1915 after acquiring New England distribution rights to D. W. Griffith's monumental 12-reel *The Birth of a Nation.*

The next stop, of course, was production. Metro Pictures Corporation was formed in January, 1915, with Mayer as secretary and Richard Rowland, a Pittsburgh supplier of theater equipment, as president. After an initial flurry of activity, Mayer withdrew when Rowland accused him of serving his own interest over the company's.

By 1918 Mayer was setting up facilities to produce on his own in California. His first star was Anita Stewart, whom he lured away from Vitagraph. He had met her, curiously enough, through a newsboy he had befriended in New York, a hunchbacked dwarf who formed a one-man fan club. If there was any superstition in Mayer, it should have been reinforced in the West. He rented space on Mission Road in Los Angeles from "Colonel" William Selig, a pioneer producer. The Colonel's studio was known as the Selig Zoo because in his travels he had acquired a mangy menagerie which he used to make films and also rented to other studios. Each morning as employees arrived, they cast a glance at the zoo's orangutan. If the fellow was playing with himself, went the tradition, it was going to be a good day. Another film colony superstition related to the large Persian rug in the lobby of the Alexandria Hotel. Before concluding a deal, stars and executives touched the Persian, convinced it would bring them luck.

Mayer's first film with Anita Stewart was called *Virtuous Wives.* A harbinger of unchanging policy-to-be, it was widely advertised as presenting "a view of high society with a moral." In Hollywood, Mayer engaged the first woman director, Lois Weber, and elaborated his view of film making.

"My unchanging policy will be great star, great director, great play, great cast," he told her. "You are authorized to get these without stint or limit. Spare nothing, neither expense, time, nor effort. Results are what I am after."

The results were not particularly extraordinary, but the modest Anita Stewart efforts made money. In 1919 a second star was added to the roster, Mildred Harris Chaplin, the estranged wife of the great English-born comic actor. Much to Chaplin's annoyance, the Mayer publicity traded heavily on the Chaplin name. The films of both these stars followed a simple pattern: poor but honest girls beset by temptation, resisting for several reels, with virtue rewarded in the end.

"I will make only pictures that I won't be ashamed to have my children see," Mayer told one of his writers. "I'm determined that my little Edie and my little Irene will never be embarrassed. And they won't, if all my pictures are moral and clean."

By 1923 the Mayer company was marching steadily on with its dramas of honor and fidelity. Players who performed for it included Hedda Hopper, wife of stage favorite De Wolf Hopper, Rénée Adorée, Huntley Bordon, Robert Frazier, Barbara La Marr (the Too Beautiful Girl), and a petite, young Canadian named Norma Shearer. Fine directors George Leane Tucker, Marshall, Neilan, Fred Niblo, and Reginald Barker worked for Mayer. Agent Edward Small brought him New York stage director John Stahl and told him there were no Jewish directors in the business and he should try this one. William Fox had earlier turned the offer down, but Mayer liked the terms and added the talented Stahl to his stable. Mayer had also signed up Harry Rapf, a simple unpretentious worker, but in 1923 he scored his biggest coup by hiring the brilliant young Irving Thalberg away from Carl Laemmle at Universal.

All in all, the Mayer company was becoming a good merger prospect. As it happened, Metro had experienced some difficulties, selling out to Marcus Loew. Loew did not inherit Rudolph Valentino, who made *The Four Horsemen of the Apocalypse* for Metro. Director Rex Ingram thought Valentino a flash in the pan. As a result, Metro president Richard Rowland allowed him to depart. In 1923 the old Goldwyn company consolidated with Metro to form Metro-Goldwyn. Marcus Loew was not satisfied with the management of this amalgamated producing firm. Lawyer J. Robert Rubin recommended upcoming Louis B. Mayer to Loew, and in April, 1924, the final merger was approved which created a new studio to be called

Metro-Goldwyn-Mayer. Mayer was to be its vice-president and general manager at $1,500 a week. Irving Thalberg became the supervisor of production at $600 a week, with Rubin as the company secretary, also at $600 a week. Nicholas Schenck of the parent Loew's Incorporated became president, making the overall business decisions from his office in New York.

The new family had its built-in tensions. Between the creative end in Hollywood and the moneymen in the East a natural friction existed. Like Mayer, Nicholas Schenck was a Russian-born Jew. He had come to the film industry after rising to the ownership of Palisades Amusement Park in New Jersey, then forming a business and personal friendship with theater magnate Marcus Loew. Full-faced, with heavy features, his imperturbable nature was in sharp contrast to the volatile and emotional L.B. To gain a point, Mayer would often stage scenes for Schenck, berating minor employees in his presence, charging them with extravagance in order to impress Nick with his efficiency. In artistic matters, Mayer usually had his way.

Mayer's relationship with the boyish Thalberg was a complex one. Thalberg was the son he had always wanted. Mayer admired his creative genius and gave him his head. At the same time, he felt competitive. Over the years the two were to wrangle and quarrel and reconcile and then wrangle and quarrel again in a tangled love-hate nexus.

Whereas Thalberg was to be in charge of the studio's major productions, Harry Rapf was to supervise the B pictures, drawing on experience gained working for Lewis Selznick and the Warners.

It was the A pictures already in the works which were the immediate object of concern. The Goldwyn contribution was Mae Murray in *Circe*—this one caused no trouble—and the irrepressible Erich von Stroheim's version of the Frank Norris novel *McTeague*. Audaciously von Stroheim cast comic actress Zazu Pitts in a serious role. He was determined to project the stark realism of the theme, greed for gold, in detail on the screen. On location in San Francisco and in Death Valley he shot reel after reel, following the book line by line, putting his actors through literal torture to gain the effects he wanted. The original budget was only a faint memory, and still von Stroheim shot on. When the amazing venture was finally completed, more than 50 reels, about 8 hours of playing time, were in the can. Von Stroheim cut them to 24 and said he was satisfied. Not so Irving Thalberg, who brought in a cutter and reduced the running time to two hours. Even in its abridged version, *Greed* is considered one of the masterpieces of the silent screen. Thalberg, however, aroused a good deal of furor by his action, prompting one critic to say, "A Thalberger is to an actual movie what a hamburger is to an actual steak."

Audiences actively disliked *Greed*, evidently disturbed by its theme that money is worthless. They laughed at the appearances of Zazu Pitts, ending forever her efforts to break out of the comic mold.

Nonetheless, Thalberg gave von Stroheim a new assignment, and an unlikely one—the direction of Mae Murray and John Gilbert in *The Merry Widow*. Von Stroheim turned the fluffy Lehár operetta into a treatise on middle European decadence, loading every scene with erotic bizarreries and perversities. Mae Murray was outraged when one aged lecher in the story was depicted sniffing her shoes in an exhibition of foot fetishism. Famed for her graceful dancing, she was further horrified when von Stroheim announced that he was dropping the celebrated "Merry Widow Waltz" from the story. The turbulent director also offended John Gilbert by letting him know how little he thought of his acting ability. Both Gilbert and Mae Murray walked off the picture and were coaxed back by Thalberg—not, however, before Mae had called von Stroheim "a dirty Hun." Although the waltz went back into the picture, troubles were far from over. For three days stars and extras in the big ballroom scene waited for an effect the director wanted —the sneeze of a trained dog. The embarrassed trainer again and again gave his cue, but the cagey canine held his spot in the limelight and refused to sneeze. The dog's footage was in any event cut by Thalberg, who also excised a good deal more. The edited film won vast favor with the public.

Many years later, when von Stroheim returned from a long European exile to play a role in *Sunset Boulevard,* director Billy Wilder recalled the MGM pictures and told him, "Von, you were always ten years ahead of your time."

"Twenty," said von Stroheim unhesitatingly.

Mayer took charge of the biggest project inherited from the Goldwyn company, a behemoth *Ben Hur* which was dragging slowly along in Italy under director George Walsh. Much like the *Cleopatra* of the sixties, the picture was beset by money and personality problems. Mayer tried to solve them by going to the scene, replacing Walsh with Fred Niblo, and putting scenarist Bess Meredyth to work on the original script of June Mathis. When results continued to be unsatisfactory, he daringly scrapped most of the European footage and brought the company back to California. Most of *Ben Hur* was reshot at the Culver City studio. The completed 5-million-dollar production starred Ramon Novarro, Francis X. Bushman, and Carmel Myers and was considered one of the summits of silent screen art.

Much to the surprise of the other companies, the merged MGM was rising to a position of prominence. In 1925 King Vidor directed playwright Laurence Stallings' screenplay for *The Big Parade.* The memorable war picture was highly acclaimed. Vidor also directed the impressive *La Bohème,* with Lillian Gish. That dedicated actress brought realism to the consumptive heroine's death scenes by going for three days without taking liquids and by putting cotton wadding in her mouth to dry her lips. Other King Vidor films were *The Crowd,* a realistic dissection of the life of a white-collar worker, and *Hallelujah,* which dealt with the American Negro and featured an all-Negro cast.

During his trip to Europe to inspect *Ben Hur,* Mayer made the greatest star discovery of his career. In Berlin to sign up Mauritz Stiller, he saw that Swedish director's latest film, *The Story of Gösta Berling.* In the second female lead was an expressive-faced girl named Greta Garbo, who made no great impression on Mayer. When he offered Stiller a contract, Mayer was therefore surprised to find he would come only on condition that she also be signed. Mayer said he thought in that event they should meet. At the Hotel Esplanade, Stiller introduced the shy, rather plump girl. Mayer was still not impressed, but agreed to offer her a three-year contract at $350 a week simply to keep Stiller happy.

Tests made on her arrival in Hollywood were more favorably received by Mayer and Irving Thalberg. Garbo was cast opposite Ricardo Cortez in *The Torrent*. "Louis Mayer can hand himself a few pats on the back for having brought this girl over from the other side," said the *Variety* reviewer. *The Temptress*, with Antonio Moreno, was followed by *Flesh and the Devil*, which teamed Garbo with John Gilbert and led to their widely publicized off-screen romance.

Garbo was quick to evaluate her box office power. Only in the second year of her three-year contract, she demanded more money. In his office, Mayer asked her how much and was startled to hear her demand $5,000 a week. When he offered half that amount, Garbo made her famous remark, "I tank I go home." Home she went to her hotel and stayed there for seven months. The long strike became a factor in the fast-growing Garbo legend, and Mayer finally ended it by capitulating.

Over the years their bargaining sessions over money and roles drew forth their best energies. Both appeared to enjoy matching wits. Mayer appreciated the Swedish star's determination and grew increasingly to admire her acting. Twice he tried to watch a Garbo picture in the making. Each time he was asked to leave the set before she would continue.

Another very intriguing actress entered the Mayer family in the twenties, the lovely, lisping Marion Davies. Newspaper tycoon William Randolph Hearst had fallen in love with warm, generous Marion when she was a chorus girl in New York. For weeks Hearst bought two front-row seats to her show, one for himself and one for his hat. Her lisp and his high-pitched voice made for fascinating conversations as he dandled her on his knee, courting her in flamboyant fashion. To make her a film star he set up his own company, Cosmopolitan, which released through Goldwyn and then through Metro-Goldwyn.

Since Hearst was a married man, Mayer may have had certain misgivings about employing his mistress. He overcame these at the thought of the prestige that would come with the association, together with the benefits of a favorable Hearst press for MGM films. On the studio lot, an elaborate 14-room "bungalow" was built at a cost of $65,000 to serve as a dressing room. When a niche over the front door was decorated with the statue of a madonna, humorous writer Dorothy Parker was inspired to write: "Upon my honor,/I saw a Madonna,/Standing in a niche,/Above the door,/Of a prominent whore,/Of a prominent son of a bitch."

The bungalow became the center of social activity for the studio. Hearst entertained there, and Mayer gave huge luncheons for visiting dignitaries, including prominent politicians. The most elaborate feasts, however, were those tendered by Hearst at the 40-million-dollar twin-towered castle he built for Marion up the Pacific coast in San Luis Obispo County. An interior swimming pool had a floor inlaid in gold foil and was surrounded by white marble statuary. A small Greek temple was reflected in the large outdoor pool. Named San Simeon, the baronial domain also boasted three marble guesthouses, again amusingly called bungalows. All these dwellings were surrounded by an acreage so vast that it took three days to traverse on horseback.

Mayer, who was gathering stars and other talent with an insatiable appetite, must have felt sympathy for the obsessive collectionism of Hearst. The publisher's agents were ransacking Europe for priceless treasures, acquiring Gobelin tapestries, shipping on Medici bedrooms, dismantling an entire twelfth-century monastery from Segovia and using 14,000 crates to convey it to its hillside home. Silver, Majolica, stained glass—shipment after shipment made its way to the bulging Hearst warehouses. On one occasion, Hearst saw a rare clock in a catalogue and asked his agent to buy it. The agent announced it was already sold. Hearst insisted he find the purchaser and buy the clock at any price. After much difficulty, the agent traced the new owner—William Randolph Hearst. Hearst was always afraid a rare object would get away. Mayer had the same fear that the contract of one of his players would expire unnoticed, and kept a close check. Despite his surveillance, a valuable young property was allowed to slip from the fold—Deanna Durbin, who went to Universal and saved that studio from financial collapse.

Like Hearst, Mayer drank little, although he served guests generously. At San Simeon, there were two rules: guests were expected to come to the main house for breakfast before eleven in the morning, taking the meal at the 54-foot table in the Renaissance dining room, and they were not to bring liquor in their suitcases. The reason was Hearst's apprehensions about Marion's fondness for alcohol. Because he was so concerned, she felt a compulsion to have her forbidden drinks. She found countless ways to outfox him. As soon as his back was turned, she would snatch the nearest drink out of a friend's hand and down it. Repetitions of the maneuver had her reeling by dinner time, and Hearst would say sadly, "Now you can see what just one drink does to her." Marion also had a device that would guarantee her a good belt even if Hearst was close on her trail. A series of servants were instructed to serve the invariable first course, beef bouillon, making sure that Marion's bowl was filled with premium bourbon. "We always have bouillon as a first course; it's her favorite," the unsuspecting Hearst would tell guests. "Marion loves it so." After dinner Marion would head for further fortification to the ladies' room, where Hearst could not follow.

Marion also maintained a house on the beach at Santa Monica, only a stone's throw from Mayer's beach house. One of Mayer's players was William Haines, inherited from the old Goldwyn company, which made a star of him after choosing him the winner of a New Faces contest in 1922. Haines also lived on the strand and noted with amusement that whenever Hearst headed for New York, where he celebrated his birthdays and certain other occasions with his family, the lid flew off at Marion's house. Dinners, parties, dancing, and drinking became the order of the day.

On one such occasion when Haines answered the call to good living and laughter, Marion was in rare form. Everyone knew that Hearst gave her expensive jewelry which she seldom wore. Why not, someone asked, and Marion with her engaging little stammer, said, "C-c-c-come with me." She disappeared into a dressing room, emerging moments later swathed from head to foot in diamonds, rubies, and sapphires, with bracelets all the way up and down her arms, strands around her neck, broaches and clips weighing down her short knit dress so that it stretched to the floor. The *pièce de résistance* was a huge pin riddled with sapphires in the shape of the American flag. "Where shall I p-p-p-p-in this?" she asked, but before anyone could answer, the dazzling piece found its place of honor over her crotch. Louis B. Mayer was not there, but he would have loved that pin. He was very patriotic.

He was also an ardent Republican, which again put him in line with Hearst. Similarly, in international affairs the two men usually saw eye to eye. In the thirties, Mayer suggested to Hearst that he visit Adolf Hitler and try to talk him out of his anti-Semitic stance. Hearst went but succeeded not a whit.

When Hearst went to France and made remarks that met with a very negative reaction, Mayer spoke up loudly on his behalf. "Loyalty to one's country and to one's flag is a fundamental emotion regardless of race, color, or creed," he declared rather grandly. "We can well understand it, and so we can thrill to know that William Randolph Hearst's patriotism is not only an inspiration to every American but to every man the world over in whose breast burns the fire of the patriot. And so it was that as we watched recent happenings, we could not help but paraphrase the lines of David Warfield in *The Music Master*—'If they don't want you, we want you. If they don't love you, we love you.'"

Hearst repaid such eulogies—usually reserved for the dead —by plugging the names of MGM players in his "society" columns and by seeing to it that powerful Louella Parsons cast a benevolent eye on the studio's films. Early in the game, Lolly made the mistake of panning one of the Metro B's. Mayer called Hearst and asked him to see the film. Hearst did so, and followed up by calling Lolly and telling her she should remember Cosmopolitan and MGM were partners.

"Does this mean I'm supposed to praise MGM pictures whether they're good or not?" asked Louella.

"I didn't say that," said Hearst. "Let's say that I suggest you temper your judgment with—judgment."

Shortly thereafter, Louella received a summons to the Mayer office. In a benign mood, L.B. explained that he had been upset earlier because a good deal of money was tied up in the film under discussion and that she should realize they were all part of the same industry. It was their duty to promote it rather than knock it down.

"Well, Mr. Mayer," Louella volunteered, "every picture can't be a good one."

"Miss Parsons, let me tell you one thing," Mayer said, fixing her with a magnetic glance. "Every MGM picture is a good one. Some pictures are better than others, but there are no really bad pictures—at any rate there are no bad MGM pictures."

It was a conviction to which Mayer held throughout his career. At a much later date, when one of his grandsons unwittingly made an unkind remark after previewing a mediocre studio product, Mayer refused to speak to him for several months. Now, as he bade Louella good-bye, he begged her to think of him as a father.

There was an abundance of boudoir scenes in Metro films, but this did not deter Mayer from sounding off against "salacious pictures," and here again the Hearst press gave his views thorough and favorable coverage. "Of course we shall have sex," they quoted him on one occasion. "As long as we have men and women in the world we will have sex. And I approve of it. We'll have sex in motion pictures and I want it there. But it will be normal, real, beautiful sex—the sex that is common to the people in the audience, to me and to you. A man and a woman are in love with one another. That's sex and it is beautiful, in the movies and in life."

In the Mayer movies, when a man and woman were in love, they got married—but Mayer was not quoted on that.

Louella Parsons was kind to Metro's efforts, but her most elaborate praise was always reserved for Marion Davies' films. These were treated in rapturous terms, with the sort of adjectives one might more appropriately apply to paintings by Rembrandt or Titian. Nonetheless, despite expensive productions and the power of the Heart press, they were not moneymakers. This was partly Hearst's fault, for he insisted that Marion play sweet young girls in pretty costume operettas rather than the more meaningful parts she sought. *Beverly of Graustark, Yolanda, Zander the Great, The Red Mill, Quality Street,* and other Davies films were saccharine fare, given a tepid welcome by exhibitors. To a reporter who asked Hearst if there was money in movies, he replied tartly, "There ought to be. I put twenty million into them!"

After a decade of cooperation, MGM and Marion Davies came to a quiet parting of the ways. Warner Brothers made overtures to the actress, who accepted. In preparation for the move to Burbank, the celebrated bungalow was cut into three parts, one division slicing into the middle of a bathroom. As the bizarre caravan moved down Washington Boulevard, a roll of toilet paper began unraveling, waving a white good-bye to Culver City and Louis B. Mayer.

Mayer came into his greatest glory in the thirties, deftly steering MGM through a maze of problems. The entire studio had to be retooled for sound, and in the process several major stars, Bill Haines and John Gilbert among them, fell by the wayside. At the height of his fame, Clark Gable was accused of fathering an illegitimate child, and careful studio maneuvering was necessary to protect his career. One of the top Metro stars was a stubborn alcoholic who had to be dried out regularly and protected from prying newsmen. Another player, a tremendously gifted former child star, took to drugs. Mayer cooperated with the Narcotics Bureau and other officials in trying to straighten her out. Still another male star was a flaming homosexual, who at one time lived with two rather disreputable men. The latter had the unfortunate habit of inviting high school boys to the house for sexual servicing. One of the boys told his mother, who told her neighbors, who told their neighbors, who drove by the star's house and tossed rocks into the window, with threatening notes attached, saying: "Perverts—get out of the neighborhood." Louis B. Mayer had to quiet the press, appease the authorities, and lecture his wayward "son" on the responsibilities of stardom. Eventually Mayer gave up on his queer star, releasing him on a morals clause in the contract.

Many a scandal was hushed up through the efforts of Mayer and his publicity chief, Howard Strickling, whose job was complex indeed, one prong reaching out to glamorize his players, the other to squelch stories of their escapades. A quiet man, self-confessedly humorless, with a stammer, he brought complete devotion to all his tasks. Mayer in turn considered him a surrogate son and stopped by his house at all hours for a chat. He and Mayer, however, could not keep one sensational story from hitting the headlines.

On Labor Day morning, 1932, a butler discovered the nude body of Paul Bern on the floor of his home, a bullet through his head. Bern was a brilliant young producer at MGM and a close friend of Irving Thalberg. He was also the recent husband of Jean Harlow, the Platinum Blonde, whose career as a cinema sexpot was reaching the heights.

The butler called the studio. Louis Mayer rushed to the scene. He saw that Bern's small-boned body was drenched in Mitsouko, Jean Harlow's favorite perfume. On her dressing table he found a note which read: "Dearest dear, unfortunately this is the only way to make good the frightful wrong I have done you and to wipe out my abject humiliation. I love you, Paul. P.S. You understand that last night was only a comedy."

Mayer pocketed the note, hoping to reduce the impact of the strange suicide. At the studio he told Strickling, who was shocked by his action. Mayer thereupon returned the note to the house.

When police entered the picture, they carefully checked the activities of Jean Harlow. She had spent the night at her mother's house, she said. There was evidence, however, that a woman had been in the Bern house. It was known that before his marriage to Jean, Bern had been living with a common-law wife. This woman had just died. There were some who suspected Jean of being involved with her in a plot against her husband. Mayer and Strickling fought hard to keep police from indicting their star on a murder charge. In this they succeeded. Jean went on to bathe in extraordinary public favor, to carry on a widely publicized romance with William Powell, and to die a tragic death five years later at the age of twenty-six when her mother, a Christian Scientist, refused until too late to allow medical aid for a curable uremic infection.

Difficulties and dangers notwithstanding, MGM swept to the heights in the thirties, becoming the largest and most successful American film studio. As its production chief, Louis B. Mayer wielded tremendous power, his position reflected by a massive ultra-modern office, designed by art director Cedric Gibbons, and by a skyrocketing salary. In 1937 his total income from salary and bonus provisions was $1,296,503, the highest in the entire United States.

Mayer tended to be of two minds about personal publicity. While at times he veered away from it, at others he found it irresistible. The celebrity-studded premieres, with their crossing searchlights and splash, were a case in point. Mayer would always hurry briskly by the radio interviewers but then permit himself to be coaxed over to the microphone. In a modest little set speech, he would welcome the audience. Similarly, Mayer liked being the top moneymaker in America, but he was also cautious about it. "Anyone who walks into my office now knows my name is good for a million dollars on a check," he confided one day to an associate. "I don't like it. It makes me feel distrustful of people, and I don't like to feel that way."

Writer Adela Rogers St. Johns feels that Mayer was foolishly wary of the press, probably because he remembered that he was a short, unread Jew who might come off badly. When she wanted to do a book on him, he refused, even though it was going to be favorable, a move he no doubt later regretted when Bosley Crowther wrote his critical account.

On one occasion, when the *Reader's Digest* sent Tom Heggen to do an interview, Mayer refused to see him until Adela interceded. All three lunched in the studio's private dining room, where Adela fed her boss cues that set him talking, about *Ben Hur* and the early days, about various players. All went well. Afterward, as she and Mayer were returning to their offices, Mayer said slyly, "Well, do you think you succeeded in making me impressive to him?" Mayer had a sense of humor, but it did not always show because the encompassing circumstances were often so imposing.

The Heggen article talked about Mayer's character and illustrated with several stories which have become classics. Mayer, it was well known, was the most outrageous ham actor on the lot, using every device in the book to win his point—threats, cajolery, insult, bribery, flattery, even real tears.

Secretaries recalled the day Robert Taylor, born Spangler Arlington Brough, angrily dashed through outer offices on his way to demand a raise in salary. For several moments his loud voice was audible. Then Mayer's mellifluous tones began to be heard. Much later Taylor emerged misty-eyed.

"Did you get the raise?" asked a secretary.

"No," said Taylor, "but I gained a father."

Red-haired Greer Garson was discovered by Mayer in 1938. Benny Thau, one of his top executives, recalls the circumstances. To take off weight, Mayer had gone to the baths at Carlsbad, stopping in London on the way home. With Thau, he decided to see a relaxing light musical, himself scanned the papers, and picked out a show called *Old Music,* which sounded perfect. When the curtain went up, Mayer flew into a rage. *Old Music* was a stark melodrama with no music at all. Fortunately a young woman in the cast, attractive, a good actress, caught Mayer's eye. An emissary invited her to join them at the Savoy

Grill for supper after the show. Greer Garson was brought to America and made her American film debut the next year in *Goodbye, Mr. Chips.*

It was 1942 when Mayer asked her to play the lead in the wartime drama *Mrs. Miniver.* Norma Shearer had already refused the part, and Mayer was unhappy when his protégée also turned it down. Garson hated the very idea of *Mrs. Miniver* because in it she was supposed to have a grown-up son in the Air Force, a role for which Richard Ney had been cast. Mayer was not to be easily countered. He began playing his symphony of moods, reminding Greer that he had made her a star, asking for gratefulness, turning aggrieved when she still refused, trying persuasion and begging her to do him a favor, switching to sarcasm to shake her, all to no avail. Finally he grabbed the script and began reading all the roles in the three major scenes, interjecting comments on her part, one of the greatest ever written, a tremendous test for an actress, likely to be the biggest success of her career if she could meet its challenge. So persuasive and energetic was the performance that it swept her objections aside. She accepted the role in a dazed condition, walked out the door, and collapsed in a faint.

English actor Henry Wilcoxon was cast as the parson in the film, and when he met Greer, he said, "May I congratulate you in advance?"

"What for?" she demanded, her antagonism for the story having by now returned.

"This picture," said Wilcoxon. "I think you'll win an Academy Award for your role."

"Mr. Wilcoxon, I have admired you in the past, but now I can no longer admire you."

William Wyler directed *Mrs. Miniver.* Because the United States had entered the war, the parson's speech at the end seemed too pacifistic at the time the film was ready for release. Special permission was granted for Wilcoxon, who had entered the Army, to get out of service for one day to reshoot it. Wyler and he sat up all night rewriting, giving the speech a Churchillian flourish, finishing at six in the morning. Wilcoxon shaved, showered, and appeared on the set at nine. The scene was finished by ten.

Mrs. Miniver won an Academy Award. Franklin Roosevelt had the final sermon reprinted in leaflet form and dropped over Nazi-occupied areas of Europe. Greer Garson married her film son-in-law, Richard Ney.

"I finally played it," she tells friends today of her role, "but Louis Mayer did it better than I did."

As Bosley Crowther was readying his book on Mayer, he called Garson with the hope of gathering anecdotes from her. She asked what kind of stories he wanted, adding that she was unwilling to help with the book if it attacked Mayer. He wanted colorful stories, said Crowther, and dropped the matter. Crowther also neglected to interview director Clarence Brown, Mayer's constant and devoted companion in his later years.

The Mayer histrionics were practiced on many subjects, with varying degrees of success. Jeanette MacDonald, one of his favorites, balked at a certain interpretation of a role, only to have Mayer drop to his knees and deliver his own emotional version of the Jewish lament, "Eli, Eli," in illustration of what he expected of her. Jeanette saw his point. At his funeral years later, she sang another of his favorites, "Ah, Sweet Mystery of Life."

With Viennese-born Luise Rainer, Mayer was seductive. "Why don't you sit on my lap when we're discussing your contract the way the other girls do?" he suggested. Luise declined. She won two Academy Awards in a row, for *The Great Ziegfeld* and *The Good Earth,* the only actress ever to accomplish that feat, but the public was not drawn to her. After her marriage to playwright Clifford Odets, she asked to be released from her contract. Mayer let her go.

Tallulah Bankhead was another holdout to Mayer's charm and persuasion. After making what she herself called "six rancid pictures" for Paramount she left that studio. In a meeting at his office Mayer offered her a considerably reduced salary but said he would build up her career, possibly giving her the role

Jean Harlow had just started opposite Clark Gable in *Red Dust*.
He thought he would have to replace Harlow, he said, because
after Paul Bern's suicide her appearance would be an insult to
the public. Tallulah, deeply offended that he would blame
Jean for Bern's act, called Mayer's attention to some of his less
savory stars and their morality, or lack of it. Mayer went right
on. In order better to act out his discovery of the dead man's
body he began to circle around his desk. Tallulah deliberately
misunderstood his maneuver.

"None of that now, Mr. Mayer," she cooed. "Stay on your side
of the desk. I can visualize the scene."

Spunky Tallulah went back to New York.

Mayer could be very expressive in talking of the value of his
people and the company. During a trying Depression year
many studios asked their employees to take a voluntary 10 percent pay cut. Mayer asked his to take 15 percent and spoke so
feelingly that not only did they accept but to a man were moved
to tears.

Mayer was always a sucker for making a speech. With his promotion head, Pete Smith, he would labor over each detail of a
prepared talk and then get off on a tangent and ignore most of
it. Florid sentimental phrases would roll from his tongue, and
if the audience did not always melt, he himself more predictably did.

Usually he was aware of the impression he was creating,
though he might at times be carried away and go too far. Director Mervyn Le Roy recalls how Mayer would shake a chubby
index finger so close to his face he feared it might enter his eye.
After one executive session, during which he pulled out all the
stops and won his point, Mayer nudged Le Roy. "Am I a good
actor?" he asked with a wink.

The ancient art of the storyteller flourished at the MGM
studio because Mayer did not read, or he read so slowly that
simply getting the content exhausted him. He hired a succession of people who could effectively recite plots of novels and

plays. Mayer had a picture sense, a visual sense. As his story-teller recited he would shut his eyes and put his hands together on his stomach, patting one with the other contemplatively. He could see the story cinematically.

One of the first of the MGM storytellers was Kate Corbaley, who came to Mayer from a scriptwriting school called Palmer Photoplay. Kate had a remarkable plot sense. Harriet Frank was herself a sound actress. When she recited a story for Mayer, a table lamp was carefully arranged to highlight her face, espe-cially to show a single tear rolling down her cheek. Almost al-ways the tear, which she had an uncanny ability to produce, made Mayer buy the property.

Lillie Messinger came to Mayer from the story department of RKO and developed her skills very conscientiously. The day before she was to outline a plot to an executive session she would be in bed by eight o'clock. She would awaken at two in the morning and from then until six study the play or novel in question, memorizing key passages in the case of plays, to give an idea of the dialogue's quality. At six she would go back to bed for an hour's sleep, appearing before the executives re-hearsed and refreshed.

Lillie felt a deep affection for Mayer and a tremendous re-spect for the qualities of his mind. To her, he always seemed a notch above the other moguls because his thinking was in terms of the entire industry, the broader picture, the wider ramifications. During the years she worked for him she often went to New York to scout properties. Mayer would call her every day, always giving her the feeling that she was missed, that her contributions to the studio were important. On her one vacation in seven years, five days at Lake Arrowhead, he again called every day. He seemed to have something akin to extrasensory perception, she felt, an ability to size people up, to understand their makeup, to get into their minds and know how they would act and react. This great penetration of their personalities enabled him to deal with them in a most effec-tive manner.

Mayer's employees were all part of his family. As his children, they were made to feel important and were drawn by a bond of loyalty which he created and exacted. When he felt betrayed in this loyalty, however, he could exact a merciless retribution. Lillie Messinger, who loved and revered him, was once the object of his wrath.

At lunch in the commissary all the talk one day was of a certain property which had been bought and which everyone found exciting. Plans were afoot to turn it into a major film. As she listened to the plot line, Lillie recalled a news broadcast of the previous day which seemed to her to point to a political parallel on the contemporary scene. She took it upon herself to see Mayer, telling him that in her opinion it would not be wise to make the picture at the moment because these political implications might produce problems. To her astonishment Mayer fell to his knees in front of her.

"Lillie, do you want to sit behind that desk?" he said emotionally. "You talk as if you knew more about making pictures than I do. Do you want to sit behind that desk and take my place?"

Alarmed, she tried to explain her point of view but only made matters worse. Mayer, withdrawing in wounded pride and pique, dismissed her. As in a medieval kingdom, everyone sensed that His Majesty had been offended. For three months no one spoke to Lillie. At the end of that time Mayer's secretary summoned her to his office.

"Did you cry this afternoon at Bernie's funeral?" Mayer asked, referring to the services for Bernie Hyman, a much loved studio executive.

"Yes, I did," said Lillie.

"Many people cried," said Mayer, "and when I die there will be people who will cry. You will probably cry at my funeral. You will cry at my funeral, but now when I need you you won't help me. You won't help me when I need you."

As the recital grew more and more emotional, Lillie, who felt she had not committed an error in the first place, began to feel herself weaken in relation to Mayer. "You will cry at my funeral," he kept repeating, "but now when I need you, you

won't help me." Already shaken by the death of Hyman, asked
to contemplate the death of Mayer, and in addition being
charged with failing that responsibility-ridden man, Lillie was
no longer able to align her emotions with her convictions. She
apologized for having stated an opinion which conflicted with
his. His benediction followed. She was restored to grace. She
left the office, rushed home, and released her conflict by becoming violently ill the moment she entered the bathroom.

The Mayer encounters could be as gripping as this, or they
could be remarkably satisfying. On one of her scouting trips
to New York, Lillie heard of a show called *On the Town* which
was being readied for Broadway. The principals arranged a
kind of backers' audition for her. Impressed, she called executive Sam Katz, who did not respond to her judgment. She
called Eddie Mannix, and he too was cool. Mayer at the time
was in the hospital, having been thrown from a horse, but she
decided to call him nonetheless. She repeated her favorable
view of the show and said they should invest in it, the sum in
question being $165,000, which would give them a sizable stake
plus preproduction rights, including first crack at a film version.

"Who's doing this show?" Mayer asked.

"You've never heard of them. Leonard Bernstein is doing
the music. You haven't heard of him, but you will. Adolph
Green and Betty Comden are doing the book and lyrics, and
they're going to be very important."

"What's the story?"

"It's about some sailors who come to New York on liberty.
But it's the way it's done that's important. This is going to be
a wonderful show."

"Something happens to your voice when you really like
something, Lillie. If you feel this strongly, I'll spend the
money."

A phone call, the quality of a trusted employee's voice, and
Mayer authorized the large expenditure, a typically daring
gamble. After the show opened, the MGM executives went to
New York to see it and brought back adverse comments on its

film possibilities. Eventually the mood at the studio changed. Arthur Freed agreed to produce, and the completed *On the Town* turned out to be a highly original and successful film.

Those who understood Mayer's psychological makeup often found him remarkably openhanded. Walter Pidgeon came from a well-to-do family in Mayer's Canadian hometown of St. Johns. A successful young securities analyst, he was launched on his entertainment career by Fred Astaire, who noted his elegant manner at the piano during a fashionable Boston soirée. At Universal, Pidgeon played second leads. At MGM he forged ahead as a leading man. When contract renewal time came up, he went to see Mayer. Their entire discussion dealt with St. Johns, the life there, the people. The subject of salary was eventually broached.

"Louis, I'm going to leave this in your hands," said Pidgeon. "As a hometown boy, I know you'll do right by me."

Pidgeon later confided to friends that no sum was ever mentioned but that when he received his contract the weekly salary was almost double what he expected.

Mayer was sentimental about pioneer film actors, signing up for bits and parts, not just as extras, past players like Barbara Bedford, Naomi Childers, Florence Lawrence, Mahlon Hamilton, Flora Finch, King Baggott, Robert Wayne, Helene Chadwick, Jack Cray, and Jules Cowles. As a New England distributor, Mayer once serenaded Florence Turner, the original Vitagraph Girl, during a convention meeting. On her return to Hollywood for a comeback in the middle thirties, he kindly renewed an earlier contract offer.

Mayer was quite capable of tearing up a player's contract and drawing up one with more favorable terms, but if an actor demanded an increase and threatened a walkout—as Clark Gable once did—he could be savage and threaten to drum the player out of the industry. His largesse at times was flamboyant. When he wanted a new property for Greta Garbo, he sent executive Bernie Hyman and his wife and writer Charles MacArthur to Egypt to "think about" a theme in that setting. With MGM footing the bill, they had a splendid time before em-

barking for Greece to see what they could come up with for
Garbo in the Greek Isles, then on to Jerusalem for further inspiration.

MacArthur and his writing partner, Ben Hecht, were very
fond of Irving Thalberg. When Mayer and Nicholas Schenck
in one situation seemed to be besting Thalberg, the two writers
played a retaliatory practical joke on Mayer and the studio.
At a Beverly Hills gas station they encountered a pleasant
young attendant with a British accent. They introduced him to
Bernie Hyman as "Kenneth Woolcott—a brilliant novelist and
playwright." Woolcott, MacArthur said, thought the movies
a lowly art form, but he had talked him into giving them a
try. The young man was signed on at $1,000 a week. At story
conferences, he registered the expressions that MacArthur advised, never saying a word, never writing a line. During the
year's run of contract no top executive, producer, or director
ever detected the fraud. To cap his triumph, MacArthur wrote
a letter over his protégé's signature.

"Dear Mr. Mayer," it read. "I wish to thank you for the privilege of working this year under your wise and talented leadership. I can assure you I have never had more pleasure as a
writer. I think if you will check your studio log you will find
that I am the only writer who did not cost the studio a shilling
this year beyond his wage. This being the case, would you consider awarding me a bonus for this unique record. I leave the
sum up to you."

The letter tripped up the hoax, which entered into Hollywood legend, alongside publicist Dave Epstein's mythical Ned
Farrington. Whenever Epstein had encountered problems in
placing a story about a client, he would wrap the item around
producer Ned Farrington, who was forever discussing properties, debating cast changes, thinking of signing up players. Epstein used the nonexistent Farrington so consistently that he
eventually tired of him. In a final fake item, he told of his
death and buried him, appropriately naming all the Epstein
clients as pallbearers.

L. B. Mayer was genuinely drawn to talent. More than any

other studio, MGM placed its stars on pedestals. If an aide reminded Mayer that so-and-so was really an s.o.b., he would say, "Yes, but remember he's *our* sonofabitch." His attitude toward writers was less positive. A classic remark variously credited to every mogul in town is most reliably attributed to Mayer. "Don't ever let that bastard back on this lot," he told an assistant, adding, "unless of course we need him."

William Saroyan served a term at MGM, where he wanted not only to write but to direct and produce. Mayer gave him a short as an experiment, which the wordy Saroyan ran far over budget.

"You're not a director or a producer, but you are a writer," Mayer told him on viewing the result. "In this short, you've got many pearls, but the pearls are unstrung."

Saroyan brooded over this, then called Mayer.

"You say the pearls are unstrung," he said. "Well, I've got news for you. The pearls are strung."

Saroyan left MGM and wrote a play called *Get Away Old Man*, which observers easily recognized as a fictional blast at Mayer.

In a short story entitled "The Missing Idol," Ben Hecht presented a producer called Mr. Kolisher, "mystically enthroned as a genius by the People," whom many felt to be based at least in part on Mayer. The description was graphic: "During the writing, acting, and producing of one of his movies by scores of other people, Mr. Kolisher charged about like one of the headless horsemen of the Apocalypse and committed almost as much damage. But not enough, however, to prevent the movie from finally appearing and being hailed as far as the hill passes of Tibet as another evidence of his genius."

Indeed, when one examines some of the great Hollywood successes, they seem to rise out of confusion, to be the end product of a series of substantial blunders. A case in point is *Mutiny on the Bounty*, a great Metro release of 1935, starring Charles Laughton and Clark Gable. It was Lionel Barrymore who first asked MGM to test Gable because he wanted him for a part in *Never the Twain Shall Meet,* which Barrymore was being allowed to direct. For the test, broad-shouldered, 190-pound Gable was put into a sarong, his hair was curled, and a flower was put behind his ear. The result was disastrous. "Good Lord, Lionel, no, no, not that," said Irving Thalberg. Only because Mayer's secretary, Ida Koverman, saw his potential was Gable given a chance. Koverman polled the female employees in the office and reported to Mayer that they thought Gable had sex appeal. Gable became a great star, but when the role in *Mutiny on the Bounty* came up, he did not like it nor did he wish to compete for his part against the English actors who were already signed up for parts. Charles Laughton said scornfully the ship had the leading role. Mayer himself thought the film was a bad idea—who would want to identify with a mutineer as the hero? Tremendous production outlays alarmed the business office in the East, where Nick Schenck arranged for a private preview. At the end, he moaned that the film was the biggest flop in the history of the studio. Because he thought it was a white elephant, it was released without fanfare. On its own it met with overwhelming public and critical favor, including an Academy Award as the best picture of the 1934-35 season.

"Mr. Kolisher alone understood the historical and spiritual significance of his product," Hecht went on in "The Missing Idol." "Mr. Kolisher knew, and knew passionately, that it belonged to the people, that every foot and phrase of it, every tear and grimace of it, was theirs. Mr. Kolisher knew that he was a Man with a Mandate. It was his duty . . . to keep the Kingdom of the Movies free from the ancient enemy of the People—Art. And how did Mr. Kolisher know, so mysteriously, what would delight the people? By knowing nothing, is the only answer I can give. By being as devoid of all subtleties, refinements, dreams, cultural equipment and talent as any of the lowliest whom he served. He was the man in the Street with bay leaves in his hair. . . ."

*   *   *

Opinions of Mayer were and are extremely varied. Part charlatan, part montebank, wrote Louella Parsons, but also creative and daring. Katharine Hepburn enjoyed her contract sessions with Mayer, canny Kate going over the documents line by line, giving and taking. Mickey Rooney called Mayer "Uncle Louis," and was often asked to accompany him on business trips, where he amused Mayer with his ebullience, with his antics.

"A dyed-in-the-wool sonofabitch," says Bill Haines even today. "A liar, a cheat, despicable." For several years, Haines was one of Mayer's top male stars, put into picture after picture, invariably moneymakers. When he sometimes went his errant way and was called in by Mayer, he resented the repeated scene, the Mayer tears, the arm thrown over his shoulder, the wail of, "Oh, my son. I never had a son. I always wanted a son." Mayer, Haines feels, was completely insincere, not sentimental but maudlin, a man who ran a complete autocracy, who thought of his players only as commodities. He finally found a way to stop the flow of Mayer's tears. He would cry, too. This dried up the Mayer ducts.

"He was a swine, an opportunist, a sentimentalist," says the elegant and cultivated actress Aileen Pringle. "I went in there one day about something, a picture I didn't want to do, I think, and told Mayer in a businesslike manner what was on my mind. He looked at me as much as if to say, 'You little worm.' He had that American flag hanging behind him and he thought of himself as the great Pooh-bah.

" 'You know, Aileen,' he said to me. 'I want to tell you that the other girls come in here and they put their head on my shoulder and they say, "Oh, Mr. Mayer, don't make me do that picture," or whatever it is. It's difficult for me to say no to them. You come in and start talking and telling me what you want, just like a man. And you know, it's very easy for me to say no to you.' "

To Aileen's house came such literary lions as H. L. Mencken and Carl Van Vechten, but neither Louis B. Mayer nor any other top studio executive was invited. Relations remained formal and somewhat frosty.

"Actually I was very fond of my superior, Louis B. Mayer, overly persuasive as he was," said director Josef von Sternberg, a man no one could accuse of being a sycophant. "He was, outwardly at least, a charming, simple and sincere person, who could use his eyes, brimming over with tears, to convince an elephant that it was a kangaroo. . . . Every aide of his was carefully selected after his merits were determined on the basis of his capacity for sincerity."

For director Clarence Brown, Mayer could do no wrong. "For me he was the second coming of Christ. I loved the man," says Brown. After 26 years of close business association, the two men became intimate friends, confidants, traveling companions.

That incomparable comedienne Marie Dressler joined the Metro ranks in the early thirties. The background for her arrival was dramatic and typically Hollywood. Marie's career on the New York stage was in temporary decline. To her friend, screenwriter Frances Marion, she wrote that she was desperate and about to take a job as a housekeeper with a family on Long Island. Her salary was to be $150 a month plus board. The news sent Frances Marion into action. She informed Irving Thalberg that her current screenplay had a part that only Marie Dressler could play. She doubted, however, that this splendid actress would leave the legitimate theater to come to Hollywood. Perhaps there was just a chance that money would talk. When Thalberg asked what sum might be offered, Frances said $2,500 a week might conceivably lure her out. Thalberg agreed. Frances called Marie, who hied to the coast.

In her autobiography Marie Dressler tells of Mayer's kindnesses. On one occasion, driving in the country, she admired a little vine-covered cottage. Mayer ordered it moved to her filming location site, where it served as her dressing room. Mayer was drawn to the elegant, witty Marie, the cynosure of all eyes wherever she went, the social intimate of many great names. He liked to have her host luncheons for special guests at the studio and visited her repeatedly during her final bout with cancer.

Claire Dubrey, who played silent leads and character roles in talkies, became Marie's closest friend and companion during those trying last years. It was her view that the comedienne was simply a commodity to Mayer, that his only concern was to learn if he could get another picture out of her. Marie's salary was never very large considering her immense popularity, and her dignity prevented her from asking for raises. On one occasion, Claire recalls, she bought herself an antique diamond ring for $5,000 and waggled it around proudly before her friends, saying that MGM had given it to her as a Christmas gift.

During Marie's final illness, Mayer would call Claire into his office to ask about her. One day, while Will Hays and half a dozen others were waiting to see him, Mayer forgot all about his pressing business and began to chat. Claire was intrigued to see him act out his descriptions of how he controlled his stars. With some he cried, he said; with others he reasoned; and sometimes he resorted to browbeating. At times he hypnotized them with his strong, brown eyes. Above all, he made each player feel that he was particularly concerned with him; when they left his office they were satisfied that he cared, and cared in a special personal way.

Adela Rogers St. Johns detected no self-interest in Mayer's attitude toward her. She came to know him as a fan magazine reporter. When her son Bill was killed in World War II, Mayer was extremely sympathetic, insisting that she come to work for him to get her thoughts away from her sorrow. At the end of a year she announced she was going back to her own work.

"Please take your time," said Mayer. "When I look at you I think of you as a sister. It's like having a sister around with you here."

A genial candor prevailed in their relationship. When Mayer became fascinated with racehorses, Adela, a baseball fan, said, "Forget the giddyups. Buy me the Chicago White

Sox. It's the thing I want more than anything else in life. Buy me the White Sox."

"I've got actors. They talk," said Mayer. "Ballplayers talk. Let me stick to horses."

Among the Mayer "sons" was newcomer Van Johnson. The red-haired refugee from Broadway played several small parts before getting a major role in *A Guy Named Joe* in 1942. One day he was driving to work along the street leading to the Metro gate in Culver City. At an intersection, his convertible was hit by another car and he suffered severe injuries. He was bleeding profusely, but no one would come to his aid because of a peculiar circumstance. The street was a double street, with the old streetcar tracks in the center. Jurisdiction on one side of the tracks lay with Culver City; on the other with Los Angeles. Both sides claimed the accident was in the other's jurisdiction. Finally a studio policeman called for an ambulance.

While Van Johnson slowly recuperated, Mayer was faced with a decision—whether or not to replace him. Mayer said that despite the cost he would hold up the picture for his injured player. The thoughtful gesture paid off. *A Guy Named Joe* made a star of Van Johnson, who went on to make a good deal of money for the studio.

One of the most talented and tormented of Metro stars, Judy Garland, resented the close supervision Mayer placed on her activities. From the time of *The Wizard of Oz* and ever afterward, Judy had a weight problem. Mayer tried to solve it by giving orders to the commissary that she was to be served the famous Mayer-recipe chicken soup, a healthy brew which did not satisfy her craving for sweets. In his office she would plead for a relaxation of restrictions. One day, as an afterthought, she said, "By the way, who's that little blonde that keeps ducking into doorways just as I get near her?"

"Her name is June Allyson," said Mayer, "and she'll get all your parts if you don't behave."

It was years later before Judy learned that with June Allyson, Mayer reversed the procedure, telling her Judy Garland would get all her roles if she didn't behave. In recent years, the magnificently resilient Judy seems to have erased any bitterness toward Mayer, explaining that most people didn't understand him.

She has perhaps heard stories like that told by Joseph Pasternak, who while producing the musical *Summer Stock* found that Judy was emotionally and physically run down. After 18 takes on one scene, Pasternak went to Mayer and said that it was simply too difficult to go on under the circumstances—Judy was sick and shouldn't be working.

"Sit down," said solemn-faced Mayer. "That little girl has made so much money for us over the years and worked so hard, and now she's in trouble. We can't just drop her out of the picture. We've got to help her and guide her out of this."

Judy finished *Summer Stock*. "The great song-and-dance actress makes this movie a personal triumph," reported *Life*. Shortly after, however, mounting pressures became unmanageable, and Judy slashed her wrists with a broken water glass in a painful attempt at suicide.

As for Judy, so for singer Mario Lanza time was a healer. "The end of it all for me came when Mayer left MGM," he told Adela Rogers St. Johns when she went to interview him.

"Why?" she asked.

"Mayer knew how to deal with people," he explained. "When I got mad I'd go into his office and I'd say what I was mad about and I'd call him a Jew sonofabitch and Mayer would burst into tears and say, 'Mario, I thought you loved me.' I'd say I didn't dislike him but he and the studio were making me unhappy with their demands on my life and he'd say he'd do something about that and exactly what was I talking about. I'd explain it to him and he'd say again he'd do something about it and I'd leave feeling a little better. Most of the time nothing ever was done about it but he knew how to handle me. After Mayer left, I'd go in to see Dore Schary and I'd call him a Jew sonofabitch and he'd throw me out of the office. Now you can't work for a man like that."

About to undergo an operation, producer Irving Asher had made all arrangements with a specialist and the hospital. Mayer checked into the matter and ordered a switch to a more expensive doctor of his acquaintance. Mayer retreated only when Asher's wife, actress Laura La Plante, intervened. She told him that while her husband's brains belonged to him, his body belonged to her and she would arrange for its well-being.

With actor Buster Keaton, Mayer was similarly authoritarian. He asked the stone-faced comedian to come to the studio on Saturday and run through some scenes for a group of visiting teachers. Keaton said he could not; he had already promised the St. Mary's College football team he would serve as their mascot that day. Mayer asked again. Keaton refused. On Monday he received a letter from Mayer saying he was fired.

Director Fred Niblo was more pliable. On a Friday afternoon Mayer told him to bring his wife and board the Mayer yacht for a cruise to Catalina Island. Niblo asked to be excused; he had promised to give a weekend party for his children. Mayer bluntly repeated the instructions for boarding the yacht. Niblo saw that protests were useless. He changed his plans.

A stocky, well-built man, Mayer would not infrequently lose his temper, causing him to rain avalanches of abuse on offending heads or, when really aroused, come at them with clenched fists. Disparaging remarks about women were certain to draw an uppercut. Erich von Stroheim was one of the first to find it out. In Mayer's presence he remarked that all women were whores, only to find himself swiftly knocked to the floor and thrown out the door. A moment later his cane flew out after him. Author Ludwig Bemelmans aroused Mayer's ire at a party by remarking of a guest that he was brave enough to have his wife and mistress in the same room.

When a *Daily Variety* editor demanded more advertising space from MGM, Mayer threatened to knock his teeth out. He also vowed to beat up a man who mimicked a noted opera singer at a party—until he was told the man was part of the act.

No one was exempt. As already noted, when fellow mogul Samuel Goldwyn was heard to impugn Mayer's veracity at the Hillcrest Country Club and refused to apologize, Mayer began swinging, landing the off-guard Goldwyn in a towel bin.

An early and famous fight pitted Mayer against comedian Charlie Chaplin. Chaplin was angry over what he considered vulgar exploitation of his name, Mayer's billing of Mildred Harris Chaplin, his estranged wife, as Mrs. Charles Chaplin on marquees. At the Ambassador Hotel in Los Angeles, Mayer heard Chaplin make remarks he did not like. Later in the lobby, he whipped off his glasses with one hand and assaulted Chaplin with the other. A local paper reported the scrape: "Charles Chaplin entered wearing gray flannels and weighing 126. Louis B. Mayer entered wearing navy blue serge and weighing 168. Chaplin led with a remark to Mayer. Mayer countered with a crack. Mayer then led with his right and missed. Chaplin swung with his left and missed. Both fell down. The decision: double TKO."

Alternately, Mayer could be surprisingly gentle. John Beck came to know him as an enterprising agent, at first independent, then as head of the motion picture division of giant Music Corporation of America. Beck got Elizabeth Taylor her first contract at Metro, and did the same for a girl named Suzanne Burce, whose name was changed to Jane Powell. Mayer was always warm and generous toward him. When the latter brought his daughter to the studio, Mayer was delighted, played with the child, and sent immediately for a studio baby carriage. He was always accessible, especially if Beck told him of some new talent he should investigate.

Beck's chief, MCA head Jules Stein, was a Chicago multi-millionaire who came to California and expanded by buying up contracts of major stars like Betty Grable. Mayer was used to telling agents what he wanted, but with the rich and powerful Stein the situation was somewhat different. He resented Stein's great wealth and social aggressiveness. For his part,

Stein was eager to please, to gain access to the Hollywood inner circle. On one occasion, when Beck had arranged a meeting with Mayer, Stein asked to go along. He wanted to get closer to this great man.

Beck took him, knowing that he was almost persona non grata at this point. In Mayer's office, he introduced Stein, whose friendly opening remark was, "Thank you very much for this meeting."

"I didn't do it for you," said Mayer briskly. "I did it for him."

There was an awkward silence, and then Mayer caught himself.

"But you must be a very nice man to have men like this working for you," he said, quickly canceling his earlier boorishness with a gracious comeback.

Stein, it was said, never forgave the moguls for the cool reception they accorded him. His retaliation came in the fifties, when MCA bought Universal-International and he himself became perhaps the most powerful man of the New Hollywood.

Whenever there are 25 candidates for a job or a screen role, the man who chooses one makes 24 enemies. Mayer chose more employees than any other mogul as he spent fabulous sums to make glossy, extravagant films built around great stars. He naturally made enemies, even without the help of his complex and demanding nature.

Still, many remember that MGM was known as the Friendly Studio, even using that motto on stationery. In addition to the many department heads and stars who stayed around for the better part of a lifetime, the sales department was a strong force in continuity. Largely Irish, perhaps a reflection of Mayer's beginnings in New England, the salespeople were goodwill ambassadors. If an exhibitor wrote to say he had bought an MGM picture with high hopes, but that a snowstorm had caused him to lose $200, an adjustment would immediately be made. Field exploitation men looked into complaints, rectified errors, and cheered their clients. Their attitude was a measure of the concern of their boss.

"You know how I'm smart?" Mayer once asked Mervyn Le Roy, and proceeded to answer his own question. "I get people around me who know more than I do. That's how I'm smart."

Mayer knew what he lacked, and he was wise enough to make up for it. His progression of secretaries aptly illustrates the point. As a New England distributor, he hired hard-working Fanny Mittenthal to write his letters and run his office. He also borrowed $1,000 from her to help finance his franchise for *The Birth of a Nation.* When the film made a fortune for him, he craftily returned the thousand on the pretext that Fanny, not being a company stockholder, could not participate in profits. Fanny was not brought along as Mayer moved up in the world. At his West Coast studio, her place was taken by a tall, polished blonde named Florence Browning. After the merger of his company with Metro-Goldwyn in 1924, Mayer took still another step upward, bringing into his employ Ida Koverman.

The stately, cultivated Ida became a tremendously powerful influence on Mayer and so on the entire studio. A widow of Scotch ancestry, she had been the secretary of Herbert Hoover during his days as a California engineer. Mayer met Hoover through her and became a dedicated supporter, later the first mogul ever to spend a night in the White House. When many Hoover supporters switched to Franklin Roosevelt in the 1932 electoral contest, Mayer remained steadfast, contributing heavily to his campaign, continuing his friendship after the electoral defeat. In politics Mayer was an archreactionary, always ready to inveigh against the evils of Communism, going so far as to invite congressional probes of Communism in Hollywood. Several sources say Mayer's dislike for his biographer, Bosley Crowther, stemmed in part from Crowther's liberal views.

Ida Koverman, who loved music and art and the finer things in life, was responsible for giving Mayer much of the polish he acquired with the years. She advised him on etiquette both at his home and at the studio, where she became the mistress of protocol, supervising elaborate luncheons for such celebrities as Winston Churchill and General Douglas MacArthur, George Bernard Shaw and Thomas Mann, the Japanese ambassador and Prince Gustavus Adolphus of Sweden and the Queen of the Netherlands. She checked his speeches for content and trained him in delivery, succeeding to such a degree that Mayer would begin orating—effectively—at the very sight of a podium. Mayer was a good listener, but to few did he listen as carefully as to Ida Koverman. He depended upon her, and she in turn guided him with a firm matriarchal hand. No one could order powerful Louis B. Mayer around but she.

In policy matters, she influenced his rule of illusion for stars, which decreed that great players must present themselves to the public as glamorous figures, wear beautiful clothes rather than casual slacks, drink not beer but champagne. As a talent scout, she contributed mightily to Metro, bringing Judy Garland to Mayer's attention and setting up the school where Judy, Mickey Rooney, Freddie Bartholomew, and Elizabeth Taylor developed their skills. Robert Taylor was one of her discoveries, and at a Los Angeles concert hall she heard baritone Nelson Eddy and led him to a film career.

"George Murphy isn't doing you much good," she once told Mayer. "You don't need him, but I do. I think he has a kind of Irish political charm that could be useful. Give him to me."

Mayer did, and Murphy spent many of his contract hours addressing political rallies for her. Her actions culminated in Murphy's shift from the make-believe of films to the reality of politics in the United States Senate.

During his early years, before dealing with an important figure, Mayer's secretaries would sometimes find him prostrate with fearful anxiety, tears streaming down his face. Ida Koverman was one of those who helped him walk among the great with a relaxed grace. He sensed the need to associate with people of class; it was what drew him to society-oriented Marie Dressler and Hedda Hopper, to sensitive artistic Irving Thalberg, to William Randolph Hearst and his exotic circle, to the conservative Old Guard Republicans around Herbert Hoover. Gregarious, exceedingly charming when he cared to be, Mayer was readily accepted.

His ability to fill his studio with good people and to draw forth their best was remarkable, with instinct and flexibility two keys to his success. When Lillie Messinger recited her first story to him, he saw at once that he wanted her to work for him.

"What do you want me to do?" she asked.

"I don't know," he replied. "People find their level."

Mayer was having trouble with a casting director when a New York friend recommended Benny Thau of Loew's. Mayer gambled and brought him out to Hollywood.

"Have you had any experience in casting?" he asked his new employee.

"None," said Thau.

"Good," said Mayer. "We'll break you in. So you make a mistake, you learn from it."

The number one executive in the world of motion picture production, Mayer hired men of top reputation, paid them top money, and then left them alone. He did not look over their shoulder, did not tell them how to do their job, usually entering the scene only in matters of policy. He had the ability to hold on to his people. Even among the temperamental stars there was only one suspension during his entire regime. Unlike other studios, MGM seldom loaned out contract players. Many department heads, top talent like Norma Shearer's brother, Douglas, the winner of countless Academy Awards for sound, spent their entire careers at the studio. On the lot, Mayer would sometimes encounter an employee who had been with him since Selig Zoo days; it would give him great pleasure to stop and talk, to ask about the man's wife and children, whose names and backgrounds he usually knew.

Although once a decision was taken, he expected argument to cease, he was himself capable of bowing to another's view. Again and again, for over a decade, he deferred to the judgment of his right hand, Irving Thalberg. Of this slim, slight, nervous man it was said he lived in a motion picture theater all his waking hours and knew instinctively whether the shadows on screen would please the public. In his head he could carry every detail of half a dozen pictures in production, sometimes holding three or four story conferences simultaneously, rushing from one to the other. His ability to prejudge material was unique, as was his gift for analyzing and solving production problems. Above all, he was superbly gifted at film editing.

: Whereas Mayer loved many of his stars and felt distant from writers, Thalberg was especially revered by his scenarists. Men as critical as Ben Hecht admired him for never putting his own name on a film. "Screen credit is valuable only when it's given you," said Thalberg. "If you're in position to give yourself credit, you don't need it." Charles MacArthur said, "Entertainment is Thalberg's god. He's satisfied to serve him without billing, like a priest at an altar or a rabbi under the scrolls."

Thalberg was in manner so boyish and unassuming that when Norma Shearer first saw him bending over a typewriter, she mistook him for an office boy. Louis B. Mayer had warned his two attractive daughters not to take interest in Thalberg because he had from childhood had a rheumatic heart condition. Constance Talmadge was unresponsive when Thalberg courted her ardently, pacing by her window night after night to see if there was a light. For a time Thalberg courted Rosabelle Laemmle, much to the distress of "Uncle Carl" Laemmle, her father, who was also aware of the heart condition. Nonetheless, the two continued to see one another until one memorable night. The occasion was an elite affair, one of the Mayfair dinner dances held once a month by ultrasocial screen society. This particular evening, at the Victor Hugo restaurant, was known as the White Mayfair because all the women were to appear in white, the men in tuxedos and tails. Lovely women arrived in lovely white gowns, and Irving Thalberg was dancing with Rosabelle Laemmle as the evening wore on. At the stroke of midnight, into this sea of white swept petite Norma Shearer, wearing a flaming red, red-fringed dress of spectacular beauty. No one could take his eyes off her, including Irving Thalberg. The courtship with Rosabelle waned.

The wedding of intense, darkly handsome Thalberg to the Canadian-born Norma was one of the great social events of the season. Norma moved into the Thalberg household, run by Henrietta, Irving's domineering mother. At their Santa Monica home, with its freshwater and saltwater pools to supplement the ocean, the Thalbergs gave small intimate parties and entertained filmdom's aristocracy.

Irving had his peculiarities, related to his health. The house was sealed and air-conditioned so that he would not have to catch a harsh sea breeze, or smell the sea, or hear the sea. Norma, too, had patterns which perplexed some observers. Next door were Douglas Fairbanks and his second wife, Lady Sylvia Ashley. Before a dinner party to be given by Norma for the Fairbanks, with guests drawn from the Fairbanks' close circle, Sylvia called to say Doug was ill. Norma withdrew the Fairbanks' place cards from the table but received her other guests on schedule at nine. A phone call at about nine thirty seemed to upset her briefly, but the party went on, dinner and dancing until the early morning. Departing guests were informed by their chauffeurs that Douglas Fairbanks had died at nine thirty in the evening. When Norma was asked about the matter, she seemed to feel there was nothing else she could have done. After all, telling the guests the bad news would have spoiled the party. At other gatherings, Norma endeared herself with her favorite party trick: balancing a full glass of water on her head, she would ease to the floor and slowly rise again, never spilling a drop.

The career of Norma Shearer, already well into the ascendant at the time of the marriage, was given a great boost by Thalberg. Top roles came her way, sumptuous productions like *Romeo and Juliet* and *The Barretts of Wimpole Street,* all guided lovingly by her husband, whose tendency to favor her did not endear her to other stars. Thalberg was not aloof from the princely art of nepotism. His sister Sylvia was on the MGM payroll as a writer, her husband, Larry Weingarten, as a supervisor, these in addition to Norma's brother Douglas, head of the sound department. Relatives often displayed great ability. Still, when various producers went independent, those who were related to studio executives became known somewhat derisively as the dependent producers, including those who were qualified by other than blood for their jobs.

Unlike Mayer, Thalberg let his busy schedule make him inaccessible, keeping prominent callers waiting not for hours but sometimes for days outside his office on what was known as the Million-Dollar Couch. Once the Marx Brothers, after a long wait, placed newspapers in a pan and lit them, letting the smoke seep under the door as a signal to Irving. Another time, when he left them in conference and promised to return in a second, he came back hours later to find them seated naked in front of a roaring fire, roasting potatoes. Thalberg, laughing, sent to the commissary for butter to go with the dish.

Thalberg told the Marx Brothers their film *Duck Soup* had more laughs than a picture needed, that with a more substantial story one needed less obvious gags. *A Night at the Opera* was his way of proving the point; it grossed as much as *Duck Soup*. On the other hand, he could also fail to see potential, as in the case of Clark Gable. Or when Frances Marion said comedienne Marie Dressler could play the drunken wharf character in *Anna Christie,* and Thalberg was certain she would only make audiences giggle. Against his own judgment he gave her the role which almost stole the picture from Greta Garbo.

Thalberg was demanding and critical, but always the aristocrat in his nature shone through. An offer of a drink would follow the most difficult session. His courteous, refined manner made numberless converts. Despite his frail nature he had great personal magnetism, long, elegant fingers that suggested an artist, and dark brown and black eyes with almost no pupils, eyes that could melt, which gave him an almost saintlike expression at times.

The overall Thalberg record was one of fantastic success, and it included such adventurous efforts as *Freaks,* a grotesque

tale of circus life peopled by fat ladies and midgets, mis-
shapen bodies and minds; gambles on opera stars Lawrence
Tibbett and Grace Moore; the Garbo pictures, along with the
more commercial Nelson Eddy-Jeanette MacDonald operettas,
the Harlow and Gable epics, and the Norma Shearer series.

Thalberg's towering reputation in Hollywood at once
pleased Mayer, insofar as he considered him his man, his son,
and distressed him, insofar as it detracted from his own glory.
The love which the rank and file of employees bore Thalberg also alternately pleased and anguished Mayer, who himself wanted desperately to be loved. Artistic quarrels sometimes nettled, and even more so, financial bickerings and
power ploys led to violent quarrels between the two men.
Only in politics, where both were relentlessly Republican and
reactionary, both ubiquitously antiunion, was there complete
agreement between them.

Intensely dynamic and ambitious, Thalberg drove himself
too hard. There were those, too, who said his marriage, long
considered unusually happy for Hollywood, was in trouble.
On September 14, 1936, at the premature age of thirty-seven,
Thalberg died of lobar pneumonia.

"I have lost my assistant of the past fourteen years and the
finest friend a man could ever have," said Louis B. Mayer's
tribute. "He was a creator, a man with vision who believed in
the mission of motion pictures . . . he was a simple man
whose greatest tribute is having in so short a span of life so
towering a monument of affection and respect."

With characteristic ambivalence, Mayer spoke not long after
to a close friend, the wife of another mogul.

"God was very good to me," he said.

"Yes, of course," said his friend. "God made you the head
of a great film studio. He made you the biggest man in Hollywood."

"No, that isn't what I meant," said Mayer. "God saw fit to
take Irving away from me."

No one ever took Irving Thalberg's place, but the man who
now handled a preponderance of producing assignments was

Hunt Stromberg, a man with his head high in nimbus clouds, with his shoelaces undone, and yet a greatly gifted picture maker. Born into the landed gentry of Kentucky, his lack of interest in the family's luggage firm led to his becoming a reporter. He was spotted by Sam Goldwyn, who brought him to Hollywood, where he served in publicity and directed before turning producer. A nonpracticing Jew married to a stunning Irish Catholic girl, also of a good family, Stromberg was socially prominent in Hollywood, a type that Louis Mayer always liked. He certainly also liked the fact that for 13 years Stromberg was a top producer of box office films in the country, a position which gave him a salary of $8,000 a week plus a percentage of the profits.

As with Thalberg, Mayer often deferred to his judgment. In London, Stromberg saw a play called *Night Must Fall*, which he wanted to buy. "We make pretty pictures," Mayer said reprovingly. "You want to make a picture in which a man carries a woman's head around in a hatbox?" Stromberg convinced him that it would be an important picture, filmed with style. It was, in effect, the first of the psychological horror movies.

Stromberg established a policy of never showing Metro executives, not even Mayer, his daily rushes or a rough cut; he showed a film only when it was completely finished. In the case of *The Great Ziegfeld* the studio heads went to San Francisco for an audience premiere. At the end of the long film, almost four hours with an intermission, Mayer watched the patrons file out and then turned to Stromberg.

"Hunt, that was magnificent," he said. "There's only one thing I didn't like and I want you to change it. At the end of the first two-hour sequence, you remember where Luise Rainer as Anna Held looks into her husband Flo Ziegfeld's room and sees William Powell, as Ziegfeld, kissing one of his top showgirls, Virginia Bruce. He doesn't see Anna; all he sees is her blowing him a kiss as she leaves. Then we see a headline: 'Anna Held Divorces Ziegfeld.' That was wonderful; that was a magnificent exit. But now what happens in your picture?

In the second sequence, almost an hour later, Anna Held comes back for that dreary telephone scene. Take it out."

Stromberg debated the matter, for Mayer had a point; to a degree it was extraneous for Anna to call up so much later to say she was glad that Ziegfeld was married and that she wished him happiness. Stromberg stuck to his original conviction that the scene was touching, dramatically viable, and when he insisted on keeping it, Mayer withdrew his objection. The film won the Academy Award for best picture of the year and another Oscar for Luise Rainer. Every critic praised the telephone scene.

Again, on seeing Clare Booth Luce's play *The Women* in New York, Stromberg immediately called Mayer to say he wanted to buy it. The reaction was violent; both Mayer and Nicholas Schenck thought it was a dirty play. "We make family pictures," they chorused. "*The Women* is dirty."

"Not the way I will make it," Stromberg insisted.

He was given his way. Norma Shearer, Joan Crawford, Rosalind Russell, Paulette Goddard, and Mary Boland headed a stellar cast directed by George Cukor. The film was one of the top pictures of 1939 and an all-time great.

With several years to go on a lucrative contract, Stromberg asked for his release in 1940. Prominent among his reasons was a policy matter. He was producing *Northwest Passage* with Spencer Tracy when the star's contract came up for renewal. "Spence doesn't like the way the picture ends," said Tracy's agent. Stromberg was used to having his way in situations of this kind; he was distressed when the nod was given to Tracy, purportedly because it was the only way to bring him back under contract.

"The first time you give an actor preference over the decision of a producer you start breaking down the whole system," warned Stromberg. When the same circumstance recurred several times, he asked to quit and went into independent production.

Mayer's personal preferences in films were pronounced. He believed in sacred motherhood and omnipotent fatherhood, the sanctity of the family over all. The virtuous should be rewarded, transgressors punished. Beautiful locales, lush sets, and good, heartwarming stories won out over grim problem dramas. A happy ending was decidedly necessary.

"I don't want any whores in my pictures," he once said. To a storyteller ending an account of a gangster plot he said, "Aren't you ashamed to tell me a story like that?" "I'll never make such pictures—those push Grandma in her wheelchair down the stairs!" he exclaimed in another setting. "If seventy-five percent of the American public didn't feel as I do about the American family, we wouldn't be here," said his summing-up.

The MGM story department, with first call on a *Cosmopolitan* story which later became *It Happened One Night*, strongly recommended it. Mayer turned it down because the millionaire father of the heroine was shown in an unfavorable light.

A clear sign of his taste is supplied by the Andy Hardy pictures, a low-budget series that turned into a big moneymaker and to which he gave his close personal attention. At one preview he watched with mounting dismay a scene in which Mickey Rooney as Andy Hardy was so preoccupied by difficulties with his sweetheart, Polly Benedict, that he pushed his mother's dinner aside. Didn't he himself have a mother, Mayer demanded of the producer, didn't he realize that no decent American boy would treat his mother in such a way? The scene was restaged so that a supercourteous Andy, mother love pouring from his eyes, said simply, "Excuse me, Mom. I'm just not hungry."

Another guidepost to the Mayer thematic taste relates to "The Rosary," the well-known song. "The hours I spent with you, dear heart, are like a string of pearls to me," Mayer would sing loudly and feelingly with his hands on his heart, and beg associates to give him a film based on the song. All through his career, he tried to drum up such interest. Just before his exit from MGM, he brought another mogul, Jesse Lasky, into the studio. One of the first things he drew to his attention was "The Rosary."

"This is such a beautiful song," he pleaded. "All we need is a story to go with it. Now why can't you smart men come up with something, you sophisticates?"

The word "sophisticates" was Mayer's ultimate term of derision. Lasky and his son actually worked up a plot for "The Rosary," but Mayer was gone before he could act on it.

Earlier, he had had better luck with another favorite song, the Navy battle hymn, "Anchors Aweigh."

"I want you to do a new musical, *Anchors Aweigh,*" he told producer Joseph Pasternak. "Everybody here wants to do it, but I think you can bring something special to it. I want you to do it."

"Good. What's the story?"

"Story?" Mayer asked with an astonished look and proceeded to whistle the tune with martial gestures.

Over the weekend, Pasternak saw a news item which told of a young lost boy whose parents traced him through his habit of whistling "Anchors Aweigh." Pasternak took the idea to Mayer. Mayer, it turned out, had told almost every producer on the lot that he wanted *him* to film the project, and each man came in with prospective themes. Gene Kelly and Kathryn Grayson eventually appeared in a version which Pasternak produced.

Over the years, Mayer was unwavering in his film preferences. "I am reminded of the late Marcus Loew always pounding home to Nicholas Schenck, to Bob Rubin, myself, and others, that the picture business was a Woolworth business where they can bring the entire family," he said in the late forties.

In 1950 John Huston's bitter, realistic probe of big-city crime, *The Asphalt Jungle,* was being filmed at Metro—Mayer allowed a good many films that he thoroughly disliked to be made at his studio. "This thing is full of nasty, ugly people doing nasty, ugly things," he said disgustedly. "I wouldn't walk across the room to see a thing like that."

Mayer's private life was not always so praiseworthy as his taste preferences might suggest. Although married, he had a keen eye for feminine beauty and courted women at a clip in keeping with his extravagant nature. The Hollywood legend says he pursued virtually every star and starlet on the lot, chasing them around the desk of his huge office with doughty determination. Considerable doubt is thrown on this aspect of his ardor when one remembers that right outside the door sat Ida Koverman, a devout Christian Scientist, a stern believer in morality and virtue, and probably the single most powerful influence in Mayer's life.

Still, the thought that he engaged in a multiplicity of courtships jibes with his nature. On train trips to the East he would play pinochle, five cents a point, at such a frenzied clip that several reserve partners were usually enlisted to make the jaunt. When in middle age his physician advised him to take up golf as a means of relaxation, he drove five balls down the green at once, wearing out a relay of caddies in the process. In later years he became an expert dancer, specializing in the rumba, and was so addicted that he would dance for two hours without stopping, tipping the orchestra to play straight through scheduled intermissions. The extraordinary energy he put into building up a fantastically successful racing stable in a single year startled every skeptic.

Mayer is known to have let his heart reach out for singer Ginny Simms and for dancer Ann Miller. He liked statuesque Jeanette MacDonald, but clever Jeanette, known as the Iron Butterfly, slipped an engagement ring on her finger and declared herself out of the running. To a very close friend Mayer confided that the woman he desired most of all was ladylike Irene Dunne, but that he knew he would never stand a chance with that well-bred and distant beauty.

One day publicist Katherine Albert was conferring with Ida Koverman when Mayer stepped out of his office. Koverman introduced Katherine to him.

"Do you want to have an affair with me?" Mayer bantered. "Because if you don't, you'd better stop batting those big black eyes at me."

The encounter gives a clue to the Mayer style. Perhaps he

did chase starlets around the room and pinch their bottoms, but somehow the picture is unconvincing. He was full of self-importance and very likely wise enough to protect his ego from trivial rejections. His worship of the image of woman was also such that he apparently pursued quite different tactics. In 1944, after 40 years of marriage, he divorced his first wife. Everyone in his circle rallied around with ideas. Louella Parsons introduced him to marriage prospects. At the beach house of agent Frank Orsatti he met other candidates. Producer Joseph Pasternak set up a date for Mayer with a starlet of his acquaintance, with whom he spoke afterward. So respectful had Mayer been that Pasternak concluded he was less carnal than in love with the idea of love.

"I don't think he wants to screw me at all," is the way the starlet put it. "He just wants to be my father."

Mayer was an intimate of great figures like Cardinal Spellman of New York, and rumors of his conversion to Catholicism were rampant, so that the friendship with Frank Orsatti, a swinger with a police record, was puzzling to many.

"Why would you have a guy like that following you around?" asked Mayer's good friend Ad Schulberg.

"He'd *kill* for me."

There was a ferocious streak in Mayer, and this came out, as revealed earlier, during his courtship of beautiful, blond Jean Howard. When Jean's affections turned to agent Charles Feldman, Mayer was so enraged that he used his influence to drive Feldman out of Hollywood. Only because he had powerful friends and a great drive was Feldman eventually able to reinstate himself in the business life of the town. Even so important a figure as Francis X. Bushman, a great star of silent pictures, was unable to survive a Mayer hate which came from his impression that Bushman had slighted him socially. And minor figures like Dick Hanley, a Mayer male secretary, had almost no way of fighting back. After Mayer fired him, Hanley for years went without work until Mike Todd came along. "If he could get along with that old bastard, he's the man for me," said Todd. Todd's wife, Elizabeth Taylor, grew fond of Hanley, and today he still works for her and husband Richard Burton.

The matter of blackballing was one of the most unsavory aspects of Mayer's character and of life among the moguls. Again and again, talented people were driven out of Hollywood because of personal spite, and often very little had to be said to accomplish it. When the name of a writer or director or star came up at an inner-circle poker party, one of the moguls shook his head negatively. It could be as simple as that. Word swiftly got around that "X" was not to be employed.

Mayer's years of bachelorhood ended in December, 1948, when he married Lorena Danker, the pretty widow of an advertising executive. For the ceremony, the couple spirited themselves to Yuma, Arizona, but alerted reporters caught the scent and pursued them in a chase worthy of a Metro comedy. When the obscure auto court where they spent the night proved not to be off limits to the press, the sheriff himself chauffeured Mayer and Lorena to a justice of the peace, who united them in a two-minute ceremony. Out the back door sped the camera-shy couple, roaring off in a taxi headed for Palm Springs. The fortyish Lorena remained married to Louis Mayer until his death a decade later.

For a man so dedicated to the family, the separation from his first wife was a traumatic experience. For the former Margaret Shenberg it was shattering. Kind, attractive, emotional, she was unable to make the transition from early poverty to regal living in Hollywood. Mayer would ask Ad Schulberg and Hedda Hopper, both stylish women, to take her shopping, to fit her with becoming clothes. Each tried, but it was difficult. When Margaret saw the price tags, she balked. If she was coaxed into a purchase, she later wore the dress only once before sending it to an old friend or relative in New Brunswick or Massachusetts. Indeed, she would collect clothes from others in the film colony and send them to those poorer souls from earlier days.

Herself unable to change, the vulnerable Margaret was aware of her volatile husband's chameleon ability to adapt. On one occasion, a cocktail party at the Mayer beach home in Santa Monica, Adela Rogers St. Johns arrived late. All the guests were gone, and Mayer had wandered off. Adela, tired after a day of writing, sat down and chatted with the hostess. The talk drifted to husbands.

"Margaret, in a way you've been lucky. You've only been married to one man," said Adela, who had had several husbands. "That's my idea of marriage, to love one man for a lifetime."

"What do you mean I've been married to only one man?" Margaret Mayer demanded.

"Well, you've told me you were married when you were very young. You've told me Louis was very young then, too, a poor struggling fellow whose hands stuck way out of his cuffs because he had outgrown his shirts and couldn't afford new ones. I know you're still married to Louis Mayer, still married to the same man."

"My dear, I've been married to more men than you can imagine. If you think that young fellow with the hands sticking out of his cuffs, poor and struggling, barely able to afford a wedding ring, if you think that's the same man who's now the head of a great film company, who has an absolutely ruthless power drive that keeps him on top, if you think those two are the same man, you're wrong. And in between there have been other Louis B. Mayers, the man fighting his way up, experiencing disappointments and failures but clawing ever upward and getting there, tough, and the man who loved sentiment and beauty and who could make lovely films like *Mrs. Miniver.* There was the man who could cry his eyes out over the work his sister Ida was doing with the Jewish old folks' home, and there was the man who could mow down an entire battalion of people at the studio if that was the way it had to be. My dear, I've been married to a dozen men."

"I had too many rabbis in the house," Margaret told Adela some time later when Mayer began staying away. "Louis might have come home more, maybe played gin rummy right here if he had felt more comfortable. But he'd come home and there'd be a rabbi visiting me. He was a devout man, but he didn't care that much for rabbis right in the house."

Margaret sought solace where she could find it. And she tried to adjust. Because Mayer liked slim women, she dieted and went too far. Her health broke down, and the mental strain also led to collapse. In a sanitarium she recuperated, her artistic nature expressing itself in painting therapy, but the recovery was not complete.

"Nothing's the same anymore," she would say sadly, and indeed nothing was, for Margaret Mayer now suffered from high blood pressure and other effects of a stroke. She would cry easily and was worn out, resentful in spite of herself.

At the end of the office day, Mayer would turn to his dependable executive secretary and say, "Ida, drive me home. I don't want to go down there alone."

Ida Koverman would drive her boss along the Pacific Highway to the Santa Monica beach house. As it came into view, Mayer would say, "The light's on. I can't go in." The car would then continue on up the coast, to Malibu and back until the light was finally out. It was all very sad and a far cry from those early days when Mayer, living in Boston, rang Margaret's bell and shouted happily, "Margaret, Margaret, see what I have for you," and proudly showed her the diamond ring he had scraped and saved to buy; or the day he had hurried to their first Hollywood home, on North Kenmore Street, and excitedly told her they were secure enough to put in a second bathroom.

In 1944 Mayer moved out of the house, and in 1947 he and Margaret were divorced after more than 40 years of marriage. The cash settlement was large. Margaret was to receive $1,250,000 on entry of the interlocutory decree, another million a year later, and a half million in each of the two following years, a total of $3,250,000. Since 3 percent interest was to be assessed on the unpaid balance, another $105,000 was eventually added to this amount. The divorced wife also received the Santa Monica beach house, valued at $250,000.

There was irony in the huge settlement. Money was never destined to bring great pleasure or balm to Margaret Mayer, who preceded Louis in death by a year, succumbing in May, 1956, of a heart ailment.

The Mayers' two daughters had been brought up under firm parental hands. Both were given $75 a month as expense allowance until they were married. Of this they were expected to save $25 and with the other $50 to cover all expenditures—clothes, hairdressers, entertainment, incidentals. When Irene tried to charge at stores where the family had an account, Mayer would reprimand her.

He did not expect the girls to venture their opinions unless asked for. As Hollywood "crown princesses," they were expected to be reserved, to behave with decorum. As a result, they were sometimes rather isolated and lonely. Irene would wander away from the beach house at Santa Monica and walk along the ocean. One day she saw a heavyset man who also seemed solitary. It was William Randolph Hearst, unpacking some of the numberless crates of art treasures constantly arriving from all parts of the world. He and Irene became friends. The two made a charming pair on the beach, he explaining his acquisitions to her while she turned bookkeeper and itemized them in a notebook.

The Mayer girls' upbringing was conservative, but that of Ivis Goulding, the sister of English director Edmund Goulding, was even more so. When Ivis turned eighteen, Irene and Edith insisted she come to their house; upstairs they giggled and gossiped and made her put on makeup for the first time in her life.

Mayer's intense dislike for Paramount's B. P. Schulberg was reciprocated by B.P., a genial punster who called Mayer the "czar of all the rushes." Mayer admired Schulberg's vivacious wife, however, a woman far ahead of the crowd, interested in progressive education, permissive with children. Budd and her two others were encouraged to speak at the dinner table, to the annoyance of the father, who was exasperated by Budd's stutter. At vacation time, Ad usually invited Irene and Edith Mayer to join her family entourage, and these excursions were a source of delight for the girls.

One of the most annoying of rebuffs came to Mayer when he tried to enter Edith and Irene in an exclusive private school. Despite his importance, they were refused because the family was Jewish. Both girls attended the Hollywood School for Girls, along with the DeMille girls and Harlean Carpenter, whose name changed to Jean Harlow when she entered films. Later, when Irene wanted to go to college, Mayer would not permit it; he thought she should train to be a mother.

Further aggravation came with the courting age. Irene blossomed into a rare beauty, resembling her mother in this respect, and adding, many said, the brains of the father. Some wags said Edith reversed the pattern, looking like her father and having the more modest mental endowments of the mother. Edith was, in fact, bright and pretty.

Mayer was mortified when David Selznick began courting Irene, largely because he was the longtime antagonist of David's father, the irrepressible Lewis Selznick. David's persistence won the day, however. "I told her not to marry him, but she went right ahead," Mayer told friends, not without humor. "Nobody realizes how important I am. Even my daughter doesn't know how important I am." Over the years, Selznick and Mayer drew close, each a tremendous admirer of the other's ability.

Edith's marriage to William Goetz, a producer at the Fox studio, was a thorn in Mayer's side which was to be more lasting. Goetz was soft-spoken but firm in his convictions, temperamentally antagonistic to his father-in-law. Mayer could be unhappy with relatives, but he would nonetheless stand by them and give them generous help. In the early thirties, the Fox studio let Goetz go. Shortly after, when Joe Schenck and Darryl Zanuck were setting up the new Twentieth Century Company, Mayer put up more than a third of a million dollars on condition that Goetz form part of the package. In addition to his financial assistance, Mayer departed from practice by loaning out several top MGM players to Twentieth. During the early years of the war, when Zanuck went into the Army and Goetz took his place in charge of production, Mayer made an effort to maintain him there, failing when Joe Schenck backed Zanuck at the crucial moment.

The dissatisfied Goetz then decided to go independent, and once again Mayer was instrumental in his success. He went to nearby Encino to see Leo Spitz at his home, called Drimmel Hill, Jewish for "nodding off." Spitz was a distinguished Chicago lawyer who had come to Hollywood to lift RKO out of 77b, the delicate legal area next door to bankruptcy. His brilliant mind impressed the entire industry, as did his modest, thoughtful nature. After his retirement to Encino many moguls made the trek there because he was superbly incisive at judging their problems and moreover gave *gornish* advice— free, that is. On his visit, Mayer induced Spitz to come out of retirement to head the new International Pictures Corporation. To Goetz he handed a check for one million dollars with which to capitalize the new firm.

Mayer's move in protecting his investment was extremely sound. Spitz played a dominant role in the new firm, and International enjoyed several years of impressive activity. Nunnally Johnson penned *Along Came Jones, Casanova Brown,* and other scripts; Sam Wood was a leading director for the company; and Gary Cooper was the top player. For the successful *One Touch of Venus,* Mayer loaned International Robert Walker and Ava Gardner, who had just made a strong impression in *The Hucksters.* Other loan-outs followed.

Goetz later worked for Universal—which Spitz merged with International—and Columbia, before turning independent. His record on his own was less than outstanding, including such films as *They Came to Cordura, Cry for Happy, Song Without End,* and *Assault on the Queen,* which a number of critics rate a strong contender for Worst Picture of All Time.

Although he accepted Mayer's assistance, Goetz was unwilling to submit to his domination. He fought with Mayer over whether he and Edith should have a small wedding or a big one, Mayer insisting on the latter. Over his father-in-law's objections, Goetz spent sizable sums on the French Impressionist paintings which today form one of the world's best collections of the genre.

Above all, he was politically antagonistic to Mayer. The boiling point came during the campaign of Adlai Stevenson. One of the ultimate terms of scorn employed by Mayer was "intellectual." Edith and William Goetz both felt great admiration for Stevenson, who certainly fell into that category. Mayer fervently backed Dwight Eisenhower. When Goetz joined Dore Schary in jointly sponsoring a benefit for Adlai, Mayer broke with his son-in-law and daughter.

Added tension came from the fact that Mayer and Schary were engaged in a latter-day power struggle at the studio. In this time of trouble the son-in-law did not rally round. So bitter did Mayer become that in his last years he would no longer speak to the Goetzes. In his will he specifically excluded Edith, "or any other member of the Goetz family," on the ground that during his lifetime he had made extremely substantial contributions to the family through gifts and financial assistance and also through advancement of Goetz's career. This accepted aid, the will stated, was to be "distinguished from that of my former son-in-law, David Selznick, who never requested or accepted assistance from me in the motion picture industry."

Following a familiar pattern, Mayer was a more affectionate, more indulgent grandfather than father. While he deeply loved his two daughters, he had hoped for sons. Edith's children were daughters, while Irene had two boys. The boys became Mayer's pets, especially the younger, Daniel Mayer Selznick, who was of course named for him, just as the older, Lewis Jeffrey Selznick, was named for the other grandfather. When Danny, a warm, affectionate child, was five, Mayer would take him to the studio and say, "This is my grandson," with a proud intonation that made clear he was his heir apparent. When the boy was ten, he would introduce him and say simply, "He's going to be President of the United States."

For his grandsons, Mayer displayed a warm sense of humor. "We're going to the zoo! We're going to the zoo!" he might exhort them; as they got to the car they would see he had brought them a pair of kittens.

Mayer hated to be *asked* to give. At Christmas, those powerful lady columnists, Hedda Hopper and Louella Parsons, were accustomed to receiving gifts from film figures in proportion to their importance. A major star who was niggling could expect the most harsh retribution—to be left *out* of the columns. One year Hedda's legman, King Kennedy, helped her unwrap presents. A large, beautiful teddy bear was among them.

"Who sent that?" asked Hedda.

"Louis B. Mayer," said Kennedy.

"I can't believe it," Hedda gasped.

She thereupon sent her secretary, Triva, for the scissors and a butcher knife. The teddy bear was ripped from end to end, but no further present was inside, no bauble or bangle. Mayer was not one to pay tribute.

Once, an associate encouraged him to contribute more to charity, saying that in any event he couldn't take his money with him. "If I can't take it with me, I won't go," Mayer replied.

Unsolicited, however, he would suddenly stop the car and buy his grandsons gifts. Or in good Jewish tradition he would say, "Let me do you a favor," and call up friends in business, telling them, "I'm sending someone over and I want you to give him the best." At his death, he had promised so many specific bequests that the Mayer Foundation, which his will established, spent a year sorting them out before it could engage in serious business.

Often Mayer would send Danny short notes on engraved cards, always of Tiffany quality. The handwriting would go in all directions, quite artistic, with fine curlicues but no full sentences and few commas, caps, or periods. It was one of the reasons that Mayer's widow and his estate executor, Myron Fox, burned all of his papers at his death, a tragic loss. They felt Mayer had already been so vilified that it was best to withdraw all source material, lest it also be misused. The hand-scrawled notes, they feared, might lead to ridicule, and worse. One of the few remaining specimens of Mayer script graces a gold watch he gave his favorite grandson when he was gradu-ated, at seventeen, from the George School in Pennsylvania: *"Danny, you have made me proud and I love you. Grandpa."*

Danny never ceased to return that love, but late in Mayer's life he spent a period actually living with his grandfather in that house filled with paintings by Grandma Moses and auto-graphed photos of the great. He saw then that Mayer was an animal philosopher, that his voice could soar, bellow, while his jowls shook, that he could be extremely tough, talking to serv-ants in a manner which was humiliating to them. When Danny confronted him, Mayer said the servants understood him and knew he did not mean to humiliate or demean them.

"You've got to be Jewish to appreciate him," Dan Selznick says of his grandfather, and it seems there was something quin-tessentially Jewish about Louis B. Mayer. The attitude toward the family, the respect for the parents, the sacred place of woman, and many other views could be traced directly to the Talmud. There was none of the detached coldness of the Cal-vinist in Mayer, who was warm-blooded, volatile, expressive, a man who hated "put-on" artists, people who were preten-tious, those who made a fuss over the temperature of wine. He often remarked on reserved people, calling them *"Kalte Zähne,"* cold teeth, and wondered out loud how they could perform with their wives. The Mayer emotionalism and con-stant bickering and fighting also seem to be frequently recur-ring racial traits.

Mayer quarreled with everyone in the family, with his daughters, Irene and Edith, with their husbands, with his wife, with his elder sister, Ida, and with her son, producer Jack Cum-mings, whom he liked to call "macher," roughly "big shot," but a term which can be used both flatteringly and sarcastically.

Disputes which began over business could turn highly per-sonal. Cummings was known at MGM as a producer of top musicals, among them *Three Little Words, Neptune's Daugh-*

ter, and *Seven Brides for Seven Brothers,* but when he came upon the script for *The Stratton Story,* he was irresistibly drawn. He went to Mayer and told him to buy this moving true account of a baseball player whose leg is amputated but who still wants to go on pitching. No, said Mayer, he didn't like the idea of a man as unrealistic as that, one who would not adapt to life. If you lost your leg you had to accept your fate, not fight it. Cummings argued that this very pluck was what gave the story punch.

"Now when this man with one leg goes to bat and hits a single and then can't run to first base, how do you think people will feel?" demanded Mayer, who had loved baseball as a child and continued to enjoy the game at studio picnics. "How will all the pregnant women in the audience feel about something so terrible? Why, if you make such a picture, *macher,* think of the miscarriages you'll cause."

The argument grew in intensity, and finally Cummings dropped it. He was surprised when he found out weeks later that Mayer had bought *The Stratton Story* and assigned Edwin Knopf to produce. He hurried to his uncle's office and reminded him he had brought the story to his attention, that Mayer had said it would cause miscarriages. Now he had bought it. Why? Mayer was evasive. It was over and done with, so why trouble him about it? Because he wanted to produce the picture, said Jack.

"Then what would I do about Knopf?" said Mayer, tossing his arms despairingly into the air.

"I'll talk to him."

"Trouble, trouble, all this trouble."

Mayer was angry, but Jack persisted. He went to Knopf, who agreed to bow out. Gregory Peck was Cummings' first choice for the lead, but he was not available. After a time, Jimmy Stewart was cast as Stratton and the picture was shot. At the preview in Santa Monica, the audience rose at the end and cheered.

Because Jack had crossed him, Mayer pouted, washing his hands of the picture, refusing even to attend the preview. He learned from Howard Strickling, however, that it was a great success. A day later he invited his friend Billy Rose to dinner and a private showing. Rose was overcome.

"I don't remember who produced this picture, but I'll tell you it's the best thing I've seen in years," he said. "Whoever produced it should be promoted and made head of the studio."

"And push me over? Never," said Mayer proudly. "That picture was produced by my nephew."

The next morning, Mayer's wife, Lorena, called and said she knew Louis would never say so but he loved the picture and was proud of him. A short time later the phone rang in Cummings' office.

"Macher, do you have a few minutes for your old Uncle Louis?"

Jack arrived at the immense office to find Mayer lingering in the doorway.

"I'll save you all the time," said Jack, thinking to avoid the embarrassment of having Mayer apologize for his coldness. "Your wife called me."

"I really can't tell you how moved I was near the end of the picture," said Mayer, ignoring the remark. "When the pitcher fields the ball and falls to the ground, and he with only one leg, and he still manages to throw the ball over to first and get the batter out."

"I'm glad you liked that."

"And I liked. . . ."

Mayer continued and for the better part of two hours acted out *The Stratton Story* scene by scene, describing his reaction to each. At the end of the recital he threw his arms around Jack and told him he had been deeply moved. The recital was his apology.

Early in the game, Cummings picked up a device that helped him immeasurably in dealing with his uncle. During the filming of *Born to Dance*, he worked with a director on loan from Twentieth Century-Fox. The man spoke so highly of Jack that Darryl Zanuck sent word that if ever he was unhappy at MGM,

there was always a desk for him at Twentieth. Mayer heard of
the offer. Thereafter, when Jack wanted to win a point in an
argument, to acquire a property, for instance, he had only to
say Zanuck was interested in it.

"Zanuck may want it, but he's not going to get it," Mayer
would say defiantly. "Buy it."

Cummings also learned that Mayer felt closer to the man
who had a failure than one with a success. He knew what a gamble a picture was and how easily it could come a cropper. At
the end of a preview he was likely to give a sympathetic handshake to the man responsible for a turkey.

In the midst of one of their arguments, Mayer gave Cummings an inscribed photo: *"To Jack, with Pride and Pro-
found Love, from Your Uncle Louis."*

Mayer wrangled with his older brother, Rudolph, a fascinating figure who was at once the black sheep of the family and
the most stylish of the Mayers. Rudolph would arrive from far
climes, smelling of exotic perfume, carrying Vuitton luggage,
and talking of French mistresses. Several times he made fortunes, always by means just a trifle shady, and lost them. Mayer
bailed him out of scrapes on the promise that he would stay
out of the picture business.

Mayer also quarreled relentlessly with his younger brother,
Jerry, whom he made the studio's general manager. So acri-
monious did these disputes become that the brothers would
stop speaking. When this happened, when Mayer was feuding,
it was difficult to get work done at the studio.

During perhaps the worst siege between Mayer and brother
Jerry, the Kaddish was near at hand, the Jewish holiday on
which it is customary for male members of the family to go to
Shul and say prayers for the dead. Nephew Jack decided
to use the occasion to heal the rift between the brothers. He
went to Jerry's wife, Reba, and said he was going to get these
two brothers to make up and go together to pray for the dead,
notably for the mother they had loved so well; she should get
Jerry into the car and park outside Louis' home in Santa Mon-

ica, and he, Jack, would go in and get Louis. Reba said she did
not think Jerry would go, but Jack insisted she use all her powers of persuasion and be outside waiting.

Jack thereupon drove to Mayer's house, where he found him
in the library, a room filled with finely bound books which he
never read. Mayer was in a contemplative mood.

"It's nice of you to come today," he said. "It's nice you
would think we could go to Shul together."

"I'm not going to Shul with you," said Jack. "You're going
to pray for your mother and ask her to accept your prayers. I
loved her, but I'm not the first line of the family. This is a day
when the male members of the family should stand shoulder
to shoulder and say their prayers as one. You should be going to
Shul with your brother Jerry."

"How dare you come here to tell me that!" Mayer exploded.
"I won't even speak to Jerry, you know that."

"I don't care what he's done or what you and he have quarreled about. This is a holy day, and you are going to say a
prayer to your mother. You are her son and he is her son, and
you should be standing together shoulder to shoulder."

"Why are you doing this to me?" Mayer turned to another
emotion, pathos. "Why did you come here? I won't go with
him. I'll never go with him, and I wish you'd get out of here
and leave me alone."

"You two are brothers, and I don't care what your quarrel
is about. You should go to Shul together. What do you want
—you go to one Shul and Jerry go to another Shul? Do you
think your mother would like that?"

"I won't go with him." Mayer gesticulated wildly. "I don't
want you to talk about it any more."

"How can you say that? You're going to say a prayer to your
mother and you think she'll accept it if you go alone? You're
going to say 'sanctified, beatified, magnified,' and all those
beautiful words of the prayer. You're going to say these words
to your mother, and you won't even speak to your own brother,
her son. And you think she'll accept your prayers? Do you think
she'll accept your prayers? Believe me, whatever your quarrel

with Jerry, you should be with him, standing shoulder to shoulder, and your mother should hear your prayers and his coming to her as one prayer."

Mayer bowed his head, and there was a long silence.

"How can we get hold of him?" he asked softly.

"He's outside," said Cummings.

Jack helped Mayer into his coat and led him out to the car. He drove the two brothers to Shul, where they prayed together. Little was said, but the breach was healed. Cummings had used the sort of emotional appeal at which Mayer himself was adept. Business at the studio could now recommence.

In a crisis Mayer sensed the need to close ranks. When he was unseated from his mighty throne at Metro-Goldwyn-Mayer, perhaps even more bitter to swallow than defeat was the fact that many of his closest associates let him down. Mayer relied for years on gifted producers like Irving Thalberg and Hunt Stromberg to carry out his giant picture program. Ironically, in the late forties, he chose Dore Schary to carry on in their footsteps. Schary was the very opposite of Mayer, intellectual, liberal, a film maker intent on conveying the messages which Mayer felt did not belong in family entertainment.

Predictably, the two men quarreled repeatedly. There was, too, the added tension brought on by changing conditions. At war's end, the public seemed to want a more thoughtful product and began buying foreign films. Television started making inroads. As they had with sound, Mayer and Nicholas Schenck fought the innovation. No television sets were allowed in MGM offices, and none could be shown in a film. In this insecure atmosphere, an underground struggle for power began to take shape. Mayer brought it to a focus when he called Nicholas Schenck in New York and said he must choose between himself and Dore Schary. To his incredulous horror, Schenck chose Schary.

After a quarter century at the helm of MGM Louis B. Mayer was out of a job. His fury now was unbounded. He stormed and shouted; he smashed the furniture. To everyone within earshot he spoke in scatological terms of the people who had betrayed him. Betrayal, disloyalty, ingratitude were constant terms, but they were the mildest that fell from his tongue. He was now Lear, dethroned but still a king.

Although he was a very wealthy man, he no longer had a base of power. As a consequence, this only recently most powerful man in Hollywood found himself dropped from social list A to social list A sub 1. The difference was keenly perceived by him. If a dinner for fifty was given for a visiting head of state, he was invited; if the dinner was restricted to ten, he was left out.

Mayer was tempted by various arrangements with other studios, but it was with Metro-Goldwyn-Mayer that his heart and entire soul lay. In an ill-advised maneuver he joined with several financiers in an attempt to regain control. He failed.

His language now became even more intemperate. At functions, he would encounter casual acquaintances and guide them to a far corner of the room, stomping back and forth before them, tirading, fulminating against his betrayers, the sessions marathon exercises in abuse. Even in rage and outrage, Mayer was outsized, a giant.

This was the theme which Spencer Tracy developed in his funeral eulogy in October, 1957, after Mayer died of leukemia. Some say Tracy was reluctant to praise Mayer, but those who were closest to the actor say he was a strong-willed Irishman who never did anything he didn't want to do. Metro aide Eddie Lawrence, who rode with him to the services, said he watched as Tracy himself edited the final version in the car. Because there is no doubt that Tracy did find Mayer difficult, his moving tribute is all the more impressive:

> It is the book of Genesis which says: "There were giants in those days." Another book tells us that "a giant is a man of great stature." There are giants in these days, too, but only rarely.
>
> There is no doubt in the minds of those who knew him that the man of whom I speak was a giant indeed. I speak of Louie B. Mayer, a man of great stature.

Now, it is one thing to be a giant, however rare, but it is not often in these days that a man may be of great stature and still know, and understand, people. Louie B. Mayer knew people better than all the other many things he knew so well. It was because he knew people that he was able to know the other many things.

Such knowledge of people is a rare privilege. Louie B. Mayer possessed it because from his early childhood he had been intimately involved with human beings in his, and their, struggles —first for existence, and after that, for progress toward being better and happier human beings.

His progress from existence to later fame and fortune came from his knowledge of people and their thinking, for the merchandise he handled was completely intangible. You could not weigh it on a scale, nor measure it with a yardstick, for it was magical merchandise of laughter and tears, of recreation and pleasure, of enlightenment and education. It was nothing more than gossamer, nothing less than a primary human need—entertainment.

It was only an optical illusion, but it could take people—all the people on earth—out of their workaday worlds, and contain them happily in a dream-world of their own selection.

In "those days" of holy writ, if you could do this, you would be called a sorcerer or a god. Louie B. Mayer was neither. He was a man—but a man who knew men, and women, and children.

In this gathering are many people who spent a third of a century in such close daily contact with him as might well bring disillusion—for giants, like gods, may have feet of clay. Yet these people, as of this very moment, say to themselves and others that they still marvel where Louie B. Mayer found his astonishing insight into the human heart and mind. He did not find it. He earned and learned it, by knowing people.

He was a man of contrasts—part sentiment and idealism, part pure practicality. At times his temper would rise in indignation when he would discover that someone he loved and trusted had taken such love and trust lightly. It was not so much because of any harm done to him, but more because of the shock to his own faith in that individual. That was the idealist side of him.

But soon the practical side would come to his rescue. He would say, "You must never be too surprised when you discover a weakness in someone you respect. This is earth, not heaven," he'd say, "and all the religions on earth are only working to make us people of earthly faults more worthy of heaven. People are only human, you know."

That was the practical man. "Besides," he'd add, "most of the people of this country must be decent and honorable or there would be no United States of America as we know it."

We all know what his fabulous career encompassed. On the day, back in 1924, when he began its greatest phase, he first addressed a group of newly acquired employees—exactly 480 of them—saying: "I have been warned that this new company starts off with a handicap. That its pictures will bear a name that can never become easy to say—'A *Metro-Goldwyn-Mayer* picture.' That we should have a short name, crisp and able to become familiar, like other studios. I can only tell you fellow workers this—if we all do our jobs as I know we will, within a year, wherever you go, when someone asks where you work, you can simply say, not three long words, but three short letters —MGM! And everyone will know you're connected with the foremost movie studio in the world."

Soon it *was* the MGM studio, but now with some 4,000 employees.

And Mayer, as widely and wonderfully known, had become the two letters by which he will be forever known in our industry—L.B.

For that industry, he fought persistently and unwaveringly. He was responsible for the Academy of Motion Picture Arts and Sciences. He conceived its original idea, and personally piloted it into existence and its first programs. Whether it was in his concept of the Academy, or his contempt for the shoddy and the opportunistic, his activities were dominated by the hope that the medium of the motion picture, and the people who work in it, would receive the respect to which he felt they were entitled. And, more than any other man, he won for the motion picture industry an esteem that was little more than a dream at the time he first envisioned the future of films.

The story he wanted to tell was the story of America—the land for which he had an almost furious love, born of gratitude

—and of contrast with the hatreds in the dark land of his boyhood across the seas. Though he never lost his love for Canada, which had given him refuge, and an opportunity that found fulfillment in the United States, it was this love for America that made him an authority on America, and his counsel was sought by men in high places.

Now, L.B. is gone from among us, gone from his beloved country—leaving as a bequest to his Lorena, his children, and his grandchildren, and his sisters the wealth of his self-respect, the swiftness of his gallant spirit, and the native treasure of his humble wisdom, for he was a man of great stature.

All the rest is history. The shining epoch of the industry passes with him.

In the future, looking backwards, one will see his head and shoulders rising clearly above the misty memories of Hollywood's past.

For the present, Edwin Markham tells it better than we can:

> When he fell
> In whirlwind he went,
> As when a lordly cedar, green with boughs,
> Goes with a great shout upon the hills,
> And leaves a lonesome place against the sky.

Index